THE
INTERNAL
COHERENCE
FRAMEWORK

THE INTERNAL COHERENCE FRAMEWORK

Creating the Conditions for Continuous Improvement in Schools

MICHELLE L. FORMAN

ELIZABETH LEISY STOSICH

CANDICE BOCALA

2017

HARVARD EDUCATION PRESS

CAMBRIDGE, MASSACHUSETTS

Second Printing, 2017

Paperback ISBN 978-1-68253-017-7
Library Edition ISBN 978-1-68253-018-4

Library of Congress Cataloging-in-Publication Data

Names: Forman, Michelle L., author. | Stosich, Elizabeth Leisy, author. | Bocala, Candice, author.
Title: The internal coherence framework : creating the conditions for continuous improvement in schools / Michelle L. Forman, Elizabeth Leisy Stosich, Candice Bocala.
Description: Cambridge, Massachusetts : Harvard Education Press, [2017] | Includes bibliographical references and index.
Identifiers: LCCN 2016052861| ISBN 9781682530177 (pbk.) | ISBN 9781682530184 (library edition)
Subjects: LCSH: School improvement programs—United States. | School management and organization—United States. | Teacher effectiveness—United States. | Academic achievement—United States. | Educational change—United States. | Educational leadership—United States. | Teaching teams—United States.
Classification: LCC LB1027 .F623 2017 | DDC 371.2/07—dc23 LC record available at https://lccn.loc.gov/2016052861

Published by Harvard Education Press,
an imprint of the Harvard Education Publishing Group

Harvard Education Press
8 Story Street
Cambridge, MA 02138

Cover design: Endpaper Studio
Cover image: iStock/© tashechka

The typefaces used in this book are Adobe Garamond, Roboto.

*To our practitioner partners in Boston, Fort Worth, Clovis, and
New York for sharing with us their wisdom of practice; and
to our colleagues at the Strategic Education Research Partnership,
especially Suzanne Donovan and Richard Elmore,
for supporting the development of our own capabilities.*

CONTENTS

FOREWORD

For the last thirty years or so, I have been interested in various dimensions of professionalism in the field of education. It always struck me, from the time I was a student in school myself, how erratic and often undisciplined teaching was as a practice and how much people in the field of education seemed to be attached to a kind of artisanal view of teaching. In this view, the complex world of learning had to be recreated from scratch each day in hundreds of thousands of classrooms. My own experience as a learner, with a rather jagged profile of competencies, was not well served by this view of teaching, from elementary school through graduate school. Could we create, I wondered, a strong, supportive, understandable learning environment that would both provide a clear and coherent theory of learning and allow for all the necessary adaptations to individual differences? Most professions grapple with this problem every day.

I began to pursue this interest in professionalism in earnest in the 1990s with a relatively simple idea: professions are distinguished from other forms of work by their shared practices; they use these practices to form a common identity and sources of social authority, to expand their knowledge, and to provide consistent approaches to diverse problems. I decided to use my position in the university to demonstrate this idea by working with practitioners to develop clinical practices that could regularly build a collective culture of improvement in the conditions of learning. My first such project was developing, with a group of colleagues and a collaborating set of schools and districts, the practice of instructional rounds. The second was the internal coherence project. The development of these clinical practices together has spanned some fifteen years.

As this book illustrates, diving deeply into the world of clinical practice requires a mastery of multiple disciplinary perspectives. In this case, the perspectives include basic theories of learning, the psychology of individual and collective efficacy, the sociology of collective learning at the team and organizational level, and multiple roles of leadership in learning. The central task of defining and developing a clinical practice is melding these multiple disciplinary perspectives into a causal framework that can guide actions, doing justice to the complexity of the underlying research, while at the same time making the implications of that research accessible to practitioners. The only way to do this is to spend time in direct discourse with practitioners and to engage them in the collaborative development of practice.

This work requires a particular set of dispositions and skills, embodied in the competencies of Michelle, Liz, and Candice, our authors. Each has a footing in a specialized field of research related mainly to influences on the development of teaching practice in school settings. Each commands a formidable battery of learning protocols that can be used to introduce and develop relatively abstract and difficult constructs into skills and behaviors that can be modeled, practiced, and used in the daily work of educators. And most importantly, each author has a broad range of interpersonal competencies that build trust and authenticity in work with practitioners. We can say that this combination of competencies is unusual among academics in research universities, but these competencies are also clearly central to the creation and development of professional practice.

For me, the internal coherence project was an important event in my personal development. As I developed my ideas around organizational coherence and clinical practice in my graduate teaching and professional development work, I realized that as my ideas became more concrete and specific, they also became narrower and less responsive to differences in context. For example, I began to use rubrics to provide feedback in my graduate courses, and that practice changed my entire mental map of what learning means and what role feedback plays in learning. I immediately gravitated toward the application of rubrics to the assessment of organizational capacity in the internal coherence clinical work. What I didn't reckon with is that the idea and practice of self-assessment is both unfamiliar in school settings and completely at odds with the dominant culture of evaluation, in which assessments are typically "done to" rather than "done with."

I finally began to understand the use of rubrics in professional development by working with Michelle, Liz, and Candice on the design and enactment of actual learning experiences for teachers and principals. In these experiences, a series of exercises designed to introduce the idea of psychological safety and focused discourse around practice preceded the use of rubrics for self-assessment. Working with skilled facilitators and designers added to my understanding and to the development of my own practice. As the book states, we learn best when people with different skills, competencies, and dispositions have to build a common product.

I have read this manuscript with a combination of pride and humility. Pride, in the sense of having been part of a collaborative enterprise that so closely approximates what I intended to do thirty-some years ago; humility, in the sense of how much of this book is the product of the authors and their dedicated persistence in the development of the practice, and not to the original ideas that spawned my involvement in it. If one were to build a profession around learning, this would a good place to start.

One of the advantages of working in a leading research university is the opportunity to work with amazing partners—leading scholars in diverse fields, talented and experienced practitioners who have returned to graduate school, public school systems representing a range of conditions and diverse student populations, and institutions charged with advancing the connection between research and practice. Another of the advantages of being a tenured professor in a leading research university is that you can choose the problems you work on and the colleagues with whom you work. In these respects, I have lived a very privileged life.

This book would not have occurred without the collaboration and support of Carol Johnson, former superintendent of the Boston Public Schools, and those initial principals and teachers in the original pilot schools in Boston. The fundamental, broad-scale empirical research of Roger Goddard and his colleagues on individual and collective efficacy were essential to this book (formerly at Texas A&M, Roger is now at Ohio State University). The book would not exist without the collaboration of senior administrators in Fort Worth, Texas, and Clovis,

California; these individuals played an active role not just in modeling the work of the internal coherence practice but also, in important ways, as codesigners of that practice. Similarly, our wonderful, energetic colleagues at California State University, Fresno, were a powerful force in building and sustaining our collective learning in the Central Valley of California.

Projects of this scope do not occur without considerable institutional support, and for us, this came through our affiliation with the Strategic Education Research Partnership (SERP) at the National Academy of Sciences, and our colleague Suzanne Donovan. SERP was explicitly designed to deepen the connection between research, policy, and practice in education and to develop the disciplines associated with this connection.

Most of all, this book would not have occurred without the powerful, persistent inquisitiveness and dedication of Michelle Forman, Liz Stosich, and Candice Bocala, all experienced practitioners who began their work on this project while graduate students at the Harvard Graduate School of Education. All three have strong, independent minds and are fiercely dedicated to deepening the connection between research and practice. Our joint work on this project was, for me, a model of what graduate study in a professional school should be about: learning together, learning from each other, asking "why not?" to divergent ideas, and taking risks in bringing unfamiliar ideas to practitioner audiences.

Richard F. Elmore
Gregory R. Anrig Professor of Educational Leadership
Harvard Graduate School of Education

ACKNOWLEDGMENTS

This book comes from a nearly decade-long journey of learning to lead instructional improvement in partnership with our esteemed colleagues in research and practice. We are grateful to have worked and learned with Richard Elmore, whose leadership of the project and commitment to developing clinical practices for the field were essential to the work described in this book. Richard has an incredible ability to cut through the complexity of organizational change and keep us all focused on how each part of the larger system connects to the instructional core. We would like to thank Roger Goddard, an early contributor to the development of the Internal Coherence Framework. Roger's research on teachers' collective efficacy beliefs has set the groundwork for describing the beliefs and experiences that educators can cultivate to transform schools into learning organizations. We are indebted to Susan Henry for sharing her deep knowledge about teaching. Su.'s framework for understanding the depth and relevance of teachers' talk is fundamental to how we support teacher teams to strengthen their collaborative work and focus on instruction. And we are indebted to Claudette Gates, the first principal to take part in the Internal Coherence Survey. In so doing, she engaged in the difficult act of leading through public learning, the work we all aspire to do.

The practices described in this book were developed, tested, and refined through research-practice partnerships supported by the Strategic Education Research Partnership (SERP). We thank Suzanne Donovan for her support of the Internal Coherence Research Project from its inception. Suzanne is a champion for developing research-practice partnerships that produce usable knowledge for the field, and her leadership has been essential for the ongoing growth of the project. We are also grateful to Matt Ellinger for contributing his eye for design to the development of the Internal Coherence Framework and website, and to Beverly Hoffmaster for her skillful coordination of each project.

We would like to thank Caroline Chauncey and the team at the Harvard Education Publishing Group for first agreeing that this book would be useful to the field and then ushering us through the process of putting these ideas into writing.

Last, we are deeply indebted to our practitioner partners in Massachusetts, Texas, New York, and California for taking a risk by trying a new way of working and allowing us to learn from them in the process. We are grateful to Ginny Boris for working her "bunnies" off to champion this work across the Central Valley. Ginny's commitment to the long journey that is required for systems change was essential for enabling the deep work of our Central Valley partnership. We are also grateful to Linda Hauser and Mabel Franks for their coaching expertise to support principals and to Rosalie Baker for staying the course with the internal coherence work, supporting it with principals and creating a place for it in her district. We could not have developed the clinical practices described in this book without the insightful feedback and incredible staying power of our Central Valley partners.

Finally, we would like to thank our families, especially:

From Michelle—to Chris, for doing everything, so I could do this.
From Liz—to Peter, who encouraged me to begin this journey and whose support has helped me stay the course.
From Candice—to Keith, for bringing balance into my life.

1

Why Internal Coherence?

Improving teaching and learning in schools and educational systems is the most important work of school leaders. Although there is no shortage of research on school leadership and organizational improvement, applying these lessons to daily work in schools presents a challenge. For one thing, educational literature and research often provide general guidance, but leaders must apply this guidance to their contexts and organizational cultures. For some leaders, weak collegial relationships among educators and low levels of trust in administrators can make it difficult to engage in the shared and public learning necessary for improvement. For others, friendly relationships among educators and relatively high levels of student performance can make the status quo quite appealing and the uncertainty that comes with improvement efforts unwelcome. Moreover, accountability policies that focus on performance status—such as whether students meet graduation or testing benchmarks—rather than continuous improvement can leave some leaders with little interest in making any changes and can leave others paralyzed by unrealistic goals. This book provides leaders at the classroom, school, and district levels with concrete practices for growing the capacity of schools and systems to support more powerful learning for both adults and students.

Researchers in the United States and internationally argue that strong internal agreement and commitment to shared goals is essential for improving learning outcomes for all children.[1] In educational systems that improve teaching and learning, educators clearly understand what they are working toward, believe that working toward this goal is worthwhile, and consistently strive to engage in the necessary learning and adaptation. Despite the many competing demands that make it difficult for leaders to focus on teaching and learning, leaders in schools that improve cultivate a culture of learning and make tight connections between their improvement goals and opportunities for adult learning in teams and as a faculty. In this way, the organization is designed to support consistent, collaborative opportunities for working toward a common goal. Organizations that improve do not simply rely on a few exceptional leaders or teachers. Instead, they deliberately create supportive conditions for ordinary educators to engage in systematic and coordinated professional learning that pushes teaching and learning to new and more ambitious levels across classrooms.

School and district leaders can work with educators to set and maintain focus on improvement and create supportive conditions for collaborative learning.[2] In many schools and systems, however, learning opportunities for educators and students are incoherent. When teachers work in isolation or rely on their individual teaching style, students experience inconsistent teaching as they move from classroom to classroom, and they encounter a spectrum of practices that range from ineffective to effective.[3] Similarly, as adult learners, teachers describe the majority of their professional learning experiences as brief, fragmented, and disconnected from their daily work.[4] Districts can exacerbate this incoherence by offering teachers a wide menu of voluntary professional development opportunities that are only weakly connected to each other and system-wide goals for improving instruction. Despite growing attention to teacher teams as structures for ongoing, job-embedded learning about instruction, many leaders encourage collaboration without providing support and guidance to ensure that teachers' learning in teams translates into organizational learning and student learning. Unless the learning activities of the faculty in a given school are coordinated, the overall result is unlikely to constitute a coherent instructional approach.

This book is designed to support you and your colleagues in working together to grow *internal coherence* for powerful learning in your organization. We define internal coherence as the collective capability of the adults in a school building or an educational system to connect and align resources to carry out an improvement strategy. Internal coherence requires educators to work in concert to assess their current status, identify existing problems of practice, commit to the implementation of a collective solution and the new learning this entails, reflect on the impact of their effort, and return to the next cycle of joint learning. In other words, internal coherence enables a faculty to coordinate the work of leaders, teachers, and teams around a shared improvement strategy, engage in collective learning about instructional content and practice to advance this strategy, and use that learning to provide all students with richer educational opportunities. As educators see that improvements in student learning directly result from their own learning and action, they build a stronger sense of collective efficacy; they believe that they have the joint capability to affect students' growth in outcomes that matter. As a result, educators are motivated to take responsibility for student success, experiment with new practices, and persevere in the face of challenges.

THE INTERNAL COHERENCE FRAMEWORK FOR IMPROVING TEACHING AND LEARNING

The Internal Coherence Framework presented in this book and the essential practices for building internal coherence draw on a rich evidence base from the fields of education, business, and psychology. This research documents strong agreement about the essential role of leaders as the drivers of change, the importance of creating a culture conducive to experimentation and learning, and the potential for teams to serve as powerful structures for learning and behavioral change. Importantly, an organization's level of internal coherence is not fixed, and the Internal Coherence Framework and essential practices are designed to form an *actionable* approach to increase this capacity from any starting point. This framework, which is based on evidence about the essential practices, processes, and conditions for enhancing teaching and learning at scale, can help leaders develop a comprehensive approach to improvement.

The Internal Coherence Framework illustrates a preliminary causal order of how schools improve, beginning with the leadership practices that foster adult learning. When principals encourage multiple perspectives, create opportunities for public discussions of practice, and work with teachers to create a shared vision for instruction, they create a safe space for learning and focus this learning on meeting collective goals. When aligned around a clear instructional improvement strategy, adult learning in professional development, faculty meetings, and teams advances these collective goals. Teachers and leaders are better able to make changes to their instructional and leadership practice, which affects how and what students learn. Specifically, teachers who learn about instructional content together can design student tasks that elicit more rigorous and complex thinking, which leads to improved student outcomes. When teachers see the improvements to student learning, they have more confidence in their shared capability to achieve the goals they set and are more committed to these collective goals. Each of the central elements of the Internal Coherence Framework is described in greater detail below (see figure 1.1).

FIGURE 1.1   Internal Coherence Framework

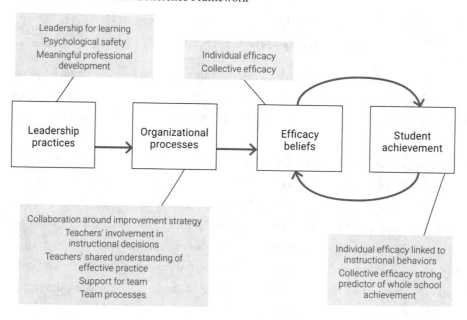

Source: Reproduced by permission from the Strategic Education Research Partnership (SERP).

Leadership Practices

The leadership practices domain of the Internal Coherence Framework draws from the extensive literature on effective leadership in the fields of business management and education.[5] This research has led to a deeper understanding of the unique role of leaders as the drivers of improvement and agents of cultural transformation. The framework shifts the focus on leadership away from general leadership characteristics, or leadership style, to the specific practices that educational leaders can use to improve instruction. This focus helps to make abstract ideas like distributed leadership and leadership for learning concrete and actionable by describing what leaders can do to share leadership (e.g., have teachers work collectively to determine professional development plans) or to encourage learning (e.g., acknowledge multiple points of view).[6] Notably, all elements of the leadership practices domain connect, either directly or indirectly, to teaching and learning. This connection reinforces the central idea that even though school leaders tend to spend less time directly involved in classrooms than teachers, they must understand how their work relates to and supports their vision for instruction.[7]

Organizational Processes

The second domain of the Internal Coherence Framework, organizational processes, draws on evidence from the scholarship about organizational learning. The evidence suggests that organizations are more successful when they build capacity for learning and leadership broadly and create a safe environment for experimentation. Teams can serve as an essential structure for supporting organizational learning. Research on organizational learning has typically been difficult to translate into practice because it is overly broad or provides inspirational rather than practical guidance. To address this challenge, we have developed the essential practices, detailed later in the book, which focus on concrete steps that educators can take to encourage learning, reflection, and feedback in the organization. This line of research is powerfully intertwined with the work of school leaders, since they have the formal authority to create opportunities for learning and can share leadership with others in the organization. For example, a principal can form a leadership team of administrators and teachers to engage in shared decision making about the vision and strategy for improving teaching and learning schoolwide.

Efficacy Beliefs and Student Achievement

Finally, the framework builds on research related to teachers' beliefs about their ability to generate meaningful student learning outcomes. The third and fourth areas of the Internal Coherence Framework, teacher efficacy beliefs and student achievement, are grounded in social cognitive literature and research connecting individual teachers' beliefs about their ability to educate students with productive attitudes and behaviors. Teachers with higher efficacy beliefs try harder, attend more closely to low-performing students, and produce more positive student performance than do teachers with lower efficacy beliefs. Individual teachers' beliefs about the collective capability of the faculty are strong positive predictors of students' academic achievement across schools. In contrast to existing research, the Internal Coherence Framework focuses not only on the effects of having positive efficacy beliefs, but also on how schools with low efficacy levels develop more positive beliefs over time. Specifically, the Internal Coherence Framework and essential practices use evidence from social psychology to suggest ways to create efficacy-building experiences, including opportunities for teachers to try out new approaches and reflect on the resulting changes in student learning.

GUIDING PRINCIPLES

Leading organizational improvement requires the coordination of many people, teams, resources, and priorities. In fact, it can sometimes feel as though you are working on everything at once: the curriculum, how teachers use this curriculum with their students, how teachers are organized to work together around curriculum and instruction, and how leaders at the school and district level manage resources and other support to advance these efforts. Improving students' opportunities to learn can take many forms, depending on your organization's unique problem of practice. Despite these differences in focus, four core principles guide the internal coherence approach to school and system improvement:

▶ Internal coherence should be built around the instructional core.

▶ Improvement is a challenge of learning, not implementation.

▶ Mastery experiences change beliefs and behavior.

▶ Clinical practices and tools make research actionable.

In the sections that follow, we describe each of these principles and how they are reflected in the internal coherence approach to improvement.

Internal coherence should be built around the instructional core. Typically, practitioners and researchers focus on one piece of the puzzle at a time: implementing a new curricular program or instructional intervention, building productive teacher teams, or preparing instructional leaders. There is growing interest in creating collaborative structures for educators to work together.[8] Yet even though leaders can create opportunities for teamwork and leadership, this attention to routines and structures can lead to a doughnut-hole problem: schools work on building organizational conditions without a strong link to teaching and learning. In other words, there is a framework—the outside of the doughnut—but nothing in the middle. For example, schools invest resources and time required for teamwork without ensuring that the teams are advancing a coherent, ambitious instructional strategy. Consequently, teachers are going through the motions of collaboration without seeing changes in instructional practice and student learning.

The complex activities of teaching and learning rely on the interdependent actions of teachers and students working with content.[9] Therefore, teaching and learning do not improve just because leaders have chosen an instructional strategy or curriculum for teachers to implement. David Cohen and Deborah Ball proposed that instructional capacity for producing meaningful student learning is a function of the interactions among teachers' pedagogical and content knowledge; the use of educational materials; and students' understanding, experiences, and engagement in the learning process—a framework more commonly known as the *instructional core* (figure 1.2).[10] While the importance of these interactions may seem obvious, the history of educational reform reflects a pattern of adopting ambitious reforms while pairing them with limited support for educators to

FIGURE 1.2   The instructional core

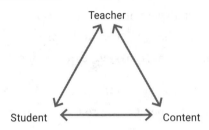

Source: Adapted from David K. Cohen and Deborah Loewenberg Ball, *Instruction, Capacity, and Improvement* (Philadelphia: Consortium for Policy Researchin Education, 1999).

integrate those reforms with their instruction and with limited awareness of how students interact with those resources.[11]

To understand the effects of reforms on student learning, leaders cannot just specify which instructional approaches are used, but must also understand how they are used and how students will interact with the approach.[12] Cohen and Ball argue that "teachers would need opportunities that were rooted in specific academic content, that explored and tested out well-designed curriculum materials for that content, and that offered convincing information about students' thinking and performance" to change their beliefs and instructional practice.[13] Leaders can play an important role in fostering such professional learning that is more comprehensively anchored in instruction.[14] When adopting new and rigorous standards for student learning, for example, teachers need opportunities to learn about and use high-quality curricular materials that align with these standards. They also need a way to gather evidence on how their students interact with those materials. If teachers lack opportunities to continuously reflect upon how the standards and curricular materials can enhance student learning, then they are unlikely to see the benefits of the new materials and may abandon them or use them only superficially.

Recently we worked with a district that had adopted a new mathematics program designed to give students opportunities to work collaboratively with their peers to solve challenging problems and justify their mathematical thinking. The new approach required students to work more independently and think at a higher level than they had with the previous curriculum. In other words, meeting the goals of the new curriculum required teachers and students to work in new and challenging ways. The district did what many districts do when adopting something new: it offered professional development workshops on how to use the new curriculum. In all the schools we visited, the teachers were using the new curriculum. However, how they did so—and how well the teachers and students understood the curriculum—varied widely.

In most schools, the teachers had adopted some but not all aspects of the curriculum, mainly focusing on the elements that more closely reflected their current practice. This was characterized by high levels of teacher direction and a focus on teaching mathematical processes rather than open-ended problem solving. In these schools, the leaders had ensured that all teachers attended professional development on the new curriculum. The leaders visited classrooms to monitor whether the teachers were using the curriculum and encouraged the teachers to work in their teams to plan together. However, there was little direction for sustained learning about the curriculum and how it could be used to raise the level of student learning in mathematics. Despite the limited understanding of the new curriculum, most teachers and leaders in these schools viewed the curriculum as something that was successfully in place at the end of the year, and they were ready to move on to a new focus. In these schools, the leaders overestimated the power of the intervention—the new curriculum—and underestimated the challenge of learning to use the curriculum in ways that would significantly change students' learning. This is a far-too-typical story in education reform. Educators adopt a research-based instructional intervention, require teachers to use it in their classrooms, move on to a new initiative, and wonder what happened when they don't see the corresponding improvements in student learning.

In some schools in this district, however, the administrators and teachers worked together to figure out how to use the new curriculum to change teaching and learning. The principals modeled challenging new practices, and the teachers jointly set goals in faculty meetings, co-planned in teams, and conducted peer observations to support learning and spread effective practices. In these schools, the administrators and teachers viewed the curriculum as representing a new way of teaching and engaged in collective learning to determine how they could use the materials with their students for more powerful learning. Schools that made greater progress in supporting students to engage in complex mathematical problem solving set shared goals for teaching and learning and coordinated the work of everyone in the organization—administrators, teachers, and teams—to meet these goals.

The internal coherence approach described in this book does not include or prescribe the use of specific instructional strategies or educational materials. Instead, the approach is designed to build teachers' collective capacity to achieve any shared goal for improving teaching and learning by aligning the work of everyone in the organization around the instructional core.

Improvement is a challenge of learning, not implementation. There is growing consensus among scholars that the success of any instructional intervention, improvement initiative, or policy is better understood as a challenge of teacher learning and organizational capacity building rather than a challenge of faithful implementation.[15] Teachers can only implement instructional practices that they already know how to perform. Asking teachers to work with students and content in new ways to produce better outcomes in student performance requires *learning*. Nevertheless, lofty goals for students, teachers, and schools are frequently matched with limited support for the learning necessary to change teachers' practice.[16] Furthermore, school and district leaders can exacerbate this problem when they frame improvement efforts as something all educators should be able to implement successfully given their current knowledge and skills, rather than something that will require new learning.[17] If educators knew how to tackle their persistent instructional challenges, they would already be doing it. Consequently, by helping teachers acknowledge and address what they do *not* yet know, leaders can guide teachers toward improvement.

One reason why others might think that improvement happens through implementation, rather than learning, is the weak connection between research on effective schools and the developmental process of transforming a school or system into a more effective organization. Research on effective schools, including high-poverty, high-performing schools, outlines the leadership practices, organizational processes, and conditions that exist at schools that outperform others. Researchers agree on the things that high-performing schools and leaders do: leaders focus on instruction and build trust, they select and use a curriculum that is aligned with content standards, and teachers collaborate around instruction. This research, however, does not document how schools develop over time into using these practices. How do schools and districts move from low-performing or stagnant to high-performing or improving?

A focus on the characteristics of high-performing schools can give a false impression that high performance is an issue of status—you have it or you don't—rather than a continuous process. This focus on status leaves lower-performing or stagnating schools with little direction on where to start and nominally higher-performing schools with little incentive to get better. Instead, we focus on a developmental approach to improvement, one that prioritizes creating the conditions for powerful teaching and learning over time.

Research from the Chicago Consortium on School Research takes a similar approach by focusing on the qualities of *improving* schools, namely, schools that initiated and maintained improvements in teaching and learning over time while performance in other schools was stable or declined.[18] The Internal Coherence Framework, described in detail above, builds on this research to provide specific guidance on the steps educators can take to generate these qualities where they are lacking and strengthen them where they exist. In the following chapters, we present both an essential practice that can be used to anchor your improvement efforts each year and additional learning experiences that can be used, given your organization's current strengths and challenges.

As educators, we believe that learning to improve is critical to advancing equity and learning opportunities for all students. While all schools have the potential to create the conditions that foster continuous improvement, schools serving large populations of students living in poverty often have the weakest levels of capacity to do so. Research shows that high-poverty schools have lower levels of capacity, on average, than do schools serving more affluent student populations, including less capable teachers, fewer opportunities for teachers to collaborate, and weaker principal leadership.[19] To ensure equitable opportunities for all students, leaders must provide direct support for developing internal coherence and improvement based on powerful learning in these schools. All students deserve to attend schools that continuously improve.

Mastery experiences, not inspiring rhetoric, change beliefs and practices. Just as it is hard to change the practices of teachers and leaders, it is difficult to change their beliefs about instruction and the abilities of their students. The phrase "all children can learn" has become a powerful and widely accepted notion in education. However, believing theoretically that all children are capable of learning is a far cry from educators' confidence in their ability to support all children's successful participation in rich, complex academic experiences. To address this more nuanced concern, schools must support the development of teacher agency, moving away from viewing teachers as implementers to viewing teachers as creators, researchers, and collaborators. Simply changing standards, curriculum, assessments, or programs is insufficient for substantially altering teaching and learning. For meaningful improvement to occur, educators need intensive and sustained opportunities for professional learning—opportunities that are aligned with school and district goals. Educators have rarely experienced the kinds of powerful learning that they are called on to produce for students. Most teachers themselves were taught in schools where lessons were delivered lecture-style and demonstrations of learning were dominated by memorizing and reporting facts. Thus, the first step toward achieving deeper learning more consistently across the sector is to raise the level of learning for educators, so that they can create these experiences for students.

It is through powerful experiences, rather than inspiring rhetoric, that adults and children change their beliefs about learning. Thomas Guskey, an expert in teachers' professional learning, argues that many professional development programs fail to change teachers' practice because they rely on developing commitment or buy-in to change teachers' beliefs before the educators have evidence that the practice, if carried out with their students, would lead to improvements in student learning.[20] This evidence—available through experimenting and reflecting on the effects of new practices—has the potential to change educators' beliefs about instruction and the abilities of their students. Guskey argues:

> Attitudes and beliefs about teaching in general are also largely derived from classroom experience. Teachers who have been consistently unsuccessful in helping students from educationally disadvantaged backgrounds to attain a high standard of learning, for example, are likely to believe these students are incapable of academic excellence. If, however, those teachers try a new instructional strategy and succeed in helping such students learn, their beliefs are likely to change. Again, the point is that evidence of improvement or positive change in the learning outcomes of students generally precedes, and may be a pre-requisite to, significant change in the attitudes and beliefs of most teachers.[21]

Many times, however, schools and systems adopt a new initiative or approach without giving teachers sufficient time or support to successfully use the new approach. This revolving door of solutions breeds cynicism among educators who have little faith in the next new thing. Continuous improvement requires an ongoing commitment to building coherence in an often changing and incoherent environment. The internal coherence approach to improvement focuses on providing educators the time and support necessary to generate learning outcomes for students beyond what the educators have previously thought possible. When leaders create the conditions to both enable and push educators to experiment with higher-level practices and offer enough support to help educators succeed, leaders can raise teachers' beliefs about what their students can do. Furthermore, when teachers improve student learning by working with their colleagues, they begin to see that powerful learning is primarily a function of the work they do with students and their colleagues, rather than mainly a function of factors beyond their control, such as students' prior knowledge or background characteristics. Close collaboration in teams can serve as a valuable process for supporting teachers in experimenting with, refining, and reflecting on new and more ambitious approaches to instruction and curriculum.[22] These collaborative experiences, in turn, can challenge teachers' beliefs about what they and their students can accomplish, including deficit views of low-performing students.

As is described in depth in chapter 8, increasing teachers' efficacy for collective improvement is both a desired outcome of the internal coherence approach to improvement and a strategy for generating higher learning outcomes over time. This book provides specific guidance for moving educators out of the role of those who implement programs with fidelity but with little investment in or responsibility for ensuring the success of the intervention. Instead, educators can play a greater role in improvement by working together to make sense of instructional interventions and challenges in their own contexts. Notably, this learning takes time and effort. It helps educators collaborate and empowers them to base changes to curriculum and instruction on their collective learning. Clearly, changing beliefs about instruction and student learning requires a collaborative, rather than a top-down, effort. The practices described in this book support the development of leadership broadly. This means not just creating leadership roles for individual teachers, but growing agency and authority among the faculty to make and contribute to key instructional decisions.

Clinical practices and tools make research actionable. Working with educators in schools and systems has deepened our conviction that educators learn to lead improvement by engaging in shared practices. As noted previously, translating evidence from research into specific actions in each unique organizational context is a complex process. We define *clinical practices* as evidence-based processes that are systematically developed and tested in the field, such that they assist practitioners in carrying out their core responsibilities effectively.

While clinical practices are a relatively new idea in education, they have a long history in such fields as medicine, law, and social work.[23] In medicine, for example, a patient would not expect a visit to the doctor to be organized according to the individual doctor's style and professional preferences. Instead, one would expect that the doctor would diagnose a patient's health problem methodically, drawing on both current knowledge from medical research to inform this process and data about the patient's current condition. The doctor would use specific tools to guide this process, such as a checklist that highlights key symptoms identified as predictors of a particular medical condition through research. Significantly, the clinical practices and tools described in this book, like those used in other fields, have been field-tested by practitioners across diverse settings.

Clinical practices and tools allow educators to apply research-based understandings to their unique school contexts. Each essential practice described in the book focuses on a key challenge of leading improvement—for example, creating supportive conditions for learning or assessing the capacity of the organization—and does so in a way that allows for schools facing unique challenges to use the practices to best meet their needs. The internal coherence approach makes the work of school improvement concrete and actionable.[24]

Presented in chapter 2, the Internal Coherence Survey is a clinical tool that leaders can use to gather information about how teachers view the current conditions in their organization. Similarly, the Internal Coherence Developmental Rubric is a self-assessment tool designed to help schools understand to what extent the practices, processes, and conditions essential for improvement are currently in place in their organization. The rubric also describes indicators for how schools grow and develop across the domains of leadership and organizational processes over time. Both the rubric and the survey are aligned with the Internal Coherence Framework and can be used to identify areas of organizational strengths and weaknesses that will support or constrain schools' ability to improve instruction and student learning broadly.

A BRIEF OVERVIEW OF THE BOOK

The book is designed to support readers with growing internal coherence in their own context. The chapters are organized according to the causal order of the Internal Coherence Framework, starting with the work of school and system leaders, moving to the importance of creating organizational structures and processes, and finally considering outcomes like collective efficacy and the corresponding effects on teacher and student learning. Each chapter provides the reader with an understanding of one area of organizational capacity, how it relates to a school's ability to improve the quality of instruction across classrooms, and a concrete practice for developing further in that area.

Chapter 2 provides a brief history of the Internal Coherence Research Project and how each engagement with practitioners led to the development of practical clinical tools: the Internal Coherence Survey, the Internal Coherence Developmental Rubric, and the professional learning series designed to support educators in understanding and using these tools.

Chapter 3 focuses on how leaders can create a climate of psychological safety and shift the learning culture in their school or district from one of individual learning to one that is a shared and public enterprise. This chapter discusses how the leadership team creates the critical conditions for developing a learning organization, including a safe space for experimenting with new practices, openness to diverse points of view, and the importance of constructive conflict within a shared purpose.

Chapter 4 presents research on the instructional core, the academic task, and a way to help leadership teams create a shared vision for teaching and learning to set the direction for an improvement strategy. The chapter includes a practice for collaboratively developing and assessing your vision to ensure that it is anchored in the instructional core and ambitious enough to require adults and students to learn in new and more rigorous ways.

Chapter 5 explains the concept of internal coherence and the connection between how the organization functions and the ability to carry out an improvement strategy to reach your vision. This chapter describes how to administer and make sense of a school's Internal Coherence Survey data, which require careful framing before they can be safely and productively analyzed by a group of educators.

Chapter 6 builds on both the ambitious vision for the instructional core established in chapter 4 and your analysis of the existing state of your organization from chapter 5 to develop a strategy to reach your vision. This chapter includes guidance for outlining the direction for teacher teams, building on organizational strengths, and tending to current organizational weaknesses.

Chapter 7 shows how leaders can better leverage opportunities for collaboration in teams to support improvements in teaching and learning. Because teacher teams are such an essential structure for executing a strategy and supporting the successful classroom experiences that change teachers' beliefs, the chapter deeply examines how leaders can elevate the relevance and depth of teachers' instructional talk in teams.

Chapter 8 describes the short-term outcome of the Internal Coherence Framework: the central role of teachers' efficacy beliefs in motivating continuous improvement. This chapter ties together all the factors in the Internal Coherence Framework by explaining how specific leadership and organizational practices help teachers adopt more rigorous instructional approaches, reflect on the efficacy of these approaches for student learning, and generate more positive beliefs about the collective ability of the organization to improve.

The book concludes with an afterword from practitioners working with the Central Valley Educational Leadership Institute (CVELI) at California State University, Fresno, and Clovis Unified School District in California. Having participated in multiple years of professional development to build internal coherence in their schools, these educators share reflections about their learning and recommend how schools might make the most of their improvement work.

TURNING RESEARCH INTO PRACTICE: KEY SECTIONS OF THE BOOK

Chapters 3, 4, 6, 7 and 8 introduce a domain of the Internal Coherence Framework, review the research base for the domain, and outline its practical implications for educators. Each of these chapters also includes three sections that make this research actionable: a *vignette* to illustrate common challenges to organizational improvement and the possible solutions; the *essential practices* or clinical practices, that leaders can use each year to set, revisit, and revise their improvement strategy; and the *foundational learning experiences* that leaders can use to help the faculty successfully carry out essential practices.

Vignettes

The vignettes illustrate common scenarios and dilemmas that schools face before they begin to organize for instructional improvement. The stories are based on what we have seen from more than five decades of collective experience in K–12 organizations.

Essential Practices

This book presents a system of research-based clinical practices and tools to support schoolwide improvement in teaching and learning. The tools have been tested and refined over ten years through partnership with educators in the field and were developed with district leaders and school leadership teams in California, Massachusetts, New York, and Texas. Throughout the book, we present actionable ways to raise the level of learning for adults and students in your school or system. These practices include methods for assessing your organization's current capacity using the Internal Coherence Survey, committing to shared learning as a leadership team, developing a vision for teaching and learning, and assessing the potential of teams' instructional conversations to realize a vision.

The essential practices described in this book provide strategies for applying what is known about effective instructional leadership to the challenges you face in leading continuous improvement. Although the Internal Coherence Framework provides the overarching guidance for engaging in improvement, each of the essential practices documents practical, concrete steps for engaging in the leadership, organizational, and instructional changes necessary for improving students' opportunities to learn.

Foundational Learning Experiences: Doing the Essential Practices Well

Because the essential practices in this book are derived from a broad base of research, leaders must understand the underlying scholarship to learn the practices. Without this deeper understanding, the essential practices can easily be reduced to a series of interesting yet disconnected activities that leave no last-ing impact. All of the authors of this book have witnessed school-improvement approaches like instructional rounds, data teams, or professional learning com-munities get reduced to a superficial level when they are adopted too quickly or, worse, become an exercise in compliance. In these cases, educators skip over the complexity of the work: "OK, now we're supposed to think of an instructional strategy to adopt. How about if all of us use a graphic organizer one time before the next meeting? Does that sound good? I'm going to write that on our commit-ment sheet. And we're done!"

We hope that the ideas and resources in this section will encourage leaders to move slow to go fast—or rather, move slow to go deep. Unlike the essential prac-tices themselves, which suggest a way for you to *do* the work of school improve-ment each year, foundational learning experiences enable you to keep the big ideas front and center and are necessary for doing the essential practice well. The foun-dational learning experiences often set the stage for the essential practices and lead up to them, but practitioners can go back to review a foundational learning expe-rience if they are having trouble with the essential practice. Although it may seem counterintuitive that the foundational learning experiences follow the essential practices in each chapter, this organization reflects the primary role of the essential practices in supporting ongoing improvement efforts. The foundational learning experiences will not require revisiting once practitioners have internalized their message, but they can be quickly referenced and used when inducting newcomers into the organization.

Finally, chapters 3, 4, 6, 7, and 8 conclude by connecting to the relevant sec-tions of the Internal Coherence Survey and Internal Coherence Developmental Rubric—two tools that readers can use to assess their strengths and weaknesses in one particular area as they undertake their work. The rubric provides a set of landmarks for practitioners to identify where they currently are and what they will see as they get better, and the survey lets teachers voice their opinion about their experience within the organization and yields data for educators to analyze when discussing current school capacity.

WHO SHOULD USE THIS BOOK?

This book is designed to support you as you take action to reach your goals for improving instruction and student learning. Teacher, school, and system leaders can all benefit from learning about the ideas and engaging in the collaborative practices presented here. Importantly, the book provides support for leading improvement broadly and is not tied to any particular instructional approach or curricular materials. We strongly recommend that educators engage with the ideas and practices in the book as part of a leadership team rather than individually. The internal coherence approach to improvement requires leadership that is shared broadly among educators at all levels of the school or system. Therefore, developing a leadership team composed of educators at multiple levels of the system, as our partners from the Central Valley Educational Leadership Institute explain in detail in the book's afterword, can play an important role in ensuring shared ownership for improvement goals. In addition, the leadership team serves as a concrete structure for supporting shared decision making. We briefly describe how school, district, and network leadership teams have used the approaches described in the book.

Schools

The internal coherence model of professional learning targets leadership teams, as opposed to principals alone, to maximize the likelihood that the model will be shared schoolwide and sustained over time, even in the face of principal turnover. The leadership team structure enables educators to actively construct knowledge both individually and through conversations among peers. In schools, this leadership team might include administrators and teachers who are responsible for setting the instructional focus for the school, seeking faculty input, and developing a strategy for improving teaching and learning in the area of focus. Teachers invited to participate in the leadership team may serve in a leadership capacity in their departments or grade levels, but this is not required: internal coherence leadership teams jointly facilitate practices and experiences with faculty, rather than sending individual members back to their respective teams in the capacity of expert. Researchers find that instruction and student learning is more likely to be high quality in schools where principals and teachers mutually contribute to leadership than in schools that lack teacher involvement in instructional decision making.[25] The practices included in this book can guide administrators and teachers who are working collectively to lead school improvement.

Districts

Leadership teams at the district level may include central office administrators who provide direct supervision to principals as well as the many district officials who support schools, such as curriculum and assessment coordinators. District leaders play a central role in supporting instructional leadership and improvement in schools.[26] A district-level leadership team can create greater coherence in the district office by coordinating support to school sites. In addition, close collaboration between district and school leaders can tighten the connection between the professional practices and improvement initiatives at the school and district level.

Networks

Networks of schools working to address common student learning challenges will also find the practices included in this book useful for coordinating their shared efforts. Networks can bring together educators within the school system and beyond. For example, as described in the chapter 2, a network of rural schools in California composed of school-, district-, and university-based educators used the internal coherence approach to coordinate their efforts to respond to the demands of newly adopted standards for college and career readiness. Developing a network can help bring together people and organizations to work on shared problems of practice and, in the process, can allow educators to share resources and access expertise that may otherwise be unavailable to them.

HOW THIS BOOK IS ORGANIZED, AND HOW TO APPROACH IT

Regardless of how you structure your learning experience, we recommend that you read the book once all the way through before beginning to use the practices and tools described in each chapter with your colleagues. While each chapter offers useful ideas and tools, the real power of the Internal Coherence Framework lies in the comprehensiveness of the approach for engaging in organizational improvement. Learning about the full model and set of essential practices will help you determine with whom you should partner, clarify the focus of your improvement efforts, and begin your work with a deeper understanding of the strengths and challenges you will face in your unique context.

The book is organized according to a recommended order, beginning with building trust and safety to engage in this work and resources for growing the foundational knowledge and shared language of the instructional core. Although chapter 2 provides an overview of the Internal Coherence Survey, you will learn how to understand and frame your survey data in your organization in chapter 5. After the initial survey administration, the "Connecting to Clinical Instruments" sections in chapters 3, 4, and 6 through 8 will become mutually reinforcing. Once you have additional years of survey data, you can refer back to selected chapters to seek guidance on challenging areas that have emerged from your data. We encourage you to draw on the ideas and practices in the book as you see fit for your own situation.

2

The Internal Coherence Research Project and Clinical Tools

The clinical tools and resources for professional learning shared in this book have been developed in partnership with school districts across the United States. This chapter introduces how the tools and practices were developed, used, and strengthened with educators in Massachusetts, Texas, and California. Specifically, we describe how we, as project members, learned from our partners in the field and how we translated those lessons into tools that other schools and districts can use. The Internal Coherence Survey, the Internal Coherence Developmental Rubric, and professional learning series support schools, districts, and networks in answering questions like these: Which schools are on the path to improvement? Why are some schools more successful than others with an instructional intervention? What actions can district and school leaders take to build the capacity of schools to improve student learning? How can our high-performing schools reach the next level of performance?

Our partnerships with school leadership teams, district administrators, and coaches have helped us acquire a deeper understanding of the organizational learning required for teachers if students are to master more demanding content with greater independence. These partnerships have been essential for developing, testing, and refining the essential practices described in this book. The chapter ends with a description of how we introduced these practices in Clovis, California, in a professional learning series that spanned two years. Hopefully, an overview of this series will help leaders envision what developing internal coherence might look like in their own contexts.

THE HISTORY OF THE INTERNAL COHERENCE RESEARCH PROJECT

The internal coherence model was first developed in 2007 as a project of the Strategic Education Research Partnership (SERP), a research and development organization designed to bring together scholars and practitioners to solve significant problems of practice in education. Recruited by the Boston Public Schools to tackle the district-identified challenge of middle school literacy, SERP tapped researchers from multiple universities, including the Harvard Graduate School of Education, to develop a comprehensive middle school literacy initiative for the district. This initiative produced new instructional materials that embedded vocabulary-rich discussion and debate into every subject area in middle schools. SERP researcher Richard Elmore observed that regardless of the caliber of the curriculum, challenges like whole-school improvement require an *organizational* response, and struggling schools often lack the structures and processes required for the organization to engage in collective learning. In fact, he argued, the Boston schools that stood to benefit the most from efforts to improve literacy instruction were likely to be those with the least capacity to respond productively to an external intervention. In response, SERP and district leaders challenged Elmore to develop a way to assess whether an individual school had the organizational readiness to make productive use of the literacy initiative and, if not, to offer ideas about how to build this capacity in schools where it was lacking. The Internal Coherence Research Project team was assembled to meet this challenge.

THE INTERNAL COHERENCE SURVEY: LEARNING FROM BOSTON

To assess a school's readiness to use an external intervention effectively, Internal Coherence Research Project researchers Elmore, Michelle Forman, and Elizabeth

Leisy Stosich, with initial contributions from visiting scholar Lasse Skogvold Isaksen, drew on research and existing surveys from the fields of education leadership, management, organizational learning, and social cognitive theory.[1] They developed a teacher survey to assess a school's existing capacity to leverage an instructional intervention for schoolwide improvement. This anonymous online survey is taken by everyone serving in an instructional capacity in a school. Initially piloted in Boston, the Internal Coherence Survey has since evolved over several iterations into its current form. Because the usefulness of clinical tools like the Internal Coherence Survey depends on their ability to measure research-based constructs and their appropriateness for a given context and purpose, one of the authors conducted a series of studies to assess and improve the construct validity and reliability of the survey.[2] These studies demonstrate that in its current form, the Internal Coherence Survey measures the conditions and processes—such as psychological safety, teachers' involvement in instructional decisions, and principal's support for teams—that the survey is designed to measure and does so reliably for schools serving diverse student populations. These studies provide compelling evidence that the survey can provide school leaders with information about specific practices, processes, and beliefs they can foster to improve instruction and student learning.

Consistent across the survey's iterations are the broad domains of leadership, whole-school and team-based organizational processes, and efficacy beliefs, as well as SERP's commitment to its use as both a diagnostic instrument and a teaching tool. Each domain of the Internal Coherence Framework is derived from research-based essential concepts that are associated with school improvement. Further, because the survey domains and items align with the order of operations articulated in the Internal Coherence Framework in chapter 1, leaders can translate their data from this survey into a logical series of steps to grow their organizational capacity as they enact a strategy for instructional improvement. This purpose serves the overarching goal of the Internal Coherence Research Project, which is designed to bridge the gap between research about what improving schools and systems do and what leaders can do in their organization given their current capacity.

The Internal Coherence Survey provides information about the elements that support or, if absent, constrain improvement efforts. Each survey item is based on specific actions school leaders and teachers can take to improve their collective practice. As described in chapter 1, the survey and the learning experiences and practices in this book are designed to be mutually reinforcing. Chapter 5 details how to administer and interpret the Internal Coherence Survey data in a school context. As leaders analyze their survey data, they will find it useful to revisit specific chapters that describe the practices and conditions assessed by the survey. Appendix A highlights which chapters contain information relevant to each set of items from the survey.

Each of the following chapters in the book will help readers understand a different domain of the Internal Coherence Survey, how survey responses can inform your improvement efforts, and the changes you may see in your survey data over time. Note that raising survey scores is not a goal in and of itself. In fact, as schools become more adept at whole-school learning and take on more and more ambitious goals for improving the instructional core, they could expect to see lower survey results in some areas. As practitioners deepen their understanding of what the conditions that support organizational improvement entail (i.e., what does a productive debate really look like?) or what actually constitutes effective practice, their standards may rise, causing their assessment of their existing capability to flag. Finally, to best understand how your survey data are connected to your instructional improvement strategy, we strongly recommend waiting to administer the survey until you have read chapters 3 through 8 and have a solid understanding of the big picture. Chapter 5 provides more detailed guidance on understanding your survey profile, as well as suggestions for anchoring your data in the larger discussion of vision and strategy with your faculty.

Using the Internal Coherence Survey with District Leaders in Boston

Once the Internal Coherence Survey had been developed, the superintendent of the Boston Public Schools employed it beyond the context of the SERP literacy intervention. At the time, Boston district leaders were concerned with building capacity in their lowest-performing schools, all of which served large populations of students living in poverty. These schools were some of the lowest-performing schools in the state and were in danger of being closed if they did not improve their students' test scores. Student performance on state assessments sent a clear message to the district that something needed to change in these schools. However, information about student performance provided little direction to principals and the district leaders who supported them about the actions they could take to improve student learning. In contrast, the Internal Coherence Survey provided a clearer picture of the strengths of leadership practice, the quality of professional development, and the level of collaboration among teachers in these schools. District and school leaders used this information to develop strategic plans for improving the conditions in these schools.

By way of example, two schools in Boston with comparable student demographics had achieved relatively similar scores on the statewide achievement test. However, a new principal in one school was beginning to establish regular collaboration in grade-level teams and provided frequent feedback on how teachers used the new literacy curriculum, a major win in a school where teachers had traditionally worked in isolation, with little input from the principal on their instruction. Since this principal had a clear vision for instruction and was making progress toward her goals for improving instruction, the district leader provided support for the principal's instructional goals by connecting her with additional resources for supporting professional learning in literacy and collaborative team practices. In addition, the district leader visited teacher team meetings with the principal to identify the next steps for supporting the work of teams, with particular attention to their work on literacy instruction. In another school, by contrast, the principal spent the majority of his time focused on student discipline with little attention to instruction. On the Internal Coherence Survey, teachers reported that the principal lacked a clear vision for teaching and learning and was not directly involved in helping teachers address instructional issues in their classrooms. The district leader worked intensively with this principal to establish an instructional focus and to create more opportunities for teachers to receive support and feedback on how they were working toward this vision.

Looking only at statewide assessment results in these two schools could have given the impression that they served similar student populations, had attained similar results for student learning, and thus needed similar support from the district. But the test scores failed to reflect the very different capacities for instructional improvement in these two schools and the implications for their next steps. Nationwide, there is a growing understanding that engaging in continuous improvement requires information not only about student performance but also about the school conditions and opportunities for professional learning that can foster student learning.[3] The district used data about the organizational practices within this group of underperforming schools, such as types of leadership behaviors or frequency of collaborative processes, to inform district support for each school's improvement strategy.

Understanding Teacher Perceptions in Boston

After administering the survey, one of the authors conducted research on how practitioners in some of the schools were responding to their data.[4] Despite the difficult implications of the survey results in one chronically underperforming school, the survey data generated excitement among many teachers because it indicated that there were steps they could take to address issues in the school at large. As they put it, their faculty had historically been given a series of classroom-based solutions for improving student learning—new curriculum, new instructional strategies, new assessments. Numerous teachers expressed frustration with this traditional reform strategy, which implied that for the school to improve, individual teachers needed to teach differently, teach harder, or teach *more*. These classroom-based solutions felt like an indictment of individual teachers' practices for bringing the school down, whereas many staff believed that they were already working heroically and to the best of their abilities within an inhospitable organizational structure. This frustration makes sense in the context of an underperforming school inundated for years with one instructional initiative after (or on top of) another.

In contrast, the internal coherence approach to school improvement recognizes the important roles that organizational culture and connected, aligned processes play in supporting the work of teachers and students in classrooms. Clearly, teachers matter for student learning, but that means that every person, structure, process, and resource in the organization needs to support teachers' efforts to succeed in the classroom. One veteran teacher in a chronically struggling school expressed her excitement at shifting the focus of the improvement strategy out of the individual classroom and into the larger organization: "When we took the [Internal Coherence] Survey . . . it [had] a lot of climate-type questions. I really got excited that we were really going to look at the climate of the building and services for the kids and student supports and how are we going to make it a stronger, safer learning environment." Although they had not previously formulated thoughts about organizational capacity or coherence in concrete terms, these teachers were aware that a sole focus on instructional strategies would never get the school where it needed to be. In Boston, we learned that in addition to providing leaders with diagnostic information about the current capacity of their organization, shifting the focus of school improvement from the work of individual teachers to the conditions that support adult learning and collaboration can reenergize schools, even those with a long history of dysfunction.

THE INTERNAL COHERENCE DEVELOPMENTAL RUBRIC: LEARNING FROM FORT WORTH, TEXAS

In 2011, the chief academic officer in Fort Worth, Texas, reached out to the Internal Coherence Research Project team to learn why some of his schools were thriving with a new district curriculum while other schools, serving comparable student populations, had been unable to make any progress with the new approach. With the addition of Candice Bocala, the team consulted with the district on improving the organizational capacity in the schools and developed a professional learning series for school and district leaders. These sessions aimed to help leaders move beyond setting goals in terms of student achievement gains and consider the changes in leadership practice and teacher collaboration that would be necessary to improve instruction and student learning. Specifically, the sessions were designed to assist the district with acting on what the past three decades of research on school leadership have surfaced: the essential leadership tasks for improving instructional quality and students' learning include articulating clear goals for instruction, coordinating instruction and curriculum, promoting teacher learning, and fostering organizational structures and conditions for teacher collaboration.[5]

The collaboration in Texas provided the opportunity to pilot the Internal Coherence Developmental Rubric, which was developed in its original form by Richard Elmore. Like the Internal Coherence Survey, the rubric focuses on the practices, conditions, and beliefs that research associates with schools that improve instruction and student learning. And like the survey, the rubric is designed to illustrate concretely how educators develop their ability to enact an instructional improvement strategy, rather than measuring the quality of school conditions in and of themselves. We have found the rubric to be a helpful tool for practitioners in several ways. It more explicitly presents the developmental orientation of growing internal coherence and clarifies what conditions in the organization will look like as they are fortified over time. In addition, the rubric has proved a more accessible entry point to the idea of organizational capacity than the more elaborate survey profile, which can feel overwhelming and abstract, particularly for those not used to thinking about schools as systems.

In its current version (table 2.1), the rubric is a preliminary tool for schools to self-assess their existing level of internal coherence before they receive their Internal Coherence Survey data. As we explain in more depth in chapter 5, the rubric helps practitioners see their survey data as a reflection of teachers' experience in the organization rather than as a measure of how much the faculty members like their principal or are satisfied with the school more generally. In addition, leaders can use the rubric to guide discussions with their faculty about specific practices and conditions essential for improving instruction and student learning at scale.

THE INTERNAL COHERENCE PROFESSIONAL LEARNING SERIES: LEARNING FROM CALIFORNIA AND NEW YORK

In 2013, the Central Valley Educational Leadership Institute (CVELI) at California State University, Fresno, reached out to the Internal Coherence Research Project team to support efforts in the region to make the instructional shifts required

TABLE 2.1 The Internal Coherence Rubric

BEGINNING	EMERGENT	PROFICIENT	EXEMPLARY
Leadership for learning			
■ Faculty perceives leadership emphasis on action and compliance. ■ Faculty prioritizes harmony and collegiality, avoids conflict. ■ Faculty fears consequences for experimentation, admitting mistakes, or questioning current practice.	■ Leaders are developing a focus on reflection, contributions from faculty. ■ There is limited faculty engagement in surfacing conflicting opinions or engaging in debate. ■ Faculty is developing comfort with discussing individual struggle with classroom practice.	■ Leaders routinely model their own learning process and solicit divergent opinions. ■ There is routine faculty engagement in productive debate over solutions. ■ Problems of practice are viewed as valuable data for collective analysis and behavioral change.	■ Leaders and teachers routinely engage in shared professional learning. ■ Leaders and teachers value rigorous interrogation of ideas to arrive at best solution. ■ Faculty perceives conflict amid community, has collective interest in moving beyond status quo.
Instructional leadership			
■ Leaders articulate vision in broad statements about vague goals. ■ Teachers describe what happens in classrooms by naming curriculum, activities, or standards separately from tasks. ■ Leadership lacks clear practice for observing or monitoring instruction.	■ Leaders articulate vision in terms of most components of the instructional core. ■ Teachers are acquiring language to describe or analyze academic tasks in classrooms. ■ Leaders have a limited practice for observing or monitoring instruction.	■ Leaders articulate vision by addressing what it will look like using all components of the instructional core. ■ Teachers consistently use language to describe or analyze academic tasks in classrooms. ■ Teachers understand which instructional decisions might raise or lower the level of task. ■ Leaders have clear practices in place for observing instruction as part of both individual evaluation and supporting collective instructional improvement.	■ Leaders articulate an ambitious vision that addresses all components of the instructional core and routinely assess their progress toward that vision. ■ Teachers understand and can routinely engage in discussion about the connection between instructional decisions and academic tasks. ■ Leaders and teachers have a shared understanding of the multiple purposes of classroom observation. ■ Teachers associate classroom observation with collective instructional improvement processes.

(continued)

TABLE 2.1   The Internal Coherence Rubric (*continued*)

BEGINNING	EMERGENT	PROFICIENT	EXEMPLARY
Organizational strategy			
▪ Leaders lack understanding of relationship between organizational structures, processes, and ability to reach instructional vision. ▪ Teachers perceive that professional learning is disconnected from the instructional vision or purpose of teams' work.	▪ Leaders are starting to connect professional learning and work of teacher teams to instructional vision. ▪ Leaders are beginning to develop a system of supports to focus the work of teacher teams. ▪ Teachers have limited understanding of connection between teamwork, professional learning, and instructional vision.	▪ Leaders clearly communicate an improvement strategy that aligns professional learning offerings, work of teacher teams, and instructional vision. ▪ Leaders clearly articulate purpose of teams' work aligned with the improvement strategy. ▪ Teachers are involved in developing the improvement strategy.	▪ Leaders and teachers routinely reflect on the improvement strategy and vision, in light of organizational data. ▪ Leaders and teachers revisit and adjust professional learning offerings and focus of teams' work according to progress toward vision.
Teacher teams			
▪ Teachers work in isolation from their teammates. ▪ Teachers rarely observe instruction or learning across classrooms. ▪ Team conversations reveal low depth of inquiry and low instructional relevance.	▪ Teams emphasize individual sharing without team expectations for commitment to action and reporting back to the team. ▪ Teachers are beginning to examine instruction and learning through artifacts such as student work. ▪ Team conversations reveal either deeper level of inquiry or increased instructional relevance.	▪ Teams have frequent tasks that require interdependent work and follow-through. ▪ Teachers have a routine practice of observing instruction and learning in classrooms or through video recording. ▪ Team conversations move consistently to deeper level of inquiry and more relevance.	▪ Teams reflect on the impact of their interdependent work on their teaching and learning. ▪ Teachers use their learning from classroom observations to revisit and revise their instructional plans. ▪ Teams have a practice for periodically examining their instructional conversations over time.
Collective efficacy			
▪ Teachers do not believe that control over what students learn lies with them, the teachers. ▪ Teachers generate beliefs about capability against individually derived standards. ▪ Teachers' perceptions of their colleagues' capabilities are informed by data peripheral to the instructional core.	▪ Teachers begin to connect instructional decisions with student learning. ▪ Teachers are moving closer to a collective standard for ambitious practice. ▪ Teachers are developing interest in observing classrooms to inform discussions of student data.	▪ Teachers have mastery experiences with more ambitious instructional practice as a consequence of learning with colleagues. ▪ Teachers consistently look to colleagues as sources of learning. ▪ Teachers interact under norms of effort, positive expectations, and persistence.	▪ Teachers' mastery experiences raise beliefs about what they, their colleagues, and the students are capable of. ▪ Teachers hold themselves and their colleagues accountable for student outcomes. ▪ Teachers view improvement as a collective challenge and peer observation as a tool for collective growth.

by the Common Core State Standards. Specifically, CVELI hoped to help principals and teachers increase their capability to engage students in Central Valley schools—characterized by high mobility rates, intergenerational poverty, and high percentages of English language learners—in rigorous academic work.

In collaboration with CVELI and local stakeholders from the district and the university, the team developed a professional learning series consisting of ten sessions to take place over two academic years. Central Valley leaders decided to roll out the series, which was titled Building Coherence for Instructional Improvement (BCII), using both team and network structures. The participants included leadership teams from all six elementary schools in a K–12 feeder system, their area superintendent, and the Central Valley leadership team from the university and county office who served as BCII coaches for the participating schools. From the outset, the intention of this collaboration was to use a turnkey approach. Therefore, after participating in the two-year series and observing how the Internal Coherence Research Project team facilitated the sessions, CVELI took over the facilitation of the next generation of the internal coherence professional learning series in other districts in the region.

The structure of the learning series brought together a network of participating school leadership teams, each composed the principal, administrators, teacher leaders, and instructional coaches, for a full-day off-site every two months. Leadership teams were responsible for actively learning the new material and for strategically applying this learning when they returned to their individual campuses after each session. BCII coaches and the area superintendent also attended all sessions and were responsible for providing follow-up support to principals and leadership teams at their school site between sessions. For each day, the morning was devoted to a short overview of the relevant research and participants engaged in text-based and active learning experiences. Each afternoon, the leadership teams and their BCII coaches convened to consolidate their understanding of the morning's work and to consider the implications of what they had learned for their particular context. Sessions concluded with the opportunity for leadership teams to present to another school their plans for applying their learning at their own school site and to open the presentation to questions and feedback.

The materials and learning experiences that made up these sessions are those that you will encounter in this book. The BCII participants analyzed the data on their own organizational conditions collected through the Internal Coherence Survey, and the leadership teams learned to engage their full faculties in the essential practices and the foundational learning experiences. From looking at data to setting a vision to ratcheting up the productivity of teachers' collaborative work, the BCII leadership teams changed the way educators worked together to improve the academic tasks in their buildings. Principals, teacher leaders, and district personnel participating in the two-year internal coherence professional learning series collectively agreed on their improvement goals. They advocated for school cultures that focus on learning and improvement rather than compliance, strengthened their professional communities, and transformed their beliefs about what they and their students could accomplish. The many insights that we gained from working with the Central Valley are manifest throughout the book, and specific lessons from this collaboration are presented by the Central Valley leadership team in the book's afterword.

In New York and California, we further developed the professional learning series through our partnerships with district leaders and Generation Ready leadership consultants in both states. As former teachers, principals, and superintendents, Generation Ready consultants provide job-embedded professional learning services to support educators with improving students' opportunities to learn. In this context, we designed foundational learning experiences to prepare district leaders and consultants to engage school leaders with the Internal Coherence Framework. In addition, our partnerships in these two states enabled us to refine our materials and practices. We improved how we help leaders understand concepts like efficacy and created opportunities for efficacy-building experiences in teacher teams.

The Internal Coherence Research Project team has worked in schools and districts with diverse environments—urban, suburban, and rural—and unique strengths, challenges, and student needs. Across these varied situations, one thing has been clear: Many of the practices we seek to influence are attached to deeply held belief systems or significant limitations in instructional knowledge and skill.

As a result, leaders cannot overlook the depth, breadth, and specificity of the learning that is required to translate research findings about improving schools into concrete action steps in a specific school situation. In *Learning to Improve: How America's Schools Can Get Better at Getting Better*, Anthony Bryk and his coauthors note: "Experiences across many different fields now caution humility about how much must be learned in order to transform successfully a change idea into new human capabilities, into day-to-day practices that work reliably, and into the redesign of organizational arrangements necessary to support all of this."[6]

The following chapters, each presenting an overview of the research, essential practices, and foundational learning experiences, are designed to successfully transform key ideas from research into new human capabilities and daily practice. We hope that your progression through these chapters with colleagues proves productive and gratifying along the way.

Committing to Public Learning

At Rockridge Middle School, grade-level teachers regularly examined student assessment data from their unit test results. The principal of the school believed strongly in the inquiry-cycle model of data analysis and frequently pushed the teachers to move from analysis of the data into concrete, actionable next steps.

Ariel, the fifth-grade team leader who taught mostly English language arts (ELA), was leading a team meeting. The team had noticed that on the most recent mathematics assessment, the students had scored poorly on questions requiring them to justify their choice of solution. Ariel suggested that it might be an issue of not understanding exactly what the question was asking, citing high numbers of English language learner students and the heavy language burden in the problems that gave students trouble. Because the group members were charged with finding a shared solution to complete their inquiry cycle and turn it in to their principal at the end of the meeting, Ariel suggested they dedicate more time in class to reading the problem. She asked the team's ELA teachers for strategies.

Another teacher on the team, Jacob, had a different idea. He had noticed that the school's current math curriculum was highly scaffolded, in contrast to the open-ended questions that appeared on the test. Not sure of his hypothesis that students fell down on these questions for lack of exposure to them over the year, and cognizant of his colleagues' desire to keep the discussion moving, Jacob kept his idea to himself and decided to check in with a friend who worked at another school.

Li, a new teacher who was struggling mightily with getting her students to do anything but say "Miss, what do I do here?" thought the root of the problem had to do more with behavior and persistence but had no idea where to begin to address it. Concerned that mentioning her struggle would not only slow down the team's work but also lead others to conclude she couldn't get her students to work for her the way the rest of them could, she also kept silent.

Conscious of the time and the fact that they had to turn in an action plan to their principal, Ariel pushed ahead with a think-aloud strategy that she was comfortable with—reading a math problem out loud and demonstrating how she would solve the problem. Since no others offered their own strategies, she proceeded to write down the strategy in the meeting notes and end the meeting. Li realized belatedly that she didn't quite understand what the think-aloud would look like in her classroom, and she resolved to ask a trusted colleague in another grade about it as soon as she could.

WHY DO WE CARE ABOUT PUBLIC LEARNING?

Turning schools whose educators learn (or don't learn) on their own into schools whose educators learn together requires a significant cultural shift. The only way to improve what students learn in classrooms is to increase teachers' knowledge of how to interact with their students around specific content. However, norms of privacy, isolation, and the tendency to attribute student outcomes to individual teaching style rather than specific professional practices have led practitioners to define positive school environments in ways that constrain organizational learning.[1] A positive work environment is often defined as one in which teachers try hard in their individual classrooms, enjoy friendly collegial relations, and have individual colleagues they can turn to without fear of judgment in a moment of need. In stark contrast to the qualities of a learning organization, ideas of trust and safety in public schools often revolve around being left alone to make sense of your own and your students' learning needs. For example, "My principal respects me as an educator and trusts me to do what's right for my students." There are benefits to working in collegial and harmonious environments to be sure, but none of them will lead to improving teaching and learning *across* the organization.

To engage in any of the essential practices or foundational learning experiences described in subsequent chapters, practitioners in schools and districts need to cultivate a shared sense of safety for learning in public. When educators feel comfortable engaging in public learning, they are more likely to admit that what they are currently doing in the classroom is not working. They feel freer to offer up ideas about teaching and learning—ideas that may be unpopular with peers— or they might take a leap of faith and attempt a practice beyond their comfort zone, despite the activity's risk of failure. When educators feel safe sharing their learning, the data on what is *not* working are considered a valuable insight to drive change. Because the Internal Coherence Framework requires educators to engage each other as learners, this chapter focuses on how leaders can turn their buildings into organizations devoted to shared adult learning. They can accomplish these goals in several ways:

▶ creating *psychological safety* for educators to engage in learning behaviors that carry a degree of interpersonal risk

▶ *modeling public learning*, so that educators learn that asking questions, examining all sides of an issue, and welcoming divergent viewpoints are valued

▶ scaffolding critical group learning practices like *constructive conflict* or *productive debate* to help practitioners push each other toward deeper engagement with problems of practice

WHAT THE RESEARCH SAYS

The Importance of Trust for School Improvement

The idea of trust holds much currency in education. Principals are charged with creating a climate of trust in schools, and well-known research on school improvement has found that an organization's level of relational trust is related to its academic productivity.[2] According to Anthony Bryk and Barbara Schneider, the authors of *Trust in Schools*, trust and student achievement are related because trust between colleagues serves as the fertile ground for technical resources, like new curricula or new standards, to take root in the organization and turn into something of value. When trust is strong, professional communities in which teachers strive for more ambitious classroom instruction function effectively, despite the risk that educators incur with behavioral change. Without this relational trust, teachers will withdraw from work that causes them to feel vulnerable, and they take refuge in the safety of their own classrooms to repeat past practice.[3]

Clearly, this willingness to be vulnerable in front of colleagues and take risks in front of a classroom of students is a prerequisite for growing internal coherence for instructional improvement. But how do leaders actually foster trust in schools? We have found that *psychological safety*, a construct closely related to trust and found in the management literature, readily lends itself to the developmental orientation of the internal coherence approach to school improvement. In other words, the idea of psychological safety has helped us to clarify the action steps required to create more positive conditions for learning in schools.

Psychological Safety for Organizational Learning

Amy Edmondson, a professor at the Harvard Business School and a scholar on learning organizations, defines a psychologically safe environment as one in which people speak up freely, unconstrained by the possibility of others' disapproval or fear of negative personal consequences.[4] Psychological safety is critical for understanding organizational learning, where learning occurs through interpersonal interactions and where individuals' concerns about consequences would otherwise shut down vital learning behaviors such as sharing information and knowledge, admitting mistakes, or asking for help. At Rockridge Middle School, for example, Li refrained from sharing her ideas or asking for help, because she feared that doing so would damage her colleagues' estimation of her abilities. Feelings of safety foster willingness to engage in improvement behaviors, including learning from failure, speaking up with suggestions to improve group process, or offering ideas that challenge the status quo.[5]

Studies in health-care organizations find that psychological safety enables teams to conduct experimental learn-how activities such as pilot projects and problem-solving cycles. These activities come with a level of interpersonal risk, including the fear of failing to achieve one's goals and the anxiety created by feelings of incompetence during learning.[6] Research also holds that feelings of safety promote individuals' willingness to participate in team learning experiences and help them overcome the anxiety and defensiveness commonly experienced when people are presented with data that may contradict their expectations or hopes.[7] Without psychological safety, teachers are more likely to act in ways that diminish learning behavior. They might withdraw from the team and its work or retreat to their own classrooms to do what they have always done.

Leadership Practices That Foster Public Learning

The management literature articulates the cluster of behaviors that leaders can employ to signal the importance of learning in an organization. Studies of leadership behaviors and their consequences for organizational learning in contexts from manufacturing to health care to the US Army suggest that many practices can indicate an appreciation for others' contributions:

- ▶ When leaders actively question and listen to employees, they prompt dialogue and debate and encourage others to engage in these learning behaviors.
- ▶ If leaders spend time on activities like problem identification, knowledge sharing, or reflections, they signal the importance of these activities and may cause them to flourish.
- ▶ When leaders press for active reasoning or creative solutions, they signal that conventional approaches require scrutiny before being adopted.
- ▶ When leaders demonstrate concern for alternative or minority viewpoints, employees whose voices might otherwise be silent feel emboldened to speak up.
- ▶ If leaders stress the importance of error analysis as a learning tool, they increase educators' sense of safety for offering up mistakes.
- ▶ Leaders who acknowledge the value of individuals' specialized body of knowledge to the shared task equalize contributions across levels of authority and promote an egalitarian atmosphere.

▶ When leaders carve out enough time for practitioners to engage thoughtfully in cycles of joint learning, they signal the importance of analytical thinking and learning from experience.[8]

Educators at every level of a system feel the pressure to *act*: to comply with external mandates, to implement initiatives to improve, to take on any programs or resources that might benefit vulnerable students. Although the specific behaviors listed above sound straightforward, leaders who privilege taking time to reflect, to examine all sides of an issue, and to honor dissenting or minority viewpoints are engaging in a radical act: granting people permission to slow down the action and think. Imagine if the task for the teacher team in the opening vignette was not to analyze the data and immediately come up with an action plan, but to analyze the data and generate a list of possible root causes driving their identified problem of practice. With the latter as their team task, Jacob and Li would have had no cause to withhold their divergent ideas for fear of disrupting an efficient process. Instead, their divergent hypotheses would have been contributions of value.

Asking leaders to engage in genuine learning amid people they traditionally supervise can also require a leap of faith. Traditional notions of a strong leader involve someone with all the answers, and the prospect of acknowledging a limitation in knowledge or expertise may feel like admitting weakness in public. However, more recent research on school improvement suggests that instruction is of higher quality and students achieve at higher levels in schools where principals create opportunities for teachers to engage in shared leadership and decision making than in schools with principals who do not engage in these practices.[9] Shared leadership is particularly important for engaging in the internal coherence professional learning experiences.

Throughout this book, we show that the value of a school's or district's progress will hinge entirely on the richness of the conversations leaders and their colleagues generate along the way, as social learning theorists Jean Lave and Etienne Wenger propose that educators learn through negotiating meaning with others.[10] Making your way together through the foundational learning experiences and essential practices in this book will position you to engage much more deeply in any instructional improvement initiative you adopt hereafter, because you will have generated a common language able to convey vast shared understandings about instructional practice and your collective improvement work. The remainder of the chapter is devoted to resources and learning experiences for you to take the first steps toward becoming a learning organization.

TURNING RESEARCH INTO PRACTICE

The essential practices in this book are designed for leaders to use with colleagues as a means to enact their improvement goals each year. This chapter's essential practice focuses on creating a psychologically safe environment to increase people's willingness to actively and honestly contribute their ideas, evaluations, or suggestions for change. Making commitments for shared learning is one concrete strategy that leaders can use to signal how seriously they take educators' willingness to engage in productive collaboration around instruction. The commitment to shared learning was developed as an alternative to a more traditional norm-setting activity, wherein participants list a set of behaviors or actions that they all agree to abide by when working together. Norm-setting activities can produce important guidelines for effective team function, but they frequently focus on appropriate ways to behave during meetings—for example, "start and end on time," "set electronic devices to silent mode," or "come prepared"—rather than on supporting each other as learners. These types of norms may not create a safe environment for high-risk behaviors like admitting confusion, asking for help, or speaking up with counter-suggestions. Whole-school improvement requires that all group members adapt their practice in response to organizational objectives. The shift from norms to commitments to shared learning emphasizes that groups should develop ways of working not just to be respectful and to use time productively, but to support each other in understanding an identified problem of practice, evaluating possible solutions, and committing to new courses of action.

Making commitments to shared learning enables participants to become more aware of their own learning needs and to practice the kind of honesty and vulnerability that builds a shared sense of safety. Once people feel like their requirements are of value to the group and will be honored by others, individuals are free to focus on collective goals rather than on self-protection.[11]

ESSENTIAL PRACTICE
COMMITTING TO SHARED LEARNING

Focusing on collective learning in teams, rather than only individual learning, is essential for schoolwide improvement. Developing and regularly revisiting learning commitments can help practitioners work together and encourage contributions from all members of the group. These commitments can foster shared learning among individuals with different perspectives, experience, roles, and preferences for collaborating. The act of discussing and then agreeing to collective learning commitments is a critical aspect of this practice. Without the learning commitments, the open sharing and reflection will have no effect on the way the team functions or the cultural norms being formed. By translating the learning needs of the individual members into implications for how the team will operate, team members make a commitment to work differently and with an intentional focus on everyone's learning.

Objective. Develop collective learning commitments, or cultural norms, that describe how you will support the learning of all members of the team.

Time: 45 minutes

1. Individual Write [5 minutes]

Respond to these questions first individually:
- What supports your individual learning?
- What shuts down your individual learning?

2. Group Share [15 minutes]

Each member of the group takes a turn sharing what circumstances support and shut down their individual learning. Each then considers the implications for their work in the team setting. The facilitator writes the group's responses related to the following questions:

- What supports and what shuts down your individual learning?
- What team conditions would support or shut down your learning in this group?

3. Chart Commitments [15 minutes]

As a group, discuss this question: What are the implications for how your group will operate? Chart (i.e., write down on large paper for everyone to view) the commitments you will make to each other to foster group learning. Synthesize, prioritize, and document the most important commitments.

4. Plan [10 minutes]

As a group, discuss the following question: When and how will you revisit these commitments to support your learning over time? Chart a few next steps or capture your plans in the notes from the meeting, and schedule a time to return to your commitments in future meetings.

By participating in this essential practice, every individual in the group has a chance to reflect on factors that both support and shut down their learning process. For example, one team member might admit to having difficulty processing written information in the moment and would prefer to receive any reading material ahead of time to review it thoughtfully at his own pace. Knowing this, the team might agree to send any reading material at least one day in advance of their meetings. Another team member might explain that she needs to think aloud when she processes new information and that she hopes her colleagues will not get impatient with her as she talks through new ideas and poses questions until she understands. Knowledge of this member's learning style might lead the team to affirm the importance of taking an inquiry stance and commit to airing all questions about new ideas as a matter of course in meetings.

Imagine if the members of the team at the Rockridge school, described at the beginning of the chapter, had made a commitment to rigorously interrogate all potential solutions before choosing one. Jacob might have felt it was his obligation to the team—rather than a drag on the team's efficiency—to voice his alternative hypothesis. During the commitment protocol, Li, the new teacher, might have voiced her anxiety that sharing a problem in her classroom would lead her colleagues to think she was a doing a poor job. Had she voiced this concern, the team might have made a commitment to understand that asking for help be understood as a desire to improve. Able to reference this promise, Li might have been bold enough to bring her problem of practice to her team members for help ("OK, I'm going to demonstrate my desire to improve here and say that I have no idea how I'd get my students to answer those questions or even how to get them to work on any problem independently. All they do is ask for my help until I've practically done it for them, and I don't know how to build their independence"). Rather than attempt to layer a new think-aloud strategy on top of her existing challenges, she might have secured some assistance from her colleagues to meet her where she was and help her build her foundational expertise.

Developing the Essential Practice Over Time

This internal coherence essential practice can be used multiple times, across each team configuration, for collective work in an organization. Psychological safety is a *local* phenomenon, which means that an individual's willingness to engage in learning behaviors in one team might be entirely different from the person's comfort in another team (e.g., a grade-level team versus a leadership team), depending on the personalities, the nature of the team's work, or the cultural norms of the group.[12] School leaders may build commitments among the faculty as a whole, but they should also advocate for individual teacher teams to create learning commitments. Similarly, district leaders are encouraged to develop learning commitments as part of the different teams with which they may work. Once schools and teams develop their commitments for learning, the promises should be recorded on a poster or in a shared document, so that the team can revisit and, if necessary, revise them regularly. Further, leaders should model the practice of referring back to commitments periodically, so that practitioners reflect on their processes for acquiring and acting on new information to ensure they are as effective as possible.

For example, at Rockridge, after completing an inquiry cycle and reviewing their team commitments, team members might pose questions like "Did everyone on the team participate in our last round of problem solving?" "Did anyone feel like he or she carried an undue burden?" "Do we need a new protocol to be sure to capture everyone's best thinking the next time around?" Through discussions like these, practitioners can see how well they have adhered to their commitments and decide if their commitments are still the best ones or could be adapted to further improve the group's productivity.

FOUNDATIONAL LEARNING EXPERIENCES

Real psychological safety for organizational learning requires more than a formal set of commitments for respecting colleagues' learning. To create an environment that encourages the best interdependent thinking from all members of group, we need to move beyond mere tolerance of different opinions or styles toward an appreciation for them. Research from a variety of fields shows the importance of conflicting opinions for promoting creativity, sparking innovation, increasing team energy and motivation, and preventing complacence.[13] However, in many organizations, outspoken individuals with opinions that differ from the majority are viewed with frustration as a roadblock to a smooth, efficient group process. If you discover—at any point—that this dynamic is an issue in your organization, we suggest spending some time with colleagues learning how differences of opinion actually provide value for group motivation and creativity. The following resources can help cultivate empathy for different work styles, an openness to divergent ideas, and an understanding that conflict among groups of people trying to solve complex problems is a sign of productivity rather than dysfunction.

Appreciation of Difference

You can use a protocol such as Compass Points, developed by the National School Reform Faculty, to help participants understand how their work styles affect each other in a group setting.[14] (For a list of protocols and readings referenced in this book, see appendix B.) Similar to a personality inventory like the Myers-Briggs but focused more narrowly on the way we work with others in teams, this protocol is both an enjoyable and a helpful exercise. Start this protocol by explaining how each direction on the compass is associated with a description of preferences for working in a group setting. A north, for example, is someone with an action orientation, someone who likes to try things right away or plunge in. An east is defined as a speculator, someone who wants to spend time on the big picture and weigh various possibilities before acting. A west needs clarification on the details before comfortably moving forward, and a south is concerned with participation and wants to ensure that all voices have been heard and feelings have been taken into consideration before acting. Participants decide which compass point most matches their preference for working in a group, and they form a group with others of the same direction. The members of each compass point group discuss the following questions, which are documented further in the full protocol:

▶ What are the strengths of our style?
▶ What are the limitations of our style?
▶ Who do we find it most difficult to work with, and why? What do we most appreciate about other styles?
▶ What do people from other "directions" need to understand about us to work with us effectively?

This protocol, which includes a full group share and some prompts for further processing, can be run in individual teams and with entire faculties. We have seen it done well in groups of seven and groups of one hundred. By the end of the experience, participants will have a better understanding of what drives their colleagues' behavior and how their own work style affects others. In addition, this protocol provides participants a safe and shared language to address some real sources of conflict that emerge in a group setting: "Forgive me! I know I'm taking a north perspective here, but we need to come to a decision in the next ten minutes. Do the wests among us need any more details before we can commit something to paper?" We have found that after participating in this learning experience, team members take a lighter touch with what can otherwise be a source of deep frustration, and they can also see the value added by colleagues whose approaches were once viewed in purely oppositional terms.

The Importance of Divergent Opinions

Another possibility for group learning extends beyond empathy for different styles to building understanding that out-of-synch contributions can contribute to our best work. Environments that support organizational learning are characterized by an openness to new ideas—the understanding that learning is not limited to solving problems from a menu of known solutions, but also involves envisioning novel solutions to move beyond the status quo.[15] When educators recognize the value of divergent outlooks for their ability to increase energy and motivation, prompt creative thinking, and prevent complacency or stagnation, groups can shift from framing outliers as roadblocks to productive contributors.[16]

To grow this shared understanding, we suggest that teams collectively read the 2012 *New Yorker* article "Groupthink" by Jonah Lehrer.[17] The article is an accessible but substantive read on the strategies able to generate the most creative or innovative solutions from a group. In brief, Lehrer recognizes that the problems we have left to solve in science—just as in education—are incredibly complex, requiring people work together to generate creative solutions or to fail alone. He presents a "scientific debunking" of the myth that brainstorming, where groups generate as many ideas as possible without any pushback or critique, is the best strategy to unleash individuals' creative potential. We recommend pairing the reading with a protocol to discuss the text like "Save the Last Word for ME," developed by the National School Reform Faculty.[18] In this protocol, participants select a section of the text that resonated with them, and each person takes a turn sharing the quotation with the group. Group members each have an opportunity to react to the quotation, but the person who shared first is the last one to speak. Using the protocol, educators will have the opportunity to reflect as a group on the Lehrer article's takeaways, such as the following observations:

▶ Exposure to unfamiliar views—even clearly wrong ones—expands our creative potential because we have to work to understand them, which causes us to reevaluate our initial assumptions and try out new perspectives.

▶ Environments that extract the most from people are characterized by intellectual diversity and a vigorous exchange of clashing ideas.

▶ Teams instructed to debate and even criticize each other's ideas generated 20 percent more solutions than those instructed to brainstorm without any negative feedback.

▶ Debate and criticism do not inhibit ideas but rather stimulate them, encouraging us to engage more fully with the work of others.

▶ The most creative teams have a mix of old friends and newcomers, which gives the teams a familiar structure to fall back on and the spark to generate new ideas—they are comfortable with each other, but not too comfortable.

After reading and discussing the article, practitioners will think differently about traditional notions of good and bad teams. Moreover, the participants who are traditionally viewed as disruptive may enjoy a more welcome reception and an enhanced sense of value in the group.

Constructive Challenge

Another excellent piece of research to share with faculty or colleagues is Betty Achinstein's article "Conflict Amid Community: The Micropolitics of Teacher Collaboration," which looks specifically at conflict in the context of teachers' professional communities.[19] Achinstein's study of two public middle schools demonstrates that how teachers suppress or embrace their differences influences their potential for organizational learning and change. Harmonious, highly bonded communities may become static settings with few opportunities for reflection or transformation. When communities privilege relationships or are based on friendship, they may limit teachers' opportunities for professional development, as like minds reduce access to alternative perspectives and do not address weakness in professional practice.[20] Communities that embrace conflict, on the other hand, acknowledge and critically reflect on their differences of belief and practice, seek out alternative perspectives and active dissent as a means to question their core values, and engage in ongoing inquiry and change.[21]

Importantly, Achinstein acknowledges both the benefits that accrue to teachers who work in a harmonious environment and the fact that engaging in ongoing conflict can be painful and frustrating. She encourages communities to develop a common, shared purpose, which will help them maintain connectedness while sustaining the constructive controversy required for learning.[22] We have developed the foundational learning experiences and essential practices in this same spirit, to provide practitioners with structured ways to express and reflect on their disagreements within the shared purpose of improving instructional decisions and student learning. When practitioners engage in lively and productive disagreement—while also maintaining predictable routines, clear instructional connections, and psychological safety—they enjoy optimal conditions for developing innovative solutions to complex problems of teaching and learning to go beyond the status quo.

In chapter 7, we focus on the idea of conflict within community as a way for teams to change from venues for voluntary individual learning to sites of collective deliberation and commitment to behavioral change. In her research on teacher teams, Susan Henry, a colleague from the Harvard Graduate School of Education, analyzed the discussion patterns of teacher teams to determine the specific qualities most likely to enhance educators' collective ability to improve teaching and learning.[23] She concluded that discussions marked by a level of "cognitive tension," where educators constructively challenged the ideas, practices, or assumptions of the group, were more likely to enhance group-level understanding. This understanding arises because educators engage with each other to synthesize information, collectively weigh options, and determine group priorities before they can develop a degree of consensus. When team members use their time together to interrogate the merits of possible solutions to problems of practice before committing to a course of action, they engage in what Judith Warren Little calls "joint or interdependent work"; this enables them to develop an understanding or devise courses of action more effectively than they could have on their own.[24]

Because norms of collegiality are so strong in our K–12 system, and because educators have traditionally learned to talk about instruction in terms of innate qualities like a teacher's style or ability to connect with students, practitioners have real trouble engaging in Achinstein's play of conflicting ideas around teaching and learning. To help educators safely partake in productive debate, we developed a highly scaffolded protocol based on the characteristics of interdependent team talk that Henry identifies. We introduce this protocol here because the ability to push back on ideas until a group of educators has arrived at the best solution is a skill that leaders should cultivate schoolwide. However, because psychological safety is a "local" quality particular to individual groups, we suggest in chapter 7 that this protocol also be conducted in the context of individual teams.

PROTOCOL
EMPLOYING CONSTRUCTIVE CHALLENGE

Conflict in teams is essential for supporting team members in challenging their assumptions, changing their beliefs and actions, and transforming their practice. Rushing to agreement can stifle creativity and innovation in teams, but subjecting possible solutions to a rigorous vetting process will take advantage of the divergent beliefs and practices of the team members. This protocol is designed to support team members in engaging in *constructive challenge*, or pushing back on group members' thinking to advance the shared goals of the team.

Time: 35 minutes

1. Read and Reflect [10 minutes]

Read the six examples of constructive challenges below. Then discuss as a group: Have you or other members of your team engaged in these kinds of constructive challenges? How did others respond? How did the challenges influence your work as a group?

- *Question interpretations.* "I hear you saying . . . Is that right?"
- *Check assumptions.* "So does this mean you're assuming that they didn't get it the first time because . . . ?"

- *Play devil's advocate, or push back on ideas.* "But if we keep scaffolding, will they ever learn to do it on their own?"
- *Surface underlying tensions.* "So on the one hand, Linda is concerned about . . . But on the other, Derek fears this might . . ."
- *Examine group hypotheses.* "OK, so what we're saying is that if we all . . . , then we will see . . ."
- *Reframe the group's collective understanding.* "So what we decided today is . . ."

2. Trying On Ways of Talking [15 minutes]

The goal of constructive challenge is to clarify a person's reasoning behind his or her proposed solutions and to push the group's thinking forward in a productive manner. There are two main roles: a facilitator and recorder. The facilitator selects one person from the group to be the problem solver, and the remaining members of the team (except for the recorder) are the constructive challengers. The recorder takes notes about the dialogue between the problem solver and the challengers and should be prepared to offer overall reflections at the end of the activity, rather than contribute to the discussion.

> *Scenario:* You are working as a team of teachers and administrators to review data from a recent argumentative writing assignment. After reviewing the student work as a team, you notice two patterns. Students generally made clear claims and documented evidence from multiple sources. However, most students provided limited and sometimes unclear justifications for how the evidence supported their claims.

Have the problem solver offer an initial solution to the problem identified in the scenario.

Next, have the others constructively challenge the proposed solution. They should use the methods suggested in step 1 (e.g., play devil's advocate, question the solver's interpretation of the problem). Encourage them to use as many of the methods as they can.

Give the problem solver and challengers five to ten minutes to engage in this productive process.

3. Reflect and Debrief [10 minutes]

At the end, have the recorder share out what he or she noticed about the discussion and what happened when these instances of constructive challenge took place. Discuss as a group:

- What was it like having that conversation?
- What felt familiar? Unfamiliar?
- Did engaging in constructive challenge influence the depth of your instructional conversation?
- How might we support this type of conversation in teams?

Like all other discussion protocols, constructive challenge is especially useful in helping educators develop enough trust in, and facility with, the strategies to engage in them naturally. Also, the protocol can be adapted in various ways to best fit your situation. To make the most of this exercise, choose a scenario that is not too complex or cognitively challenging, because the participants should spend most of their mental energy trying on the various ways of talking to each other rather than actually solving an important problem. Further, depending on the participants' level of anxiety with pushing back on their peers, consider how close the scenario is to their real work. The experience becomes more high-stakes the closer the scenario gets to an actual problem of practice, so using a platform that is divorced from reality may make the exercise easier at first. For example, the group might debate a solution to the problem of congestion in the parking lot at dismissal or come to agreement on which character from a current television show would make an ideal superintendent in their district, and why.

A final suggestion comes from our California partners, who were extremely invested, initially in maintaining collegiality. Leaders can scaffold the experience even more dramatically by printing each constructive challenge prompt on an index card and requiring participants to draw one from the deck. With this adaptation, folks have even less personal responsibility for using this difficult language, which may facilitate their willing participation.

Imagine how the discussion in the Rockridge teacher team might have been different if their educators were well versed in the language of constructive challenge:

ARIEL: So, we're seeing that students are doing poorly on the questions that require them to show solutions and to justify their choice of solution over another, right? You know what I'm thinking? When I look at these problems, I see a heavy language burden, and I'm guessing that our students, especially our English language learners, are falling down on just understanding what the problem is asking. We should probably spend more time with them on hearing mathematical language. What if we did think-alouds in math like we do for ELA? We could use that as our action step.

JACOB: OK, so I hear you saying that you think the reason they're falling down is primarily an issue of reading and not mathematics. Is that right?

ARIEL: I'm not sure. I'm just noticing the language in these problems, and I know this is an area of struggle for our kids.

JACOB: They definitely struggle with the reading, but I was also thinking about our curriculum. We almost never use problems like this during the year. At least in my class—if people are doing it differently, let me know—I feel like we usually *give* them the procedure for finding the solution, and then they just have to do the procedure. When they have these questions on the test, it's totally new for them.

LI: I'm a little embarrassed to say this, but given what's happening in my class, even when I tell them what strategy they should be using to solve a problem, they still don't get anywhere. They just keep asking for more and more clarification. I feel like they're just trying to get me to do the work for them. I can't imagine them ever being able to do what a problem like the one on the assessment is asking.

ARIEL: So, you are saying . . . ?

LI: I don't know exactly, but maybe we need to help them be more persistent in general. Or to care more about their work. They just want to do the bare minimum to get credit.

ARIEL: OK. So we have three ideas on the table. One is that they are getting tripped up by reading and understanding what the problem is asking. Another is that our curriculum doesn't include problems that ask what these test questions ask, so the kids are not prepared. Another is that they lack persistence or don't care enough to stick it out. Is that what we have so far?

JACOB: I need to push back a little on the idea of persistence in general or the idea of them caring. I mean, I agree that we see kids giving up in the middle of problems, but I doubt it's because they fundamentally don't care, right? It's more of a function of what we're doing and how we're teaching. Because if you look at some of the kids who lack engagement during a math class when they're in ELA or in sports after school, they might be super engaged. I think we need to understand their actions as a consequence of what's happening in the class, because otherwise, we have no way to change anything.

ARIEL: All right. It seems like what we've decided is, we don't exactly know what's driving their trouble with these types of questions. And the problem may be different in different classes. Should we agree as a next step to discuss how we might understand what's really going on?

CONNECTING TO CLINICAL INSTRUMENTS

As we show throughout this book, no one builds a learning organization in "five easy steps." The essential practices, learning experiences, and other resources in this chapter are necessary to get traction in this long-term work. If you and other leaders can make commitments to one another by working on the recommendations in this chapter, you will have a strong foundation for the experiences in the upcoming chapters. You can more safely and candidly discuss your current performance in relation to a vision for the future, and you and your colleagues will feel comfortable enough to voice issues of concern about, for example, the way teacher teams are currently functioning or the relevance of the professional learning program to the real challenges in the classroom. In addition, as you progress together through the following chapters, supporting teachers' efforts to bring their ideas and their struggles into the collective sphere, psychological safety and faculty trust in leadership will grow.

The Internal Coherence Developmental Rubric provides a set of landmarks for practitioners to identify where they currently are and what they will see as they get better. The first line of the developmental rubric describes how a school faculty might progress as the faculty cultivates leadership actions and beliefs that support public learning and psychological safety.

The Internal Coherence Developmental Rubric: leadership for learning

BEGINNING	EMERGENT	PROFICIENT	EXEMPLARY
▪ Faculty perceives leadership emphasis on action and compliance. ▪ Faculty prioritizes harmony and collegiality, avoids conflict. ▪ Faculty fears consequences for experimentation, admitting mistakes, or questioning current practice.	▪ Leaders are developing a focus on reflection, contributions from faculty. ▪ There is limited faculty engagement in surfacing conflicting opinions or engaging in debate. ▪ Faculty is developing comfort with discussing individual struggle with classroom practice.	▪ Leaders routinely model their own learning process and solicit divergent opinions. ▪ There is routine faculty engagement in productive debate over solutions. ▪ Problems of practice are viewed as valuable data for collective analysis and behavioral change.	▪ Leaders and teachers routinely engage in shared professional learning. ▪ Leaders and teachers value rigorous interrogation of ideas to arrive at best solution. ▪ Faculty perceives conflict amid community, has collective interest in moving beyond status quo.

Once you have administered the Internal Coherence Survey in your organization, a process covered in chapter 5, you may wish to return to this chapter for strategies to bolster safety for public learning if either domain below is cause for concern.

Internal Coherence Survey Items: Modeling Public Learning

These survey items name specific actions that the research associates with leaders who promote organizational learning. When leaders collect and make public the faculty perceptions of their leadership behavior, they demonstrate openness and vulnerability, which in and of itself can be powerful for increasing faculty willingness to do the same. Data on this factor provide leaders with concrete next steps and an opportunity for reflection, especially if the faculty's perception of the leader's engagement in the behaviors differs from the leader's own views.

ASSESSING PUBLIC LEARNING

▶ The principal invites input from faculty in discussions about teaching and learning.

▶ The principal asks probing questions about teaching and learning.

▶ The principal listens attentively.

▶ The principal encourages multiple points of view.

▶ The principal acknowledges the limitations of his or her own knowledge or expertise.

Internal Coherence Survey Items: Psychological Safety

When leaders engage in the types of learning behaviors and facilitate the experiences and essential practice in this chapter, the faculty will eventually feel safer assessing with others the strengths and weaknesses of their instructional practice.

ASSESSING PSYCHOLOGICAL SAFETY

▶ People in this school are eager to share information about what does and does not work.

▶ Making mistakes is considered part of the learning process in our school.

▶ If I make a mistake at this school, it will not be held against me.

▶ In this school, teachers feel comfortable experimenting with untried teaching approaches, even if the approach might not work.

▶ In this school, it's easy to speak up about what's on your mind.

▶ People in this school are usually comfortable talking about problems and disagreements about teaching and learning.

In the following chapter, educators will embark on shared and public learning with colleagues about the instructional core and the academic task. The goal is to set a vision for instructional improvement grounded in observable classroom practice.

4

Developing a Vision for the Instructional Core

Rachelle, a second-year teacher at Skyview High School, was looking forward to the full faculty meeting that afternoon. The calendar indicated that the topic of the meeting was "developing the qualities of a Skyview graduate," and Rachelle felt in need of some direction in this area. Fully committed to the school's vision of graduating deep thinkers and engaged, active learners, Rachelle was struggling with how to generate these outcomes in her life sciences and biology classes.

At the meeting, the faculty broke into groups to discuss what teachers needed to do to produce graduates with higher-order thinking skills like application, questioning, and critical analysis. When the faculty members came back together, they looked at the trends across the groups and came up with a master list that included the following: empathy, cultural competence, going the extra mile, high expectations and high support, energy and passion about academic content, and rigorous and relevant teaching tasks.

As always, Rachelle appreciated the opportunity to work with colleagues, but as she left the meeting, she realized that she felt even more discouraged than when she had walked in. She was confident in her high expectations, worked hard to support her students by meticulously scaffolding her lessons, and spent the first ten minutes of each class on an open discussion of how the topic might connect to their everyday lives. In spite of her efforts, she still felt like she was working much harder than her students ever did. And while she wholeheartedly agreed with the school's vision, she wished the faculty could get more explicit about what higher-order skills actually looked like in practice and how teachers could teach to them. Rachelle was sure that if this became the primary focus of their professional development sessions, the staff was talented and dedicated enough to make it happen.

WHY ANCHOR THE VISION IN THE INSTRUCTIONAL CORE?

There is growing agreement among the education community that students must be involved in meaningful and rigorous academic work. But there is less agreement on what, precisely, meaningful and rigorous academic looks like in classrooms. This lack of clarity is often evident in the vision or mission statements that leaders set for their schools, as in the following examples:

"All students will reach their full potential as learners."
"Each student will gain the skills to navigate a culturally diverse world."
"Students will graduate as critical, ethical, and engaged thinkers and learners, prepared for college or career."

Although these statements sound powerful, they take the form of aspirations that are disconnected from the academic work required for their production. This disconnect makes it difficult to know how to translate the statements into teaching and learning interactions. To create a vision that can set the direction for an instructional improvement strategy, practitioners must anchor their vision in the instructional core. The framework of the instructional core holds that student learning results from the interactions between teachers, students, and content and is summarized in chapter 1 (see the "Guiding Principles" section). The essential practice in this chapter is designed to help leaders set a vision that addresses all three components of the instructional core, not only articulating desired student outcomes but also generating ideas about what teachers will be doing with students and content in classrooms to achieve them.

Anchoring a vision in the instructional core is real intellectual work, because at the start of a new improvement cycle, no one in the building may actually know which teaching competencies are required to reach the vision. Nevertheless, by collectively agreeing on the interactions that best indicate success with ambitious teaching and learning, you and your team will have a jumping-off point for an improvement strategy. Understanding the distance between where teaching and learning in your organization is now and where you want it to be enables you to home in on the particular knowledge and skills the faculty must learn together to improve student learning and generate teacher efficacy for instructional improvement over time.

Although setting a vision is the focus of this chapter's essential practice, the ability to talk in terms of the instructional core is foundational knowledge required for every facet of instructional improvement work. Educators at all levels of a system need a solid, shared understanding of how to identify, analyze, and discuss the learning experiences that students are truly having in classrooms. Therefore, the research and foundational learning experiences in this chapter do a deep dive into the instructional core and the academic task, the latter defined as the work students must do to successfully complete what is asked of them in any given lesson. As the experience of the Skyview High teacher illustrates in the chapter opening, it is one thing to believe in the importance of students' acquisition of skills like critical thinking, but it is entirely another to figure out the specific instructional interactions that will generate them.

This chapter will help leaders set a clear direction for instructional improvement. It will describe these required steps:

- ▶ establishing a *focused and specific vision* for learning
- ▶ grounding this vision in common language based on a *shared understanding of the instructional core and the academic task*
- ▶ supporting educators to learn how to *observe, analyze, and discuss the level of academic task* in classrooms

WHAT THE RESEARCH SAYS

Articulating a Vision

Articulating a vision is an essential leadership practice related to improvements in instruction and student learning.[1] School leaders articulate a vision to set a direction for the school and to exercise influence.[2] Because most schools are highly compartmentalized, with individual teachers working in specific grades or subject areas, school leaders often have little direct control over teaching and learning. Therefore, the leaders influence instruction indirectly by setting a vision for improvement and creating structures and conditions to foster professional learning and collaboration. Furthermore, instruction consists of many complex relationships—between teachers, students, and content—not easily manipulated by top-down directives.[3] To most directly influence teaching and learning, leaders can set the expectation that the faculty talk about, analyze, and consistently reflect on the level of academic tasks present in classrooms. Rather than prescribing desired student outcomes or performance targets, leaders begin this work by articulating a schoolwide vision that specifically describes how teachers and students will interact around content.

Internally coherent organizations establish collective expectations for high-level academic work.[4] Schools develop collective expectations when teachers use commonly understood terms to articulate widely held beliefs about what students can do and what the organization's goals are. Organizational scholar Peter Senge referred to these collective expectations as "common mental models" about how things are done.[5] Without these collective models or expectations, leaders spend additional energy establishing a unified direction and clarifying how initiatives or priorities relate to other work across the school.[6] For internal coherence, the vision must be grounded in a shared understanding of the instructional core and academic task.

Instructional Capacity

In *Instruction, Capacity, and Improvement*, education scholars David Cohen and Deborah Ball introduce what we now commonly refer to as the instructional core.

They propose that the main driver of student learning lies in the interactions between teachers and students around educational material or content. Instructional capacity, which the authors define as the ability to produce "worthwhile and substantial" student learning, depends on all three elements of instruction (student, teacher, and content), because each element shapes capacity by the way it interacts with the other two. Instructional materials that students are engaged with (e.g., texts, problems, questions, and media) influence instructional capacity by constraining or enhancing opportunities to learn and teach. Students' experiences, interests, and prior knowledge shape how they respond to teachers and materials. Teachers' intellectual and pedagogical resources are particularly critical, because they shape how teachers understand and use student contributions and content materials.[7]

In our experience, many districts still primarily focus their improvement efforts on what curriculum teachers are using or on teachers' knowledge of instructional strategies or tools. Teachers are asked to swap one math curriculum for another, incorporate formative assessments into their lessons, or ask higher-order questions. But the teacher is only one component of the instructional core, and the interactive model of capacity reminds us that a new curriculum or instructional strategy alone will not enhance student learning. Rather, educators need to pay attention to all three in concert: How will students' roles and responsibilities for learning change with this new curriculum? How meaningful is the particular content knowledge or skill that students have to demonstrate on a formative assessment? What opportunities do students have to grapple with a higher-order question once it has been asked, and what other representations of content will the teacher direct them to if they can't figure out an answer?

The Academic Task

Once educators develop the habit of considering all three elements of the instructional core in concert, they can effectively intervene in the instructional process and make better decisions about how students will interact around content. We describe this as raising the level of the academic task, thereby deepening the learning experiences that students are having in classrooms. According to Elizabeth City and her coauthors in *Instructional Rounds in Education*, the academic task is the "critical heuristic," or approach to problem solving, for understanding the effects of instructional practice on student learning.[8] In contrast to a topical description of what students are learning (algebra, the Industrial Revolution, dividing fractions, persuasive essay), the model of the academic task focuses on the inherent learning demands embedded in a curriculum, as generated by the interactions in the instructional core. In his important article, "Academic Work," Walter Doyle suggests that the intellectual demand of a given task is defined by (1) the product that students are required to complete, (2) the cognitive processes required to generate this product, and (3) the resources available to students during production.[9] Doyle argues that students will learn whatever a task leads them to do; that is, they will acquire the information and practice the operations that are necessary to accomplish the tasks they encounter.[10]

Each school will have its own process and frameworks for defining the levels of tasks, but when we refer to high-level academic tasks, we often consider whether the task

- ▶ is consequential, or has real-world meaning beyond the classroom;
- ▶ requires what are often referred to as twenty-first-century skills, such as complex communication, collaboration, and problem solving;
- ▶ meets criteria for rigor, as established by learning frameworks such as Bloom's Taxonomy, Marzano's Taxonomy, or Webb's Depth of Knowledge; and
- ▶ addresses essential learning content and practice standards set forth by professional educational associations.[11]

When faculty can use the instructional core and the academic task to diagnose and describe what is happening in classrooms, their instructional discourse improves. Imagine if the faculty at Skyview High had used the model of the instructional core and academic task when setting the vision for their students. In considering what critical thinking would look like in her classroom, Rachelle might have posed her question to her colleagues and generated some productive insights, even while the faculty was still developing its understanding of the interactions in the instructional core required to reach its vision:

RACHELLE: I could use some input from everyone on how to teach to these skills and abilities we want for our students. I feel like I'm doing everything we've talked about in the faculty meetings. I spend the first ten minutes of every class letting students discuss how the day's topic might relate to their own lives to promote relevance. I support every child's success with what I consider pretty rigorous work by scaffolding it as much as they need, and I am passionate about this content. I still feel like I'm dragging them through the lessons and that what I have taught doesn't show on their assessment results. Honestly, I could use some help.

COLLEAGUE: Wait—you have ten minutes in every class for them to discuss how it's relevant to their lives? How does that work? Do they journal? Do they know enough about the topic to make meaningful connections? Give us a sense for what happens during that time—because that's a lot of time!

RACHELLE: They don't journal. We have a whole-class conversation. I wanted it to be more of a fun, nonstressful time. And they know a little bit about the topic because I give a little intro, like, I might define *evolution* and then they might talk about why certain animals have unique characteristics because of natural selection, or bring up the scientific relationships between humans, apes, and monkeys, or things like that. Sometimes they come up with interesting ideas.

COLLEAGUE: So they don't actually have to turn anything in?

RACHELLE: It was more to authentically generate interest and help them see why they should care about what we're studying. I didn't want to make it into graded work, because I thought it would become a chore.

COLLEAGUE: I understand that impulse, definitely, but let's think about this. If your class is like mine, I'm guessing there are a handful of kids who would talk all day and about twenty others who are more than happy to sit back and let them do all the work. Right?

RACHELLE: Pretty much!

COLLEAGUE: It seems like it would help to have some accountability for all the students to participate in some way.

RACHELLE: Like handing in a journal?

COLLEAGUE: That could be one way. But even before we talk about that, if your goal is to get students to reflect on how the science is relevant to them, does it make sense to do it when you introduce a topic? Would it make sense to do it at the end of class, when they have more to work with? Also, how often do we need them to think about relevance? Does it need to be a daily thing? Maybe at the end of a unit?

Without this basic understanding of the academic task, Rachelle's colleague could not have dug into Rachelle's dilemma so productively. Taking Rachelle's initial assessment of her situation at face value—that she is providing rigorous work, scaffolding success, and spending time explicitly on the connection between the material and students' lives—Rachelle's colleague would have had difficulty figuring out how to support her and would have been more likely to offer commiseration than concrete ideas for change. The ability to think in specific terms about what we are truly requiring of students makes a tremendous difference in how educators understand and talk to each other about what happens in their classrooms.

The Stated Versus the Enacted Task

In our experience, it is very common to walk into a classroom and encounter a rich, consequential objective written on the board and simultaneously observe students engaged in very basic activities. Education scholars make a distinction between the *stated* task—often what a teacher thinks he or she is teaching—and the *enacted* task, or what is really required of students for success on the task as a consequence of the interactions taking place as a lesson unfolds.[12] For example, a social studies teacher, believing that he is supporting his students to "think like historians," might have a posted unit objective that students will be able to "use information to draw conclusions and make arguments about the transition from an agrarian society to an industrial society in the United States." The unit might involve students reading several primary sources, including newspaper clippings, political cartoons, and essays from the late 1800s. However, imagine that if after the students complete this reading, the teacher gives a lecture on the "top three reasons the United States became an industrial society" and asks students to write a paper explaining these three reasons using the primary sources. In this scenario, the teacher has transformed the stated task from "use information to draw conclusions and make arguments" to the enacted task of "use information to illustrate the teacher's argument."

Consider Rachelle's impulse to provide her students with both high expectations and high support. Efforts to scaffold challenging problems often mean that teachers turn a rich, complex task into something more accessible for students, rather than letting the students grapple with ambiguous or challenging ideas. This instinct, particularly given the pressure on educators to differentiate their lessons across a broad range of student ability levels, is both rational and well intentioned. However, such efforts can very easily bring down the level of *cognitive demand*—or the kind and level of thinking required for successful completion—dramatically, in an instant. Doyle proposes that the cognitive or intellectual demand of a task is defined by the products students are actually required to turn in and the mental processes (e.g., application of a known procedure, creation of an original hypothesis, justification of the correct approach) required to complete them, taking into account the resources at students' disposal as they do so.[13] Resources can include tangible artifacts like a graphic organizer, a model to work from, or a calculator, but they can also include less obvious supports like the ability to work with a partner or the example a teacher does with (i.e., for) the students at the board before releasing them to work independently. Once the faculty members at Skyview High gain facility with this level of nuance, they would be positioned to analyze the impact of Rachelle's scaffolding and distinguish between supporting students to learn complex material and reducing the level of what students are really being required to accomplish.

Maintaining the Level of the Stated Task

Because high-level tasks are difficult to implement well, they frequently become lower-level tasks during instruction.[14] Despite teachers' best intentions, and often because of them, teachers diminish the level of challenge in what they require of their students. Table 4.1 draws on research about instruction across content areas

TABLE 4.1   Actions teachers take to support or diminish the level of academic task

ACTIONS SUPPORTING THE LEVEL OF THE ACADEMIC TASK	ACTIONS DIMINISHING THE LEVEL OF THE ACADEMIC TASK
▪ Ask open-ended questions that encourage student thinking rather than requiring only recall. ▪ Keep description of task open enough to allow for students to make their own judgments about how to accomplish the task. ▪ Build on student responses, asking follow-up questions that support deeper content understanding. ▪ Draw frequent conceptual connections. ▪ Press for justifications, explanations, and meaning through questioning, comments, and other feedback. ▪ Give students the means to monitor their own progress toward accomplishing the objectives.	▪ Focus on procedures rather than content understanding (e.g., grammatical rules rather than meaning in English; algorithms rather than conceptual understanding in math). ▪ Specify the steps students need to complete for a complex task, rather than asking students to determine the steps themselves. ▪ Shift the emphasis from conceptual understanding to the correctness or completeness of the answer. ▪ Plan a lesson that does not allow enough time to wrestle with the demanding aspects of the task, or give too much time so that students drift into off-task behavior. ▪ Do not hold students accountable for high-level products or processes (e.g., ask students to explain their thinking, but accept unclear or incorrect student explanations).

Source: Adapted from Walter Doyle and Kathy Carter, "Academic Tasks in Classrooms," *Curriculum Inquiry* 14, no. 2 (1984): 129.149; Martin Nystrand and Adam Gamoran, "Instructional Discourse, Student Engagement, and Literature Achievement," *Research in the Teaching of English* 25, no.3 (1991): 261.290; Mary Kay Stein and Margaret Schwan Smith, "Mathematical Tasks as a Framework for Reflection: From Research to Practice," *Mathematics Teaching in the Middle School* 3 (January 1998):268.275.

and grade levels to list common practices that support or diminish the level of the academic task during instruction.

In this book, we use the phrase *instructional decision*. The myriad instructional decisions teachers make in a single class period will maintain or reduce the level of the academic task. Observing for these decisions requires looking beyond the stated objective on the board or the title of the students' worksheets to the interactions unfolding among the components of the instructional core. How do students demonstrate what they have learned? Do they get credit just for trying, or are they held to reaching a certain standard? How do teachers respond when students are stuck—do they sit down and do the beginning of the problem with (or for) the students or offer a different way of looking at the problem? Do teachers allow pairs of students to hand in a single product with both the children's names on it? Does the teacher provide an essay for students to use as a model when they write their own? Does the teacher give five or ten minutes for students to make sense of a difficult question before bringing attention back to the board?

Observing for the Real Academic Task

We often use the phrase "task predicts performance" from instructional rounds, which is the idea that students will acquire the knowledge and skills that teachers have them use on a daily basis.[15] However, not all educators have the training to tease out the stated from the enacted task in real time or describe what the task in a classroom on any given day actually is, so that they can identify what knowledge or skill is truly required of students for its completion. For example, two teachers might be observing the same writing lesson. One teacher who has not deeply internalized the concept of the academic task might report back that students were "using the four-step writing process to compose an essay," but another teacher with a more nuanced understanding might explain, "Students are independently writing single sentences on a graphic organizer but not combining them into paragraphs." Doyle's definition of the task, above, can serve as a helpful set of guidelines for deciphering what the enacted task in a classroom really is—thereby predicting what student performance will look like as a consequence of participation. When observing a class to determine the task or what students must actually do to be successful, consider the following:

- ▶ What are the products that students are truly being held accountable for generating?
- ▶ If students generated this product with no support, what types of thinking or cognitive processes would be required?
- ▶ What resources or givens are made available to the students while they generate the product, and what are the implications for the level of cognitive demand?

The Impact of Tasks over Time

The cumulative impact of the types of academic tasks children encounter day in, day out is profound. According to one study, in classes that consistently engage students in high-level mathematics tasks, children achieve at higher levels than in classes with lower-level tasks.[16] Beyond their impact on assessment data, academic tasks have been shown to influence students' level of *engagement* in learning. When students take on tasks that they view as meaningful, such as those that connect to the real world or that offer students a sense of ownership and purpose for their work, students are more likely to be motivated to put forth the effort needed to be successful.[17] We have seen many schools and districts direct an improvement strategy at increasing student engagement in the abstract, as though engagement were a quality intrinsic to the children. Rather than ask whether their students are engaged, teachers need to look closely at what they are actually asking students to engage *in*. Many lower-level tasks put kids into a passive role related to the content that the teacher provides. Higher-level tasks can put students into a more active role as they build, illustrate, or synthesize content, with teachers providing facilitation and support.

Consider the following description of two teachers teaching "the same thing." If the task in each classroom was emblematic of the types of tasks students encountered in each of their classes most days, imagine the implications for students' engagement in their learning:

Prompt: "In the prologue of *Romeo and Juliet*, what relationship does Shakespeare establish between love and hate? How do his specific word choices illustrate this relationship? Use text evidence to support your answer."

Classroom 1. The aforementioned prompt is written on the board. The teacher asks the students to get out their text and take five minutes to jot down notes to prepare to discuss the questions in small groups. The students discuss the questions in small groups. In one group, the students disagree about how to interpret a line. They reread it and discuss the meaning. The teacher brings the students together for a whole-group discussion and asks, "What relationship does Shakespeare establish between love and hate? What word choices illustrate this relationship?" The teacher and students build on each other's responses. For homework, the teacher has the students write a paragraph explaining why they think Shakespeare chose these words to begin the play.

Classroom 2. The teacher says that the class is going to have a discussion about the relationship between love and hate in the prologue. The teacher asks, "Who is fighting? Who hates each other?" A student answers that there are two households fighting. The teacher takes notes on the board during the discussion, and students copy these notes. The teacher goes on to ask who is in love and how these lovers and fighting households are related. After each response, the teacher moves on to a new question, with one student answering at a time, and all students copying what the teacher writes on the board. For homework, the teacher has the students write a paragraph explaining how Shakespeare establishes the relationship between love and hate.

In their casebook for analyzing instructional tasks, *Implementing Standards-Based Mathematics Instruction*, Mary Kay Stein and colleagues argue that "the cumulative effect of students' experiences with instructional tasks is students' implicit development about the nature of mathematics."[18] Extending this observation across subject areas, consider how students' roles in their daily classroom tasks influence their ideas about the nature of school. Imagine the different experiences of two students, one assigned to classroom 1 and one to classroom 2. What would be their understanding of what it means to learn about literature? How engaged would they be in the learning process in this subject? Why?

Would the discussions in your school or district reveal similar important differences in the kinds of tasks students encounter in their classrooms? It is essential to focus your instructional improvement work directly on the interactions that generate the academic tasks students encounter every day. Once the educators in your organization feel comfortable with these constructs, you will be better positioned to create a vision for the learning that you aspire for your students and to engage in the instructional conversations required to realize this vision.

TURNING RESEARCH INTO PRACTICE

The essential practice in this chapter—developing a vision for the instructional core—is designed to help educators set a vision for the ambitious academic tasks they hope to see in classrooms. The vision incorporates desired student outcomes, what teachers will be doing with students and content, and the role that students play in their own learning. This essential practice asks educators to predict what success would look like in five years. We set a vision this far into the future to reinforce the principle that improvement requires sustained adult learning and not a more expedient implementation of a new program or instructional strategy. Furthermore, we have learned that asking teachers and leaders to think this far into the future can remind them that improvement means learning to do things they don't yet know how to do. This future orientation can also free educators of the impulse to constrain themselves to a "land of nice," where they hasten to point out what is already positive in the organization. The vision should be ambitious enough that practitioners understand the need to work and learn together to accomplish it over time.

ESSENTIAL PRACTICE
CREATING AN AMBITIOUS VISION FOR THE INSTRUCTIONAL CORE

To create the vision in this essential practice, educators need to include all three components of the instructional core. They should articulate not only the desired student outcomes but also how they expect to see teachers interacting with students and particular types of content.

Objective. Develop an ambitious vision for teaching and learning anchored in the instructional core.

Time: 1 hour

1. Identify a Focus [10 minutes]

As a group, discuss the following question: What are you trying to improve in terms of instruction and student learning? Spend up to ten minutes collecting ideas about what your school is trying to achieve—goals related to student learning. If there are several possible goals, write them all down, and then come to a consensus about where to focus your attention for the next few rounds. If possible, return to the other goals later. Commit your focus to chart paper.

2. If We Succeed, What Will We See in Our Classrooms? [20 minutes]

Draw the triangle for the instructional core on chart paper. Using markers or sticky notes, write down your ideas for what classrooms will look like if you succeed in your goals. Align your written ideas with each component of the instructional core and the interactions between these components, using the following prompts:

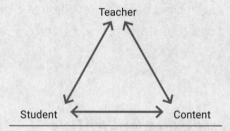

Source: Adapted from David K. Cohen and Deborah Loewenberg Ball, *Instruction, Capacity, and Improvement* (Philadelphia: Consortium for Policy Researchin Education, 1999).

If we succeed . . .

- What will we see students doing?
- What will we see teachers doing?
- What will the instructional content look like?
- How will students interact with teachers? How will students interact with content? How will teachers interact with content?

3. Assessing the Audacity of Our Vision [20 minutes]

After committing your vision for the instructional core to paper, discuss the following questions:

- Is our vision ambitious enough that it requires adults and students to learn to work in new ways?
- Would making this vision a reality result in meaningful improvements in student learning?
- Is our vision observable and grounded in the instructional core? Would we be able to see if students and teachers were working in ways that reflected this vision?
- Be specific. What would our vision look like? What would it feel like? What learning would it require? How would it improve learning?

4. Revise and Commit to Paper [10 minutes]

In light of your discussion, revise your vision for the instructional core, and write your final ideas on chart paper. Post your final ideas for each component of the instructional core—teacher, student, content—and the interactions between them.

Developing the Essential Practice Over Time

The essential practice described above asks you to imagine what you will see in classrooms across a school or district. Hopefully, you and your team will revise the initial vision statement as you engage in instructional improvement, because the ongoing examination and revision of where you want to go and how you will get there is the stuff of organizational learning. The essential practice sets up a long-term vision for the instructional core, which in turn will uncover a series of more immediate action steps as the learning cycle unfolds. For example, the Skyview High faculty's long-term vision for the instructional core might include students' proficiency at pushing each other's thinking through discussion and debate, rather than a complete dependence on the teacher as a source of knowledge. If this proficiency were part of the vision, the faculty might, during the first wave of task analysis, discover that group work in the organization currently consists of students seated together but doing individual work. This observation would set the stage for the next short-term cycle of learning, in which the faculty gathers resources on how to structure real collaboration in the various content areas, discusses how the resources might play out, and commits to trying some of them.

Leaders support the development of internal coherence when they use their vision as an instructional roadmap and a shared commitment to refining practice in service of its goals. By defining what high-level instruction will look like and returning to the collective drawing board as each consecutive step emerges, you will ensure that the vision is a dynamic force in your organization, rather than an aspiration with no clear guidance for teachers or a thirty-page document that sits untouched in a binder.

FOUNDATIONAL LEARNING EXPERIENCES

If a vision for the instructional core is to successfully chart the course for an improvement strategy, some fundamental shifts may be required in your organization. Most immediately, practitioners must internalize how to talk about the instructional core, academic task, and instructional decisions when they come together to make sense of student learning outcomes. The importance of moving the discussion from the stated to the enacted task is underscored by the case study of two teachers, Fran and Kevin, teaching the same mathematics lesson they developed together, with enactments that lead to dramatically different results for students.[19] At this point in the internal coherence professional learning series, educators often realize the importance of getting into each other's classrooms to gather data on what truly drives student learning: the specific interactions between the students, the teacher, and the instructional content as a lesson unfolds in real time. The moment when teachers shift from viewing classroom observation as something done *to* teachers by administrators for the purpose of evaluation, to something done *by* teachers with colleagues for their own professional growth is a critical one, and we continue to reinforce this shift in the upcoming chapters. In this section, we provide a learning experience for use with the Fran and Kevin case study, additional readings, and other guidance on how we think and teach about the instructional core, the task, and a vision that can inform an improvement process.

Anchor Texts for Group Discussion

To engage most powerfully with the essential practice for creating an instructional vision, we recommend that educators spend some time making sense of the research that anchors this chapter. Specifically, we recommend pairing each of the following readings with discussion protocol to engage with text, such as Patricia Averette's "Save the Last Word for ME" (see appendix B for full reference) to structure a collective reading experience.

> ▶ *Academic Work*, Walter Doyle, 1983. This is dense academic writing, so we recommend reading a short excerpt, beginning at "The Intrinsic Character of Academic Work" (p. 160) and stopping at "Types of Academic Tasks" (p. 162). The beginning of the article explains why a topical description of a curriculum does not capture the intellectual demands placed on students. It also introduces Doyle's framework for the task as the products, cognitive processes, and resources of instruction and spells out exactly why task predicts performance.
>
> ▶ *Instruction, Capacity, and Improvement*, David Cohen and Deborah Ball, 1999. [Recommended excerpt: "Introduction" (p. 1) through "Capacity Not Fixed" (p. 4).] This research report outlines a framework for those engaged in comprehensive school reform and focuses on instruction and the environments required to improve it. The short section "Capacity and Instruction" outlines the interactions between teachers, students, and instructional materials, now commonly referred to as the instructional core. The whole article is worth reading, but the first four pages will provide a solid foundation on why teachers need the opportunity for practice and sustained reflection with colleagues—and not simply a new curriculum—if they are to deepen what students learn.
>
> ▶ *Implementing Standards-Based Mathematics Instruction*, Mary Kay Stein et al., 2009. [Recommended excerpt: chapters 1 and 2.] This book of cases for professional development is an outstanding resource. It includes the

Fran and Kevin case that anchors another foundational learning experience, below. For a text-based discussion, we also highly recommend the first two chapters of the book. Chapter 1 provides description and learning experiences on the how and why of analyzing the cognitive demand in math tasks. The very short chapter 2 provides an in-depth look at how the level of a stated task is maintained or allowed to decline in the evolution of a lesson. Though focused on mathematics, the implications for all other subject areas are clear.

The Impact of Instructional Decisions

Another approach we take in our professional learning series is to use scenarios and discussion prompts to push practitioners to consider the impact of instructional decisions on student learning.

> *Prompt 1:* "Imagine two students of similar ability in two different classes in the same school, with teachers who were teaching a lesson on the same thing (e.g., *Romeo and Juliet*, fractions, or the Civil War). Could the two students emerge having learned very different things? Why, or why not?"

When we pose this question to teachers before they have learned about the instructional core and the academic task, they tend to agree that the two students could have learned different things. However, they often cite reasons intrinsic to the teachers or their style (e.g., "Some teachers might connect better to their students" or "Some teachers might have background knowledge that enables them to teach differently"). Other participants might make a general reference to "the way they taught it." These common responses lead into the importance of following up with prompt 2, which pushes educators to think more specifically about instructional decisions that influence what students learn.

> *Prompt 2:* "Consider this elementary school mathematics problem: Lucia is baking apple pies, and she puts 4 apples in every pie. If Lucia has to bake 13 pies, how many apples does she need in all? Lucia has to remove the seeds from each apple before she puts them into the pie. If each apple has 8 seeds,

how many seeds does she have to remove to bake all 13 pies? Explain your reasoning using words, numbers, or pictures."[20]

Class 1. Teacher 1 gives students seven minutes to work alone and record their work, then seven minutes to work in pairs to come to their final solution. The teacher calls on students of her choice to explain and justify their final solution for the class. Together the class uses the work of their peers to determine the problem's best solution or solutions, which they write up in their notebooks.

Class 2. The individual work times and paired work times are the same as in class 1, but teacher 2 calls only on the students who volunteer present their work, and after the presentations, the teacher writes on the board his own idea for the best solution. The students then write down this solution in their notebooks. Rather than collect daily work, the teacher collects and reviews their notebooks on a weekly basis.

Class 3. Again, the work times are the same as in class 1, except teacher 3 pairs what she feels are her strongest students with the ones she feels are her weakest. She lets the students pick who presents, and the students hand in a joint product at the end of each class.

After posing these three enactments of the same stated task, we ask educators to discuss the following:

1. What cognitive processes does the apple pie problem, as stated, require for successful completion? What are all the things a student would need to know or do to answer the question correctly?

2. Is this level of cognitive demand from the problem as stated maintained by the enactment in class 1? Explain.

3. What are the implications of the decisions made by teacher 2 for the level of the task? By teacher 3? What must students do to successfully complete what is required of them in each classroom?

Before posing the preceding questions, we are careful to remind participants to focus their ideas about student learning solely on the information provided. In our experience, educators quickly come up with questions about information the prompts *don't* tell them, such as "What was taught the day before?" or "Do the students have a rubric?" By acknowledging ahead of time that there are many legitimate questions to which there is no clear answer, it is possible to circumvent this discussion and remind participants that the purpose of this exercise is to compare the impact across classrooms, given only what the group *does* know from the information provided. The questions participants come up with are important in the real world of classrooms, but this is a learning experience designed to focus on the implication of the specific details that are given.

Once the participants have engaged in this initial discussion, we emphasize that many of the instructional decisions that inadvertently diminish the level of the task are both rational and well intentioned. For example, the teacher's instincts in class 2 both to create a safe learning environment by never cold-calling and to make sure that students don't leave with a "subpar" solution make perfect sense. However, the impact of these decisions is to reduce the level of the academic task dramatically: the true task in this classroom becomes simply to wait until the teacher writes the "correct" answer on the board and then copy it into a notebook. Similarly, the practice of asking students who are strong in one area to help struggling peers can be a powerful one. But without a means to hold those struggling students accountable for learning the material themselves, only the strong students are required to meet the cognitive demand in the task as stated. In contrast, every student in class 1 may be called on to explain what they've done and why.

After this initial discussion, we ask participants to consider the impact of these various teaching decisions on learning and engagement as they accrue throughout an entire academic year. This is done by considering the importance of examining tasks over time by using prompt 3.

Prompt 3: "Presume that by and large, the teachers in classrooms 1, 2, and 3 consistently introduce problems in a similar fashion over the course of a year (i.e., teacher 1 consistently calls on her students to explain their work, teacher 2 always puts up his idea of the best solution on the board, and teacher 3 consistently pairs what she perceives to be stronger and weaker students to develop a joint product)."

Given these conditions, have participants discuss the following questions:

1. What assessment data would you expect to see for each class at the end of the year on questions requiring students to show and justify their work on other mathematics problems?
2. What patterns of student engagement would you expect to see in each classroom? How might students in each class understand what it means to learn mathematics?

This discussion provides another opportunity to emphasize the importance of having educators engage with evidence of classroom practice at this level of specificity when considering the root causes of student performance. For example, imagine if the teachers in these three classrooms were asked to make sense of the differences in their student's assessment data in their team meeting. What sense might they make of the strong performance of students in class 1, the relatively poor performance of students in class 2, and the bimodal performance of both the stronger and the weaker students in class 3, with only the students' assessment scores to go on? Especially given that all three teachers were, to the best of their knowledge, teaching the exact same lessons? Or, how might the participants assess the students' high opinion of teacher 1 or frequency of student misbehavior in teacher 2's classroom? By posing these questions, we continue to push the idea that groups of educators can use observation data to advance their collective practice and to shift away from the view of observation as a tool for evaluating individual performance.

Stated Versus Enacted Task Experience: The Case of Fran and Kevin

In *Implementing Standards-Based Mathematics Instruction*, Stein and coauthors note that the purpose of their case studies is to demonstrate the most prevalent ways that cognitively challenging math tasks devolve during a lesson. They explain these processes in ways that will resonate with the world of teachers and students in classrooms, "where intention, uncertainty, chance, and judgment prevail."[21] In the case of Fran and Kevin, two teachers concerned with developing their students' conceptual, rather than procedural, understanding of the multiplication of fractions develop a lesson plan together. As the case unfolds, the reader becomes a fly on the wall, first in Fran's classroom as she enacts the lesson in real time; then in her team meeting, where she gives her team a brief report on the lesson; and, finally, in Kevin's classroom, where his various instructional decisions lead to a totally different set of learning outcomes for his students.

As Rosalie Baker, Virginia Boris, and Linda Hauser attest in the afterword of our book, the Fran and Kevin case study is an invaluable example for educators concerned about growing coherence around the instructional core, and the examination of this case should not be rushed. Consequently, we spend a full teaching day on this case study and pair it with the protocol we developed specifically for the case.

The protocol we developed to structure the case study experience (see appendix C) asks educators to individually analyze Fran and Kevin's written lesson plan and the specific student learning challenges that the lesson was designed to address. Groups of educators then read the case and "observe" the two teachers in their separate classrooms conduct the lesson they designed together. Participants then map the various decisions made by Fran and Kevin as specific interactions between the elements of the instructional core. Comparing the two lessons, participants might note, for example, that Fran asked her best student to demonstrate to the class how she solved the problem, to show a perfect solution with no mistakes. Kevin, on the other hand, had a student who initially got the wrong answer hash out his solution with another student and then demonstrate to the class where he had initially gone wrong and how he had ultimately solved the problem.

Because this case study contains so many important implications for how we think and talk about what drives student learning, we reference it again under the foundational learning experiences for chapter 7, as a way to revisit the implications for team-based conversations anchored in the instructional core. By the end of this experience with the case study and the protocol (appendix C), participants will come away with the following shared understandings:

▶ Because of the specific decisions each teacher makes, the students in the two classes are concerned with accomplishing very different things: Fran's students pick up on the need to get the correct answer, whereas Kevin's decisions keep students focused on what they are doing conceptually.

► Fran had every intention of keeping a focus on students' conceptual understanding, but in the moment felt the pressure to keep her students moving
   toward an end product—an instinct many teachers can relate to.

► This is not a case of a good versus a bad teacher. But after observing the two
   enactments, the participants should recognize that Fran's colleagues might
   be able to offer concrete suggestions to help her if they had the opportunity
   to watch her teach. Her report alone would provide little of the information necessary for her colleagues to help her maintain this high-level cognitive task.

Generating Ideas for an Instructional Vision

Once all the members in your organization have internalized the framework of
the instructional core and the stated and enacted academic task, you are ready to
set a vision to drive an improvement strategy. Setting a vision based on how teachers will interact with students and content is a way for leaders to create coherence
among teachers' various mental models of what students are capable and the standard to which adults should be held accountable. The essential practice in this
chapter leads you through this vision-setting exercise, but before talking about it
in teams, each educator may need to spend some time independently generating
ideas about this vision for the future. What qualities, skills, or knowledge do you
hope to cultivate in your students? What do you know from your pooled experience and expertise about how to develop these qualities, skills, and knowledge?
What tasks would be required to generate these benefits? What have you done
thus far that is related to this vision? What do you not yet do well? Where do you
need to supplement your existing knowledge with research?

As we mentioned in the introduction, the Internal Coherence Framework
does not include a particular instructional approach or set of materials. However,
some visions for teaching and learning will generate richer learning experiences for
your faculty than others. Here are some questions you might ask yourself when
determining the value of a vision for instruction:

▶ Is this vision ambitious enough that it requires adults and students to learn to work in new ways?

▶ What do we need to learn that we don't know now?

▶ Does this vision address higher-level skills in learning taxonomies, such as Bloom's or Marzano's Taxonomies, Webb's Depth of Knowledge criteria, or measures of cognitive demand?

▶ Does this vision help us address important learning standards for content and practice, as defined by professional associations or adopted by state education agencies?

CONNECTING TO CLINICAL INSTRUMENTS

Educators' ability to talk in terms of the instructional core and the stated versus enacted academic task and to truly understand the impact of discrete instructional decisions on students' learning experiences underlies every subsequent facet of the internal coherence professional learning series. These ideas are accordingly embedded throughout the domains of the Internal Coherence Survey and Internal Coherence Developmental Rubric.

The second line of the rubric illustrates a developmental progression for establishing an internally coherent vision that refers to shared understanding of the instructional core and the academic task.

The Internal Coherence Developmental Rubric: instructional leadership

BEGINNING	EMERGENT	PROFICIENT	EXEMPLARY
▪ Leaders articulate vision in broad statements about vague goals. ▪ Teachers describe what happens in classrooms by naming curriculum, activities, or standards separately from tasks.	▪ Leaders articulate vision in terms of most components of the instructional core. ▪ Teachers are acquiring language to describe or analyze academic tasks in classrooms.	▪ Leaders articulate vision by addressing what it will look like using all components of the instructional core. ▪ Teachers consistently use language to describe or analyze academic tasks in classrooms.	▪ Leaders articulate an ambitious vision that addresses all components of the instructional core and routinely assess their progress toward that vision. ▪ Teachers understand and can routinely engage in discussion about the connection between instructional decisions and academic tasks.

The Internal Coherence Developmental Rubric: instructional leadership (*continued*)

BEGINNING	EMERGENT	PROFICIENT	EXEMPLARY
• Leadership lacks clear practice for observing or monitoring instruction.	• Leaders have a limited practice for observing or monitoring instruction.	• Teachers understand which instructional decisions might raise or lower the level of task. • Leaders have clear practices in place for observing instruction as part of both individual evaluation and supporting collective instructional improvement.	• Leaders and teachers have a shared understanding of the multiple purposes of classroom observation. • Teachers associate classroom observation with collective instructional improvement processes.

Internal Coherence Survey Items: Leadership for Learning

As in chapter 3, there are multiple survey items that assess the principal's leadership. The following survey items are those most directly connected to the ideas about setting an ambitious vision that is grounded in the instructional core.

ASSESSING LEADERSHIP FOR LEARNING

▶ The principal is knowledgeable about effective instructional practices.

▶ The principal communicates a clear vision for teaching and learning at our school.

▶ The principal is directly involved in helping teachers address instructional issues in their classrooms.

The next two chapters focus on developing a strategy for organizational learning to enable you to reach the ambitious vision you have articulated for the instructional core. Chapter 5 looks specifically at the connection between strategy and the current state of the structures and processes in your organization, and chapter 6 helps you develop a plan to strategically align all the components of the organization with the vision for ambitious teaching and learning in every classroom.

Assessing Organizational Capacity for Instructional Improvement

As Evan, the principal from Lakeside Elementary, walked with Anita, the district supervisor, around the school, he talked about the improvement strategy for the current year, stopping into classrooms to provide evidence of the strategy in action. "The main aspects of our improvement strategy are rolling out the district's new math curriculum and the Word Generation curriculum in English language arts," he said. "Specifically, we're focused on supporting students in engaging in discussion and debate as part of both of them. Our grade-level teams are using the data-team structure one meeting per month. We've also partnered with the university to get two interns to work with our faculty on rolling out a multitiered system of supports, or MTSS, model to address student academics and behavior."

As they moved through the hallways, Anita asked, "How do you think it's going with the new curricula? Do you think your teachers are internalizing the switch from the old programs in math and ELA? The emphasis on asking open-ended questions and having students develop arguments to convince their peers is a pretty big switch from our past programs. I know other schools are struggling with this." They stopped in front of a classroom where the teacher was sitting with a group of six students at a small table working on writing. The rest of the children in the class were writing in their notebooks in response to the prompts on the board:

Students [should/should not] be required to wear uniforms to school.

The main reason supporting my opinion is . . . [state your primary argument here].

In addition, . . . [state 1–3 more arguments from the list on the board].

In conclusion, . . . [powerful example, phrase, etc., to convince reader of your position!].

As Evan stuck his head into the classroom, the teacher came to the door.

"How's it going with the Word Generation curriculum? " Evan asked. "Did they do the debate?"

The teacher nodded. "Yes! We debated for about ten minutes, and then we wrote a list of possible ways to support each side of the argument on the board. They had to choose a side and pick supporting arguments from the list, and now they're writing about it. I'm differentiating the writing task by letting them use two to four supporting arguments in their writing that they'll hand in. The kids sitting with me need a little extra help with their writing, so I'm working with them while everyone else finishes on their own."

"Great," Evan said. "Will you use their writing as evidence in your data team?"

"Maybe next cycle," the teacher said. "At the moment, we're focused on MTSS, deciding how to assign students to the right interventions during the academic support block."

HOW DOES ORGANIZATIONAL CAPACITY RELATE TO INSTRUCTIONAL IMPROVEMENT?

In education, as in many other sectors, doing more new things is often confused with getting better. At Lakeside Elementary, for example, the teachers and administrators are working hard to implement two new curricula, a new behavior program, and a routine approach for using data in teams. In addition, the school is using its current systems to support student learning. All of these programs and processes have the potential to improve student learning, but each initiative is likely to further fragment teachers' time and attention unless the initiatives are coordinated. For meaningful improvement in instruction and student learning, the school or district as a *system* must be organized to support connected and reinforcing opportunities to reflect on and improve how students learn and how teachers work.

There is a great disconnect in many schools between the ambitions espoused for students and the learning experiences the organization is designed to produce. For example, there is widespread support for preparing students to be twenty-first-century learners who think critically and can work with peers to solve complex problems. However, walking into many classrooms, you will see students working in isolation on tasks that require them to merely recall information or apply simple procedures—tasks that are much less demanding than the goals espoused by educational leaders. Why is this the case? For one, improvement efforts are often focused on only one part of the entire system at a time: adopting new curricula, training teachers, building teacher teams, improving school culture, or preparing leaders. When we work with leaders, we urge them to move away from a narrow focus on the strengths and weaknesses of individual people or structures within the organization and begin to question the very design of the larger system that has contributed to the current state of teaching and learning across classrooms. This holistic approach is what the research terms a *systems perspective.*

Consider a common challenge faced by many schools and districts: when instruction is not responsive to the specific learning needs of students, some students can fall further and further behind as teachers continue to move forward in "covering" the curriculum. Typically, leaders may view this challenge as a matter of teacher training or teacher buy-in to the schools' focus on instructional strategies for differentiation. Although opportunities for professional learning are likely to be one piece of the puzzle, a systems perspective encourages leaders to think more comprehensively about the way the organization is designed (or not designed) to produce the outcomes it seeks: instruction adapted to each student's unique learning needs. What opportunities are there for teachers to learn about the developmental needs of their students and plan instruction based on their needs? Are teachers left to do this work alone or with the support of colleagues? What incentives are presently encouraging teachers to focus on curriculum coverage over instruction tailored to students' needs? What messages are teachers receiving from leaders about what good instruction looks like? Each of these questions addresses one aspect of the larger system. When brought together, these questions can help paint a clearer picture of the organizational changes needed to more tightly align the way the organization works with the goals for student learning.

A systems perspective would be helpful for the leaders at Lakeside Elementary. The shift to two new curricula that emphasize student discussion and debate represents a significant change in how teachers interact with students around educational content. However, the teacher in the vignette appears to have adapted the new English language arts curriculum into his traditional approach: rather than letting students develop their own arguments from what they heard in the debate, the teacher has provided a list of arguments to choose from and provided sentence stems. This instructional decision, which reduces the level of the task from the new curriculum, may not be hard to understand, considering the system in which this teacher operates. For example, where, when, or how does the organization give teachers time to focus sustained attention on what they need to be doing differently? Are they able to try out practices that may be beyond their comfort zone or, with their colleagues, evaluate the impact of these changes on student learning? In short, does Lakeside Elementary as an organization have the ability to support teachers in making real changes to the interactions in the instructional core?

This chapter introduces the clinical tools and foundational learning experiences to diagnose the current capacity of your school or district to improve teaching and learning at scale. Each of these tools can provide specific information about the extent to which your organization, or system, is currently designed to improve teaching and learning. The tools can help you understand the implications of creating a strategy realistically aligned to your organization's current capacity and the steps you can take to strengthen this capacity. Educational leaders can use the tools and practices to diagnose their current systems, understand their development over time, identify and address problems of practice, and coordinate the organization to support meaningful and widespread improvements in teaching and learning. This chapter focuses on three steps for assessing the current capacity of your organization for meeting your improvement goals:

- ▶ understanding the concept of *organizational capacity as internal coherence* and how it relates to your ability to improve teaching and learning at scale
- ▶ *seeing the system*, so you can design the system to produce the desired results
- ▶ *collecting and using organizational data* to inform your improvement efforts

WHAT THE RESEARCH SAYS

Organizational Capacity

We define a school's level of organizational capacity as its level of internal coherence—the collective ability of the faculty to connect and align resources to improve instruction and student learning throughout the organization.[1] As illustrated in the Internal Coherence Framework (see figure 1.1), a school's capacity to improve instruction and student learning is influenced by the leadership of the principal, the involvement of teachers in school improvement efforts, the structures and processes that support collaborative learning among educators, and the knowledge, skills, and beliefs that educators bring to their work with students and colleagues. Figure 5.1 articulates what occurs at each level of the organization—classrooms, teams, faculty, leadership—when a school has reached a level of high coherence and is well positioned to enact a strategy to reach its vision for the instructional core.

In some schools and districts, the goals for improving teaching and learning are clear and focused. However, walking around some of these schools on any given day, an observer might find it difficult to figure out what the educators are doing to meet these goals. One reason for this disconnect between the goals for improvement and the daily work of schools is the failure to integrate the improvement strategy in the internal processes of the organization. The strength of the relationship between organizational processes and the improvement strategy is reflected by the extent to which teachers feel that improvement goals are realistic, measurable, and aligned with the programs, initiatives, collaborative structures, and curricula that are already in place.[2] In schools and districts with high internal coherence, the responsibilities of educators at all levels—central office

FIGURE 5.1   Building coherence for instructional improvement

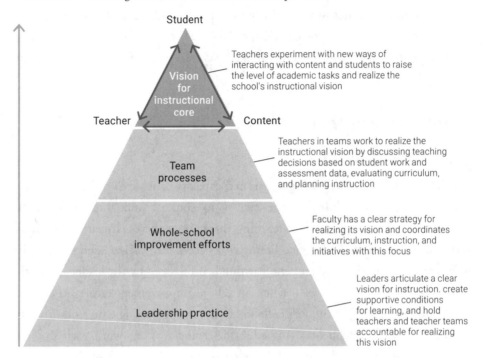

administrators, principals, coaches, teachers—and the organizational processes in which they engage, such as classroom observations and collaboration in teacher teams, serve to both monitor and support the progress of the improvement strategy.

Rather than simply hire capable individuals to support student learning or adopt promising programs, high-capacity organizations make coordinated efforts to improve teaching and learning across people and structures. For example, if Lakeside Elementary had a higher capacity to improve students' ability to develop evidenced-based arguments, its teachers and leaders would work together to identify curricula to support this goal, and the school would have teachers form grade-level or departmental teams to learn how to use these curricula effectively with their particular student population. Moreover, administrators would use classroom observations as an opportunity to provide feedback to teachers in supporting student argumentation.

Systems Thinking

In organizational improvement work, there is an implicit recognition that every system is perfectly designed to achieve the results it gets.[3] In an educational context, this means that schools and districts are perfectly designed to continue producing the same results for students they have for generations. Systems thinking has been viewed as a powerful approach to organizational change.[4] In education, systems thinking involves considering how the many interrelated parts of the larger organization, whether it is a school or a school system, contribute to the larger process that influences student learning. A systems perspective to educational improvement suggests that to improve results for students, one must understand how schools and districts are organized and interrelate as physical structures, human relationships, and ways of working. Adopting such a perspective is not easy. Tools like the Internal Coherence Survey and the Internal Coherence Developmental Rubric are designed to help you see the system, and the essential practices and foundational learning experiences help you develop a plan that connects each larger unit of the system to the smallest unit of teaching and learning in every classroom.

Through school surveys such as the Internal Coherence Survey, leaders can assess the current strength of the essential processes and conditions for improvement, such as how well administrators have created a safe environment for teachers to talk openly about instruction and whether teacher teams have processes in place to support not only the sharing of ideas but also collective decision-making.[5] This information, in turn, can be used to develop a strategy that is well matched to the current capacity of the school. For example, a principal who had recently taken over a school with high levels of turnover and a faculty of all novice teachers, including many first-year teachers, described his strategy for improving writing instruction. The strategy relied primarily on schoolwide professional development led by outside experts and reinforced by frequent informal observations and feedback from the principal and assistant principal. Although this principal recognized the potential for teacher teams to serve as an important structure for teacher learning, he also recognized that teachers had little, if any, experience working in teams and brought limited pedagogical content knowledge to their work with colleagues. In contrast, a district that had made a three-year investment in developing the capacity of teacher teams, including training all teachers in team inquiry processes, and had relatively experienced and stable faculties in most schools described teacher teams as a key structure for supporting teachers in analyzing student work and adjusting teaching practice to meet district goals for improved student learning.

Scholars argue that the search for one right strategy or solution for improving teachers' practice and student learning is misguided because this approach fails to address the powerful influence of context.[6] Instead, educational leaders can develop promising strategies for improving student learning by taking into account the unique context of their school or district.

The Intersection of Organizational and Instructional Improvement

The relationship between the *organizational* data provided by tools like the Internal Coherence Survey and Developmental Rubric and a school's *instructional* focus on mathematics or academic talk has proven confusing to our partners in the past. Initially, when asked what they were working on, our California school partners would talk about an instructional improvement agenda and then their separate focus on building organizational coherence. In reality, we work on both instructional and organizational improvement, in tandem. First, reaching your vision for the instructional core requires aligning the leadership practices, collaborative structures, and whole-school and team processes to advance this vision. If organizational conditions such as psychological safety or team processes are worked on in isolation, the school will not be equipped to summon an organizational response to its learning challenge. In addition, leaders do better when they can take honest stock of where they are as an organization *now* (e.g., "I currently have a faculty full of novice teachers," or "I currently have a highly developed system of teams"). When developing their improvement strategy, they are better able to take advantage of existing strengths and are realistic enough about existing weaknesses that the strategy has a chance of success.

Finally, the relationship between organizational and instructional improvement is one of mutual reinforcement. You can only work on essential organizational practices like setting a vision, establishing a purpose for the work of teacher teams, or supporting high-level instructional talk if you are focused on a goal for ambitious teaching and learning. You can use your instructional focus as the platform around which you develop practices like constructive challenge, commitments to shared learning, or the generation of efficacy beliefs. And in turn, your attention to these organizational practices increases your ability to reach more and more ambitious instructional goals, as you become more adept at collective learning over time.

Internal Accountability

Schools and districts function as unique systems that are shaped by their own context, teachers' and administrators' individual ideas of responsibility, the collective expectations for teaching and learning, and the structures and processes that hold everyone accountable for meeting these individual and collective expectations. Research from Richard Elmore and colleagues on internal accountability suggests that each school or district has some degree of agreement about the kinds of learning opportunities they are expected to create for students and the role of individuals and groups in supporting these learning experiences.[7]

Analyzing differences in school internal accountability systems, Elmore and colleagues find that "schools are likely to have more powerful internal accountability systems . . . if the values and norms embodied in these systems are aligned with individual conceptions of responsibility and collective expectations in the school."[8] In other words, schools and districts have more influence over the daily actions of teachers and leaders when individual beliefs about instruction, collective expectations, and the structures and processes that support the work of educators are closely aligned around a common goal. When these elements are not aligned, there is likely to be a greater discrepancy between the espoused goals of the system and the actions of individuals within this system. The internal coherence approach to improvement builds on this research, providing tools and practices that educational leaders can use to more tightly align individual and collective goals and expectations for ambitious teaching and learning.

USING CLINICAL TOOLS TO SUPPORT INSTRUCTION: THE INTERNAL COHERENCE SURVEY AND DEVELOPMENTAL RUBRIC

In education, professional standards call on leaders to "collect and use data to identify goals, assess organizational effectiveness, and promote organizational learning."[9] However, most data available to educational leaders focus on student performance, not the leadership practices or organizational conditions that support continuous improvement.[10] Although information about student performance is critical, school and district leaders have little direct influence on student learning. Instead, educational leaders influence teaching and learning indirectly by developing a clear vision for instruction, working collaboratively with teachers to realize this vision, and developing supportive conditions for teacher learning.[11] The Internal Coherence Survey helps educational leaders gauge the degree to which the practices, conditions, and beliefs that matter for improving teaching and learning are currently in place in their schools and support them in diagnosing areas for intervention. Data from the survey can reveal a school's current capacity to successfully carry out a collective strategy for improvement. Specifically, it provides information about how teachers—those responsible for carrying out instruction each day—view the organization's conditions.

Schools and districts can use the Internal Coherence Survey to inform their improvement efforts by administering it annually. We do not recommend administering the survey more than once a year, since the conditions assessed by the survey are not easily changed by short-term interventions. For example, improving the level of psychological safety, including the faculty's comfort with new approaches, would require much more than administrators' verbal encouragement of experimentation in classes. Instead, teachers would need to experience positive feedback and support from administrators and colleagues when they experiment with a new approach, even when their attempts fail at first. And like the entire orientation of the internal coherence model, the orientation of the survey is developmental. It is not designed to rate schools as high or low. Nor is it meant to be used as a basis for sanctions or to rank schools against one another. Leaders should not be concerned with trying to improve survey results as an end unto itself, but should be concerned with developing more positive conditions in the organization to support instructional improvement.

Similarly, the Internal Coherence Developmental Rubric can be used by administrators and teachers to assess current organizational capacity and to identify areas for intervention. As described in the foundational learning experience in this chapter, we recommend using the rubric before administering the survey. The process of locating the school or district along the continuum of the rubric's domains allows leaders to draw on their knowledge of the organization. In addition, the rubric can serve as a tool for engaging in shared discussions about the current capacity of the organization.

ADMINISTERING THE INTERNAL COHERENCE SURVEY

The Internal Coherence Survey is an online appraisal that takes approximately twenty-five minutes to complete. It should be taken by every person serving in an instructional role in a school. The respondents would include teachers, assistant teachers, and paraprofessionals but would exclude principals, guidance counselors, or anyone in a purely administrative or other noninstructional role. The latter group of professionals is excluded because all of the survey questions are closely related to the structures, processes, and conditions that support teaching and learning, as a means to capture the existing capacity of the organization to systematically raise the level of the academic tasks in classrooms schoolwide. (For the full text of the survey and instructions for accessing it online, see the chapter 5 appendix.)

Careful framing of the survey data is of the utmost importance. Before they take the survey, teachers must be assured that it is anonymous and confidential. The survey asks teachers to assess the leadership of their principal and their relationships with colleagues, and for this information to be useful teachers must feel safe answering honestly. Using an online survey platform with a single link for all faculty members can ensure that responses are anonymous and can encourage honest answers. Leaders can also make clear that the purpose of the survey is to support internal, ongoing improvement. Specifically, survey data will provide a candid snapshot of the current strengths and weaknesses in the organization to inform the development of an appropriate strategy and will not be used to evaluate the school or lead to sanctions. Overly positive responses will hide areas of weakness that, if not taken into consideration, will hinder improvement.

Since the survey is designed to capture the unique perspectives of each member of the instructional faculty, it is important that almost all teachers take the survey. Specifically, we recommend ensuring that at least 80 percent of teachers participate. Response rates lower than this threshold, especially in schools with fewer than twenty faculty members, can compromise both the anonymity and the accuracy of the organizational data. In our experience, leaders have the most success obtaining high response rates when they dedicate thirty minutes of a full faculty meeting for all instructional staff to take the survey. Because the survey link must be anonymous, trying to boost response rates by tracking down who did and did not take the survey is not possible. Finally, we highly recommend that you do not administer the survey until your leadership team has a solid understanding of the entire Internal Coherence Framework and the professional learning series as a whole. This understanding includes how this assessment of organizational capacity relates to your current improvement strategy and how each of the survey domains and items relates to the practices in the upcoming chapters.

Developing the Internal Coherence Survey Profile

By synthesizing the unique perspectives of all educators who are responsible for instruction, the Internal Coherence Survey provides an overview of the capacity of the organization to improve instruction and student learning. Thus, the survey data should be presented in a way that helps to communicate the differences in how teachers experience the organization. In other words, teachers' overall rating of the school's organizational capacity is important, but the areas where educators' experiences vary, and the potential reasons for these differences, are also important. We have developed an Internal Coherence Survey Profile to present the survey data in a clear and accessible format.

The profile includes two kinds of graphs: average factor scores and individual survey item response rates, both presented below. The first kind of graph shows average factor scores for an individual school from one year to the next (see, for example, figure 5.2). A survey factor is made up of multiple individual items that relate to the same underlying idea. For example, the factor "teacher involvement in instructional decisions" includes items that ask about teachers' involvement in planning school improvement, professional development, and curriculum. As shown in figure 5.2, the score represents the average response of all participants on all items related to this factor. This information can help members of the school community understand the experience of educators collectively and be used to measure progress over time.

By contrast, individual survey item response rates can show how teachers' perspectives vary while the profile results protect the identity of all survey participants. Specifically, figures 5.3 and 5.4 report how many educators chose each response option. As you can see, teachers in this school differed greatly in whether they believed teachers were involved in determining professional development needs and goals (figure 5.3). However, most teachers agreed that teachers were involved in discussing effective instructional practices (figure 5.4). This detailed information can help identify important areas for discussion and action. Most importantly, survey item response rates can illustrate differences in individual perspectives while protecting the identity of all survey participants.

FIGURE 5.2   Average teacher score in response to statements that each of two factors related to whole-school processes (collaboration around improvement strategy and teacher involvement in instructional decisions) is in place in the school (where 1 = highly inaccurate and 6 = highly accurate)

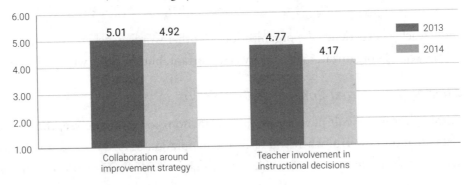

FIGURE 5.3   Survey Example: "Teachers in this school work collectively to determine professional development needs and goals"

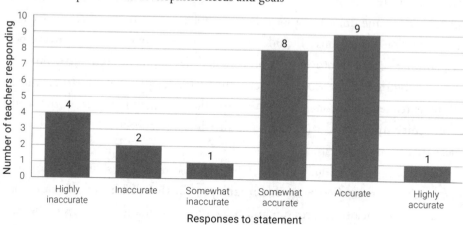

FIGURE 5.4   Survey example: Teachers' response to survey statement "As a full faculty, we work toward developing a shared understanding of effective instructional practices"

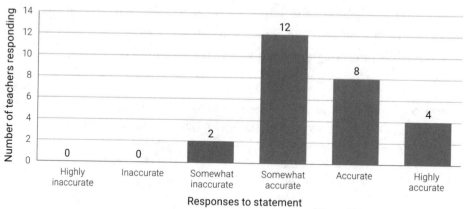

Sharing the Internal Coherence Survey Profile

Although it is difficult not to jump to explanations for what you see, the survey data are most powerful when you resist the temptation to do so. For example, we have seen leadership teams try to identify which individuals in their organization were responsible for the more negative responses. Administrators and teachers may make assumptions about why these individuals have more negative views of the school—they have been rated poorly in their evaluation, are planning to leave the school, are nearing retirement, or were involuntarily transferred to the school. The desire to understand a respondent's motivation is understandable. But responses cannot be accurately linked to specific respondents, and it is unhelpful to dismiss some teachers' responses as unimportant for the school's ongoing improvement efforts. Some leaders move quickly to offer solutions. This is also an unadvisable approach because it hinders dialogue about the data (e.g., "Teachers feel like they don't have a say in professional development? Well, my door is always open. I hope that, moving forward, people will know that they can express their views to me about what we should do in professional development. What do you think?").

To put the Internal Coherence Survey Profile to best use, leaders need to stay at the level of understanding and analysis. Instead of jumping into a solution for teachers' perceptions around professional development, for example, the Lakeside Elementary leaders might investigate the response patterns and gain the following insight: when Lakeside teachers struggle with a new curriculum, they have no formal channel for seeking support because team meetings are not devoted to analyzing the curriculum. Over time, candid conversations about the Internal Coherence Survey Profile can help reveal the conditions that are driving the response patterns and, when contextualized within the full series of essential practices described throughout the book, can lead to more substantive solutions.

Taking a step back to see the system that is driving the response patterns takes discipline and patience. The essential practice, below, as well as the foundational learning experiences at the end of the chapter, are designed to help you dig into the data to understand their implications for your current strategy and next steps for growth.

TURNING RESEARCH INTO PRACTICE

The Internal Coherence Survey provides extensive information about your organization's capacity to develop and carry out an instructional improvement strategy. Carefully considering these data can help you develop a deeper understanding of the ways people and processes in a school serve to support or hinder instructional improvement. The following internal coherence essential practice can help you to spend time digging into your Internal Coherence Survey Profile data and considering how each domain of the survey helps you to better understand your organization's overall level of capacity for improving teaching and learning. As described above, the survey includes questions about essential yet sensitive topics such as teachers' perceptions about their ability to support student learning, principals' openness to multiple perspectives, and whether team members hold each other accountable for following through with collective commitments. The essential practice can help leadership team members to avoid personalizing these data and, instead, focus their discussion on the implications of the data for organizational improvement.

ESSENTIAL PRACTICE
ANALYZING CURRENT ORGANIZATIONAL CAPACITY

This essential practice is designed to be used with an Internal Coherence Survey Profile created for an individual school and can be used annually to reflect on the current capacity in the organization and to understand the changes over time. Taking time to reflect on the detailed information provided by the Internal Coherence Survey Profile can help schools identify organizational strengths and areas for growth that leadership teams can target when they are developing plans for realizing their vision for instruction.

Objective. Reflect on the data in your school's Internal Coherence Survey Profile

Time: 1 hour

1. Assessing Your Organization's Capacity [45 minutes]

Discuss how the Internal Coherence Survey Profile and your knowledge of your organization relate to your plans for improving instruction and student learning. Consider using figure 5.1 to support this discussion. Have a facilitator record the group's responses on chart paper or a shared document, adding to and revising the group's initial ideas.

Teachers

- How confident are teachers in the ability of the faculty to support student learning?
- Are there specific areas in which teachers feel more or less confident about the abilities of the faculty (e.g., supporting underperforming students)?

Teams

- How do teachers view their teacher teams?
- Do teachers see these teams as supporting their learning?
- How do administrators support the work of teams?

Faculty

- Is there a clear strategy in place for improving instruction and student learning?
- Are teachers involved in instructional decisions at the school?
- Do teachers view professional development opportunities as meaningful?

Administrators

- How are administrators supporting teacher learning?
- Do teachers feel safe experimenting with new approaches?
- How will administrators involve teachers in developing shared expectations for realizing the instructional vision?

2. Summarizing Your Organization's Capacity [15 minutes]

As a group, document a summary of observations from the Internal Coherence Survey Profile on chart paper or a shared document. Discuss with the group the following questions:

- What are our current organizational strengths? How might we take advantage of them when we develop our strategy?
- What areas for growth will we need to address to reach our improvement goals? What challenges should we be aware of when we develop our strategy?

FOUNDATIONAL LEARNING EXPERIENCES

From our partnerships with leaders across the country, we have learned that making sense of the idea of organizational capacity and its relation to improving teaching and learning is not intuitive, particularly for teachers used to thinking in terms of a classroom rather than a whole school as a system. Therefore, it is essential to provide opportunities for the faculty to learn about what the data actually mean before sharing the profile with them. To build this understanding, we recommend using the Internal Coherence Developmental Rubric before administering the survey and analyzing the data from the Internal Coherence Survey Profile. The Internal Coherence Developmental Rubric; the exercise described in "Survey Preparation: Mapping the Organization," below; and the Active Learners Elementary case study in chapter 6's appendix have all proven very helpful for setting the stage when sharing survey data with faculty.

Educators with different roles and experiences are likely to see the system differently, and uncovering these different perspectives can create a more accurate picture of how the organization works. For example, teachers and administrators may view the current capacity of the organization differently, given their unique roles. Discussions that explore these different perspectives can help leaders develop a shared understanding of the current state of the organization. Candid conversations about the current capacity of the organization require an environment that supports collective learning and productive debate. Chapter 3 provides concrete guidance for developing or strengthening the conditions that support shared learning in your school or district. Before engaging in discussion about the Internal Coherence Survey Profile, be sure to undertake the essential practice and foundational learning experiences in chapter 3 to actively develop a safer and more trusting environment for learning in the leadership team.

Survey Preparation: Internal Coherence Developmental Rubric

Leaders and teachers can use the Internal Coherence Developmental Rubric to build their understanding of organizational capacity. Although we recommend beginning conversations about the rubric with the leadership team, eventually all faculty members can use the rubric as a first pass at assessing the degree to which their organization is currently designed to support continuous improvement in teaching and learning. (For the full text of the rubric, see chapter 2.) Shorter and more straightforward than an Internal Coherence Survey Profile, the rubric provides an overview of the specific behaviors, beliefs, and practices that are part of each domain of the Internal Coherence Framework.

The rubric also reinforces the developmental orientation of the professional learning series by providing information about how each of the key domains of the Internal Coherence Framework looks in schools where the practice is beginning, emergent, proficient, and exemplary. In contrast to a checklist approach that might provide information about what high-performing schools do, the Internal Coherence Developmental Rubric is intended to support schools at different stages in their improvement journey. Consequently, the rubric can support leaders in both reflecting on their current status and identifying next steps for improvement. In this way, the rubric becomes a tool for seeing the system and considering whether and how the current practices and processes in place support the goals of the organization.

For all educators, using a rubric to assess the organization's capacity allows them to draw on their extensive knowledge of the organization to better understand how the many elements of the system influence students' opportunities to learn. Leaders—including teacher leaders, principals, central office administrators, and charter school network directors—are constantly collecting data on their organizations by visiting classrooms, sitting in on teacher and leadership team meetings, planning and delivering professional development, reviewing student work, and other practices. The rubric can help educators to bring these different streams of data together to tell the story of their school or district.

It can be helpful to reflect individually about one's perceptions before sharing them with others. The protocol below supports individual reflection about where the organization might fall on each domain of the rubric. Engaging in this reflection protocol independently can help educational leaders to both learn more about the domains in the Internal Coherence Framework and how they connect to the current practices and conditions in their unique school or district context.

PROTOCOL

ASSESSING THE CAPACITY OF YOUR ORGANIZATION WITH THE INTERNAL COHERENCE DEVELOPMENTAL RUBRIC

The goal of the rubric is to help you identify where you are as an organization along a developmental continuum, so that you may better leverage your strengths and identify next steps for building capacity for improvement.

Objective. Reflect on the current capacity of the school or school system to support improvements in teaching and learning.

Time: 15 minutes

1. Individual Reflection [5 minutes]

Independently review the rubric, focusing on the content of the key domains and how they develop over time.

Locate where your school or district falls on the rubric. Place a circle around statements that reflect the current conditions and practices in the organization.

2. Document Your Reflection [10 minutes]

Write down your responses to the following reflection questions:
- Why did you place your school or district where you did?
- What data or experiences influenced your decision?

Survey Preparation: Mapping the Organization

Another experience that will help groups of educators better understand why their survey data look the way they do is a mapping exercise, in which practitioners map all of the improvement initiatives in play in the organization and the degree to which they are coordinated or mutually reinforcing.[12] Using the protocol below, practitioners write on individual sticky notes each improvement effort that requires new learning or sustained attention in the organization. Preexisting practices that are now a matter of course, like a homework policy or an existing curriculum, do not need to be included. In chapter 6 you will have the opportunity to impose order on everything you uncover here, when you develop a strategy for how all the puzzle pieces in the organization *should* fit together. But to scaffold practitioners' ability to make sense of the data, the goal here is to reflect on everything that's happening in the organization exactly as it is.

Once you have surfaced and posted on sticky notes each discrete improvement effort that requires new learning or teachers' sustained attention, take out some markers and begin to map out the relationships between them—or the lack thereof! Is a new curriculum that teachers learn about in professional development supposed to affect what happens in a classroom? Will it be considered in teacher teams? Is the work of teams connected to an overarching strategy? Is it aligned to student assessments, and what are the teachers supposed to do with the data they obtain? Do administrators provide feedback on the teachers' use of the curriculum and assessment data? Draw question marks where opportunities for learning are missing, and annotate what is actually taking place in teacher teams. The purpose here is to be candid and to get as messy as possible. Do not strive for a tidy diagram or feel any pressure to overemphasize what's going well. Doing this honestly will allow you to examine what the experience of working in your organization feels like. These perceptions drive the response patterns you will see in your survey profile.

This protocol can also be used at the district level to better understand how district-level actions influence the experiences of teachers in schools. This same protocol can reveal how the many initiatives put in place by different district departments relate—or don't—to district-wide goals for teaching and learning.

PROTOCOL
MAPPING YOUR ORGANIZATION

This protocol can help schools or districts understand the connection or lack of connection between initiatives, departments, or activities occurring within the organization.

Objective. Reflect on the current capacity of your school or school system to support improvements in teaching and learning.

Time: 40 minutes

1. Brainstorm [10 minutes]

- What are all the improvement initiatives currently under way in your school? Write down each on a sticky note and place them on your poster.
- Consider each of these aspects of your school or system: curriculum focus, new standards, professional development, collaborative practices, interventions, and discipline.

2. Map [20 minutes]

- On your poster that is now covered with sticky notes, group together the related initiatives, and develop categories. Draw arrows or other diagrams to indicate relationships among categories.
- How are the categories related to each other?
- Where are teachers learning to do new things?

3. Infer [10 minutes]

- What do you notice?
- What does it feel like to be a teacher in this school? A coach? An administrator?
- What do we say we are trying to achieve? Is this goal aligned with how we are currently working?

Exploring the Internal Coherence Survey

After participating in the mapping exercise and reflecting on what it would feel like to work on teaching and learning in the context of your organization, practitioners are well positioned to think about what they will see in their Internal Coherence Survey data. Before looking at the actual results, you should read through all the domains, factors, and items on the Internal Coherence Survey and predict what you would expect to see in your data, in light of what you know of your situation and the discussion generated during the mapping exercise. When educators reflect on what they expect to see in the Internal Coherence Survey data before administering it to teachers, they can begin to identify some of the differences in how educators with different roles experience the organization and what questions or concerns these different perspectives raise for working collectively to improve teaching and learning across classrooms.

The Internal Coherence Survey describes key factors related to improvement in actionable ways, so educational leaders can apply this information directly to their practice and school structures. In this way, the survey can act as a tool for bringing research-based understanding to bear on improvement efforts in schools.[13] Toggling back and forth between the map that practitioners have organically generated and the items and factors in the Internal Coherence Survey can also help you clarify how the survey data relate to your school or district. Using the Internal Coherence Survey in this chapter's appendix, consider the following questions and reflect on the meaning of the survey items in the context of your organization:

▶ What do you notice?

▶ What do you predict you will see in your survey data, given your knowledge of the organization?

▶ What questions does this raise?

After engaging in the framing, administration, and analysis of the Internal Coherence Survey, as well as the various foundational learning experiences, you should have a solid understanding of the current state of your organizational capacity and the implication of this capacity for developing an appropriate strategy. In the upcoming chapter, you will build on your assessment of existing organizational strengths and challenges when you develop an initial strategy appropriate to your context.

Internal Coherence Survey

DIRECTIONS FOR ADMINISTERING
THE INTERNAL COHERENCE SURVEY

The Internal Coherence Survey is designed to be administered to all faculty members who work directly with students in an instructional role (i.e., teachers, assistant teachers, paraprofessionals). You can access the survey online, at http://ic.serpmedia.org/surveys.html.[14] It asks about the conditions that help teachers learn to improve their instructional practice to better support student learning and includes items regarding support from the principal and their work with fellow teachers. Thus, the survey should not be administered to anyone serving in an administrative role (e.g., principal, coach). As described earlier in this chapter, participants' responses must be *confidential*. Thus, we recommend using an online platform such as Survey Monkey to administer the survey using a single link. To maintain participants' anonymity, you should not collect any personal information (e.g., name, e-mail address, role in the organization). Note that in the following survey, the only personal information requested is the name of the school where the individual works. Even this information is necessary only if the survey is being administered at more than one school.

The response choices are the same for most of the survey items, which assess the extent to which a practice, process, or condition is in place at the school by using choices ranging from "Highly Inaccurate" to "Highly Accurate." In addition, some items ask the frequency with which certain practices occur in teacher teams. The survey has been piloted with these response choices, and we highly recommend using these same response choices rather than replacing them with such common survey response choices as "Agree" and "Disagree."

As described above, each factor in the survey uses multiple items to measure a larger idea:

- leadership for learning: items 1–8
- psychological safety: items 9–14
- meaningful professional development: items 15–19
- collaboration around an improvement strategy: items 20–23
- teachers' involvement in instructional decisions: items 24–30
- collective efficacy: 31–36
- teams' shared understanding of effective practice: items 38–41
- support for teams: items 42–46
- team processes: items 47–52

Only teachers who participate on an instructionally relevant teacher team (i.e., grade-level, content team) should answer survey questions 38 through 52. However, all teachers should answer questions related to collective efficacy, that is, items 31 through 36. When administering the survey using an online tool, you can use skip logic with question 37 to ensure that teachers who do not participate on a team do not answer questions related to teamwork.

Understanding which survey questions relate to which factors is essential for developing the Internal Coherence Profile. As described in chapter 5, the profile should include graphs that display average factor scores. You can obtain these scores by simply calculating the average of all responses on all items included in the factor. For example, the leadership-for-learning factor includes eight items. Each item includes responses that are weighted from 1 to 6 (1 = Highly Inaccurate; 2 = Somewhat Inaccurate; 3 = Inaccurate; 4 = Somewhat Accurate; 5 = Accurate; and 6 = Highly Accurate). Thus, the factor score is an average of all responses to all eight items that measure leadership for learning. You could either use an online survey platform or import the data to Microsoft Excel or a similar program to graph the average factor scores and individual item scores for the Internal Coherence Profile.

INTERNAL COHERENCE SURVEY

Please indicate the school where you work: _____

LEADERSHIP FOR LEARNING

Please indicate how accurately each of the following statements describes your **principal,** in light of your experiences **in your school this school year.**

	Highly Inaccurate	Somewhat Inaccurate	Inaccurate	Somewhat Accurate	Accurate	Highly Accurate
1. The principal invites input from faculty in discussions about teaching and learning.	○	○	○	○	○	○
2. The principal asks probing questions about teaching and learning.	○	○	○	○	○	○
3. The principal listens attentively.	○	○	○	○	○	○
4. The principal encourages multiple points of view.	○	○	○	○	○	○
5. The principal acknowledges the limitations of his or her own knowledge or expertise.	○	○	○	○	○	○
6. The principal is knowledgeable about effective instructional practices.	○	○	○	○	○	○
7. The principal communicates a clear vision for teaching and learning at our school.	○	○	○	○	○	○
8. The principal is directly involved in helping teachers address instructional issues in their classrooms.	○	○	○	○	○	○

PSYCHOLOGICAL SAFETY

Please indicate how accurately each of the following statements describes your experiences **at your school this school year.**

	Highly Inaccurate	Somewhat Inaccurate	Inaccurate	Somewhat Accurate	Accurate	Highly Accurate
9. People in this school are eager to share information about what does and does not work.	○	○	○	○	○	○
10. Making mistakes is considered part of the learning process in our school.	○	○	○	○	○	○
11. If I make a mistake at this school, it will not be held against me.	○	○	○	○	○	○
12. In this school, teachers feel comfortable experimenting with untried teaching approaches, even if the approach might not work.	○	○	○	○	○	○
13. In this school, it is easy to speak up about what is on your mind.	○	○	○	○	○	○
14. People in this school are usually comfortable talking about problems and disagreements about teaching and learning.	○	○	○	○	○	○

MEANINGFUL PROFESSIONAL DEVELOPMENT

Please indicate how accurately each of the following statements describes your **professional development experiences on your campus this school year.**

	Highly Inaccurate	Somewhat Inaccurate	Inaccurate	Somewhat Accurate	Accurate	Highly Accurate
15. My professional development experiences this year have been closely connected to my school's improvement plan.	○	○	○	○	○	○
16. My professional development experiences this year have included enough time to think carefully about, try, and evaluate new ideas.	○	○	○	○	○	○
17. My professional development experiences this year have been valuable to my practice as a teacher.	○	○	○	○	○	○
18. My professional development experiences this year have been designed in response to the learning needs of the faculty, as they emerge.	○	○	○	○	○	○
19. My professional development experiences this year have included follow-up support as we implement what we have learned.	○	○	○	○	○	○

COLLABORATION AROUND AN IMPROVEMENT STRATEGY

Please indicate how accurately each of the following statements describes your experiences **at your school this school year.**

	Highly Inaccurate	Somewhat Inaccurate	Inaccurate	Somewhat Accurate	Accurate	Highly Accurate
20. Our school has an improvement plan, of which we are all aware.	○	○	○	○	○	○
21. We focus our whole-school improvement efforts on clear, concrete steps.	○	○	○	○	○	○
22. We coordinate our curriculum, instruction, and learning materials with our school improvement plan.	○	○	○	○	○	○
23. The programs or initiatives we implement connect clearly to our school improvement plan.	○	○	○	○	○	○

TEACHERS' INVOLVEMENT IN INSTRUCTIONAL DECISIONS

Please indicate how accurately each of the following statements describe **teachers' work at your school this school year.**

	Highly Inaccurate	Somewhat Inaccurate	Inaccurate	Somewhat Accurate	Accurate	Highly Accurate
24. Teachers work collectively to plan school improvement.	○	○	○	○	○	○
25. Teachers work collectively to select instructional methods and activities.	○	○	○	○	○	○
26. Teachers work collectively to evaluate curricula and programs.	○	○	○	○	○	○
27. Teachers work collectively to determine professional development needs and goals.	○	○	○	○	○	○
28. Teachers work collectively to plan professional development activities.	○	○	○	○	○	○
29. As a full faculty, we work toward developing a shared understanding of effective instructional practices.	○	○	○	○	○	○
30. As a full faculty, we regularly revisit and revise our thinking about the most effective instructional practices we can use with our students.	○	○	○	○	○	○

COLLECTIVE EFFICACY

Please indicate how accurately each of the following statements describe the **teachers in your school this school year.**

	Highly Inaccurate	Somewhat Inaccurate	Inaccurate	Somewhat Accurate	Accurate	Highly Accurate
31. Teachers are confident they will be able to motivate their students.	○	○	○	○	○	○
32. Teachers have the skills needed to produce meaningful student learning.	○	○	○	○	○	○
33. If a child doesn't learn something the first time, teachers will try another way.	○	○	○	○	○	○
34. Teachers believe that every child can learn.	○	○	○	○	○	○
35. Teachers are skilled in various methods of teaching.	○	○	○	○	○	○
36. Teachers have what it takes to explore new instructional approaches to help underperforming students meet standards.	○	○	○	○	○	○

37. Do you participate in a grade-level or content-area team? (*Please select all that apply.*)

○ Grade-level team   ○ Content-area team   ○ Other (*Please describe.*) _____

○ I do not participate in a teacher team. (**Skip to the end of the survey**.)

If you participate in more than one team, please choose **one** team on which to base your answers to the following items.

TEAMS' SHARED UNDERSTANDING OF EFFECTIVE PRACTICE

Please indicate how often have you worked with members of your **team** to do each of the following **this school year.**

	Almost Never	2–3 Times a Year	Once a Month	2–3 Times a Month	Once a Week	More than Once a Week
38. How often have you worked with members of your team to discuss teaching decisions based on student work?	○	○	○	○	○	○
39. How often have you worked with members of your team to discuss teaching decisions based on student assessment data?	○	○	○	○	○	○
40. How often have you worked with members of your team to evaluate curricular or assessment materials?	○	○	○	○	○	○
41. How often have you worked with members of your team to discuss lesson plans or specific instructional practices?	○	○	○	○	○	○

SUPPORT FOR TEAMS

Please indicate how accurately each of the following statements describe the **principal in your school this school year.**

	Highly Inaccurate	Somewhat Inaccurate	Inaccurate	Somewhat Accurate	Accurate	Highly Accurate
42. The principal provides teacher teams with the right balance of direction and independence.	○	○	○	○	○	○
43. The principal gives teacher teams a clear and meaningful purpose for their time together.	○	○	○	○	○	○
44. The principal provides adequate time for teacher teams to meet.	○	○	○	○	○	○
45. The principal ensures that teacher meeting time is protected and maintained consistently throughout the year.	○	○	○	○	○	○
46. The principal supports teacher teams in following through on instructional decisions made by the group.	○	○	○	○	○	○

TEAM PROCESSES

Please indicate how accurately each of the following statements describe your experience on your **team this school year.**

	Highly Inaccurate	Somewhat Inaccurate	Inaccurate	Somewhat Accurate	Accurate	Highly Accurate
47. Our team meetings have an agenda, which we do our best to follow.	O	O	O	O	O	O
48. There is always someone who has the responsibility of guiding or facilitating our team discussions.	O	O	O	O	O	O
49. When our team makes a decision, all teachers on the team take responsibility for following through.	O	O	O	O	O	O
50. Our team meetings include productive debate.	O	O	O	O	O	O
51. All members of the team are actively involved in our collective learning.	O	O	O	O	O	O
52. Team meetings connect to each other and the overarching purpose for teamwork.	O	O	O	O	O	O

Source: The Internal Coherence Survey, reproduced by permission from the Strategic Education Research Partnership (SERP). Copyright © 2010, 2015 by SERP.

Developing a Strategy for Organizational Learning

The agenda for the first meeting of the Sun Valley Middle School leadership team was to develop a presentation for faculty explaining the school's improvement strategy for the coming year. To open discussion the principal, Marianne, asked each member of the team to write down on individual sticky notes what he or she thought were the key components of what the school was working on. After a few minutes, she invited the participants to put their notes on a whiteboard, take a moment to reflect on what they saw, and narrow down their observations to the key initiatives in play. When the twelve-person team finished the exercise, the team was left with the following: promoting student explanation and justification of mathematical thinking orally and in writing, incorporating formative assessments into daily lesson plans, response to intervention, data-based decision making in teams, an instructional strategy for English language learners focused on oral debate, and the incorporation of smart-boards and clickers in every classroom.

"OK!" said Marianne. "We've got our components! Now, how do we explain them so the faculty understands that they're all part of a unified strategy?" This proved to be a good question, and it kept the team of teachers and administrators talking for almost twenty minutes.

Ultimately, the team members concluded that all of the initiatives would contribute to their goal of preparing their students, a large proportion of whom were English language learners, for higher-level learning. Specifically, they determined that the new math curriculum and the debate strategy in ELA supported their focus on formative data collection because both required students to explain and justify their thinking. They also thought that the use of clickers synched with computer projection technology would benefit the English language learners who didn't feel comfortable raising their hands in class to communicate their ideas. The technology would thereby improve the teachers' ability to collect meaningful formative assessment data in real time. These data would in turn drive their ability to successfully implement response to intervention and drive their data-based decision making in teams. To present its strategy to the faculty, the team captured its improvement strategy as a series of arrows, each labeled as one of its initiatives, all leading to the team's vision for a student-directed, discussion-rich classroom.

WHAT IS THE ROLE OF ADULT LEARNING IN A STRATEGY FOR INSTRUCTIONAL IMPROVEMENT?

Strategy is often mentioned in discussions of leadership, and for good reason. Educational leaders face the important and difficult challenge of connecting and coordinating the work of individuals and teams across the school or district to advance a shared vision for instruction and student learning. However, because teaching and learning is made up of the complex relationships among the components of the instructional core, developing an effective strategy for improving instruction requires much more than setting goals for student outcomes and identifying instructional approaches or programs for all teachers to implement. Real change hinges on practitioners learning to interact with students and content in new ways. Therefore, developing a strategy requires not only a vision for the instructional core but also a plan of action for the professional learning and collaboration required for realizing this vision.

The diagram created by the Sun Valley leadership team made it clear that all of the school's initiatives were designed to meet the same goal: classrooms characterized by all students able to explain and justify their thinking, with a particular focus on English language learners. However, like many leadership teams, Sun Valley's framing of its improvement strategy as a series of initiatives all focused on the same ends lacked some critical information. The strategy provided little information about *how* these initiatives would support the deep adult learning necessary to change teachers' practice and students' academic experience. As Richard Elmore argues, "Organizations that improve do so because they create and nurture agreement on what is worth achieving, and they set in motion the internal processes by which people progressively learn how to do what they need to do in order to achieve what is worthwhile."[1] The internal processes by which people learn to do new things are the cornerstone of a coherent strategy for instructional improvement. They act as the bridge between what you hope to accomplish for students and where you are now. Nevertheless, these processes often receive little attention in discussions of strategy.

At Sun Valley Middle School, math and ELA teachers were asked to teach in ways that required students to explain and justify their thinking, a significant shift from the more traditional forms of instruction that were prevalent in classrooms. Sun Valley's vision for the instructional core required teachers to change their classroom practice in new and challenging ways. However, the leadership team failed to address several important questions as part of their strategy: How and where will teachers have time to work together to understand the real differences between their current practices and the school's vision for teaching and learning? How will teachers learn to use these new practices with the students they serve? What actions will administrators take to support this learning among teachers?

Improving teaching and learning throughout the organization requires a plan of action for how the adults in a building will work together to deepen their collective knowledge and ability to enact more ambitious academic tasks. This chapter will help you use information about your organization, including the Internal Coherence Survey data described in chapter 5, to develop an effective strategy for how the adults in your organization will engage in the learning required to realize their vision for instructional improvement. The essential practice in this chapter will draw on both your vision for the instructional core and your assessment of the capacity of your organization. It will ask you to develop a strategy for reaching your vision that is focused on adult learning and aligned with your existing organizational strengths and weaknesses.

Specifically, this chapter considers how to develop a strategy to advance an instructional vision. It recommends you take the following steps:

▶ Develop a strategy based on your understanding of *the current capacity of your organization.*

▶ Create opportunities for *professional learning* that are aligned with the school's vision, strategy, and resources.

▶ *Involve teachers in decision making,* so they see themselves as agents of change.

▶ *Coordinate the work of teams* to focus on goals for schoolwide improvement.

WHAT THE RESEARCH SAYS

How the Puzzle Pieces Fit Together

Typically, discussions of educational improvement strategies focus on goals for student outcomes and the specific instructional strategies that teachers will use to meet these goals for improved student learning. When these discussions focus exclusively on changing teachers' instruction to improve students' outcomes, the solution that educational leaders often arrive at is a simple one: teachers need professional development to learn how to change their practice in ways that will improve student learning. However, professional development alone is insufficient for making meaningful and widespread changes in teaching and learning.[2] Real improvement requires alignment among opportunities for professional learning, signals from administration, collaborative practices in teams, and the curriculum and resources used in classrooms.[3]

As leadership scholar Stacey Childress explains: "Strategy is the set of actions an organization chooses to pursue in order to achieve its objectives. These deliberate actions are puzzle pieces that fit together to create a clear picture of how the people, activities, and resources of an organization can work together to accomplish a collective purpose."[4]

The puzzle pieces in place at Sun Valley Middle School—a new math curriculum, new ELA strategy, response to intervention, formative assessment, technology, and data-based decision making in teacher teams—all represent worthwhile methods to improve teaching and learning. However, the leadership team's existing strategy lacks a clear picture of how the people will work together on these activities in the context of existing organizational structures to accomplish their vision for the instructional core. When an organization takes into account the existing structures and processes, and their strengths and weaknesses, it can more accurately determine how the many puzzle pieces—people, structures, resources— could be used strategically to advance the group's goals.

Creating Opportunities for Professional Learning

Historically, opportunities for teachers to advance their own learning have been fragmented. Because there is only a weak infrastructure for sustaining professional learning in many schools, teachers have limited opportunities for in-depth learning about content and pedagogy and receive little support for applying their knowledge directly to their classrooms.[5] Furthermore, there is no clear consensus in education about what and how teachers should be learning.[6] Therefore, schools need a clear strategy that is well adapted to the schools' own circumstances. The strategy should help teachers develop into thoughtful practitioners who make reasoned and responsible instructional decisions, apply them in the classroom, and assess their impact on student outcomes.[7]

Researchers widely agree that professional development that occurs on the job, focuses on content, is coherently linked to other curricular or instructional initiatives, and is ongoing is the most effective way to improve teachers' practice.[8] Specifically, to affect teachers' practice and student outcomes, professional development should have the following qualities:

- ▶ Be directly focused on content knowledge and pedagogy, allowing teachers to deepen their disciplinary understanding and to convey content to students.
- ▶ Engage educators in active learning that allows them to make meaning of new practices and skills.
- ▶ Be strategically aligned with other school learning goals and be linked to the district's priorities for supporting and evaluating educators.
- ▶ Be based on the use of data and assessment results.

► Occur in a continuous, work-embedded model, where teachers have the opportunity to practice new learning over time.

► Occur in a collaborative environment, where teachers can work together and receive support from coaches and mentors.[9]

More recently, there has been a move toward expanding the traditional concept of professional development to the term *professional learning*.[10] This perspective places less emphasis on teachers "being developed" through single workshops or courses and more emphasis on collaborative, job-embedded learning that is grounded in teachers' day-to-day classroom experiences.[11] This type of learning is essential for internal coherence since it is connected to the goals of the organization and encourages collective responsibility for improvement.

When leaders use the essential practice in this chapter (see "Essential Practice: Developing a Strategy for Instructional Improvement" on page 127) to develop a strategy based on how teachers will learn what is necessary to achieve their vision, they begin to create the kind of professional learning experiences deemed most effective in the research. Specifically, they will work to align teachers' professional learning opportunities with larger goals and will anchor this learning in the collaborative work of teacher teams.

Connecting Strategy to the Work of Teams

Scholars in organizational learning argue that organizations improve when they build capacity for leadership and learning broadly and deliberately focus on the learning of the group, rather than the individual.[12] Teams—leadership teams, content teams, grade-level teams, and so forth—are essential structures for supporting collective learning and improvement in schools. They can help break down the figurative walls between classrooms and contribute to the development of shared instructional practices and improved student learning.

In order for individual teacher teams to advance collective goals, leaders must explicitly incorporate the work of teams into their improvement strategy, align the work of teams with school goals, and coordinate learning and action across them.[13] One of the most important things a school leader can do for a team is to provide a compelling direction, or a clear and meaningful purpose, for the team members' time together. When school leaders create a strategy for how adults will learn to work with students and content in new ways, teachers' work in teams is a primary structure in which teachers can engage in active and ongoing learning about content and pedagogy with peers.

The next chapter details how to support teams' internal processes and, specifically, their interdependent learning about the instructional core. Leaders do this when the direction they set for each team's work is clearly connected to the overarching school strategy and when they articulate learning goals that are relevant and challenging enough so that the team feels inspired to work together toward these goals.[14] Often, the stated purpose for teams is quite general, such as planning instruction, using data to differentiate instruction, or engaging in an inquiry cycle to address an instructional dilemma. In a strategy that focuses on how all the pieces fit together, the teams' purpose should tightly connect to the learning and actions necessary to move a faculty from the status quo to where it needs to be. Table 6.1 shows how a teacher team working with a new curriculum that encourages students to explain and justify their thinking in mathematics has better aligned its instructional goals.

Involving Teachers in Developing Strategy

To encourage teachers to collectively commit to a shared vision for the instructional core, leaders must involve them in developing a strategy to reach this vision.

TABLE 6.1   Aligning team goals to specific instructional needs: an example

TYPICAL GOAL	ALIGNED GOAL
Plan for instruction	Investigate the instructional shifts necessary so that teachers can use the new math curriculum to support students' opportunities to explain and justify their thinking
Look at data	Design a formative assessment to see how well students explain and justify their thinking, and learn how student performance is changing in response to the instructional shifts made by teachers
Provide student support	Use assessment data to provide differentiated support to students in explaining and justifying their thinking in math

Examining leadership from the perspective of teachers, Susan Moore Johnson and colleagues find that teachers are more invested in school improvement efforts when they have opportunities to contribute to instructional decision making rather than simply being expected to implement the instructional changes determined by the principal.[15] Principals empower teachers as "agents" rather than "objects" of change when they engage teachers in identifying and solving problems of practice.[16] Leaders do this by engaging in *shared instructional leadership*, or involving teachers in sustained dialogue and decision making around issues central to teaching and learning while retaining their authority as the central change agent.[17]

Principals who work in partnership with teachers to improve teaching and learning may be more successful in realizing their vision for instructional improvement than those who rely on their positional authority to compel teachers to carry out their strategy. Indeed, scholars argue that instruction and student learning is more likely to be of high quality in schools where principals and teachers mutually contribute to leadership than in schools that lack teacher involvement in instructional decision making.[18] In addition, research shows that teachers have more positive beliefs about their ability as a faculty to influence student learning—a stronger sense of collective efficacy—when they can influence instructionally relevant school decisions.[19] By giving teachers authority to influence important decisions about the curriculum and instruction, principals authorize teachers to act as change agents and, in doing so, strengthen their beliefs about their ability to improve student learning.[20] These stronger beliefs can encourage teachers to engage in behaviors that support schoolwide instructional improvement, such as frequent collaboration around instructional goals.[21]

Involving teachers in instructional improvement requires more than seeking their feedback as part of an annual strategy session. Instead, teachers can act as partners in identifying and solving problems of practice as these challenges arise during ongoing efforts to reach the school's vision. Furthermore, leaders can create opportunities for all teachers, not just those who serve in formal leadership roles, to contribute to ongoing efforts to revisit and revise the strategy for improving instruction and student learning. These opportunities enable teachers to raise concerns about what they and their students find challenging and to identify the kinds of professional learning that could address these challenges. The Internal Coherence Survey includes specific questions on how teachers contribute to decisions about professional development, curriculum, and other instructional matters.

TURNING RESEARCH INTO PRACTICE

There is growing interest in the potential for leadership teams—teams of administrators and teachers—to support active collaboration around instructional improvement.[22] Emerging evidence, however, suggests that principals may be more likely to use leadership teams as a venue for sharing information about their plans for the school rather than sharing decision making with teachers.[23] Developing a strategy for system-wide improvement in instruction and student learning is an essential leadership practice that is most productive when done in collaboration with teachers. The essential practice and foundational learning experiences described in this chapter can support leadership teams' shared decision making around the development of a strategy, a vital practice for authorizing teachers to act as leaders in instructional reform.

The following internal coherence essential practice—the development of a strategy for instructional improvement—can help leadership teams work together to reach their vision for the instructional core through a strategy well matched with the current capacity of their school or district. In this practice, participants will consider ways to make their existing organizational structures and processes stronger to advance their instructional goals. The group will consider factors like the way the principal invites input from teachers, the purpose of teams' work, and how teachers experiences as individuals and in teams will drive decisions about future professional learning. Through this essential practice, educational leaders can aim to strengthen both instruction and organizational capacity concurrently, better preparing themselves and their organization for addressing their next improvement challenge. The practice assumes that improving instruction and student learning across classrooms requires much more than simply identifying a new initiative to implement. Instead, the practice focuses on (1) identifying the learning that must take place for teachers and students to work with content in more powerful ways and (2) the way schools and districts can be better organized to support this learning.

When developing a strategy for adult learning to reach an ambitious instructional vision in the context of a specific organization, you will answer questions such as these: What do educators need to learn to move from their present situation to one in which they can enact their vision for the instructional core? How will that learning happen? What is the role of administrators in supporting this learning? How will the work of teacher teams be aligned with the learning that teachers need? What current activities or practices in the organization are taking time or focus away from where it needs to be?

This essential practice builds on the ambitious instructional vision you developed in chapter 4 and the information you observed about your organization in chapter 5. Specifically, the data on organizational strengths and current challenges from the Internal Coherence Survey and Developmental Rubric will be used to develop a strategy that is well matched to the current capacity of your school.[24] The foundational learning experience of mapping the organization (chapter 5) will also help you with the essential practice by surfacing everything that is currently happening in the organization. In this essential practice, you begin to think about what *should* be happening in the organization if you are to reach your organization's vision for the instructional core. This is the opportunity to identify, cull, and reorganize the puzzle pieces that need to be in place for you to develop a more deliberate plan of action. (See page 127 for essential practice.)

Developing the Essential Practice Over Time

Leaders often develop a strategy for school or district improvement at the beginning of each year, only to set aside the effort and return to it at the beginning of the following school year. This approach to strategy development raises two problems. First, the strategy is not a central driver of the day-to-day decisions made in schools. Second, this annual focus on strategy can give the false impression that there should be a new improvement strategy each year. Rather than consider strategy setting an annual activity, we encourage educators to regularly revisit and revise their plan of action as new challenges or needs for professional learning

ESSENTIAL PRACTICE
DEVELOPING A STRATEGY FOR INSTRUCTIONAL IMPROVEMENT

This practice requires your leadership team to have developed a vision for the improvements in instruction and student learning you want to see in your organization (see chapter 4) and to have done some form of assessment of the existing areas of capacity and challenge in the organization, such as administering the Internal Coherence Survey or using the Internal Coherence Developmental Rubric (see chapter 5). The practice is designed to help your leadership team identify the specific learning you need to reach your vision and the specific structures, practices, and processes that you can put in place to support this learning.

Objective. Develop a strategy for reaching your vision for the instructional core that both draws on and strengthens your organization's existing capacity for improving teaching and learning at scale.

Time: 1 hour, 30 minutes

1. Revisit Your Vision [10 minutes]

Review your vision together as a team. How do you hope to see students and teachers engaging with content? Use the document you created to describe your vision in chapter 4 to support you in speaking about the specific changes you expect to see as they relate to teachers, students, and content.

2. Individual Reflection [5 minutes]

Consider how teachers are currently engaging with students around content. What do teachers need to learn to realize your vision? On separate sticky notes, write each instructional approach or idea that your teachers would need to learn.

3. Group Share: Building a Learning Bridge [20 minutes]

Each member of the group shares his or her sticky notes about what teachers need to learn to realize the vision for the instructional core and why. Place the sticky notes about what the teachers need to learn as a bridge between the current work of the organization and the vision for the instructional core.

4. Prioritize and Map Your Strategy for Instructional Improvement [30 minutes]

In light of your understanding of the learning that is necessary and the current capacity of your organization, create a strategy map that addresses each element below (have a facilitator record the team's responses):

- the specific learning experiences adults will need to realize your vision
- where this learning will happen
- who will support this learning
- how these learning opportunities are connected

5. Assess and Revise Your Strategy [15 minutes]

Discuss the questions below to revise and strengthen your strategy for improving instruction and student learning. Again, have a facilitator record the responses.

- Does our strategy have a clear focus? Are there too many areas of focus?
- Is the strategy tightly connected to the ways teachers interact with students around content?
- Does our strategy have focus areas that are complementary and mutually reinforcing?
- Does it provide opportunities for teachers to deepen their knowledge of content and pedagogy?
- Does our strategy foster ownership among the faculty?

6. Reflect [10 minutes]

What are your next steps for putting your plan into action? When and how will you revisit and revise this strategy as you move forward? Again, have a facilitator record the responses.

emerge. The Internal Coherence Survey asks whether practitioners revisit and refine their collective understanding of best practice, and this ongoing feedback loop can turn a simple protocol for putting a strategy to paper into a driving force for improvement in your school or district.

Were the leadership team at Sun Valley Middle School to use the essential practice in this chapter to develop its strategy, the group might conclude that its main focus, in both math and ELA, was to improve students' ability to articulate and justify their thinking, with a particular focus on the school's English language learners. Identifying a singular focus might help the team begin to prioritize how the teachers should spend their time in meetings. Such a focus might also help the team set the direction and purpose of teamwork around key learning goals, use faculty meetings to share individual team learning with the rest of the school, and focus observational feedback from administrators on the instructional decisions made in teacher teams to support students' ability to justify their thinking. Each cycle of collective investigation and analysis at Sun Valley would yield new insight into the instructional decisions that had a positive impact on students' ability to explain or justify their thinking, and each cycle would generate clarity on the next step required for fostering the professional learning necessary to advance the faculty toward its long-term goal.

To monitor and refine your strategy in action, members of the leadership team might visit classrooms to collect data about the progress being made toward the vision. Additionally, they might ask the faculty about how any new or existing learning opportunities were supporting teacher learning and how these opportunities could be strengthened. They could also create opportunities for teachers and teams to report back about the successes and challenges they had when they were trying out new instructional approaches in their classrooms. Administrators could visit teacher team meetings to learn whether and how these meetings were advancing the strategy. District leaders who visit school leadership team meetings could learn about whether teachers on the leadership team have opportunities to engage in shared instructional leadership and to identify areas where the principal could work more collaboratively with teachers. Each of these actions could help provide more information about how to adapt your strategy to better address your organization's unique goals and context.

FOUNDATIONAL LEARNING EXPERIENCES

Developing a strategy that fosters meaningful and aligned learning experiences for teachers toward a shared vision for instruction and student learning presents a major challenge for leaders and teachers. This requires acknowledging the limitations of current practice, considering the current capacity of the organization in relation to instructional goals, and careful coordination of learning across individuals and teams. In our experience, many leaders and teachers find it difficult to engage in candid conversations about current practice and how it would need to change for students to achieve at a higher level. Furthermore, leaders can find it challenging to involve teachers in identifying these learning needs. The following resources can help you identify the learning that needs to take place for you to reach your vision and develop a strategy that takes into account your unique school and district context.

Determining Where You Are Now, Instructionally

For a leadership team or any other group of educators to engage in the essential practice above and visualize a learning bridge from where they are now to where they want to be, everyone participating in the exercise needs to have a sense of where classrooms currently are. This may prove challenging for members of leadership teams or teachers who do not have the opportunity to observe other classrooms or learn with any detail about what is happening instructionally across the school. In preparation for creating the learning bridge that will inform the schoolwide strategy, the leadership team can collect from a wide sample of classrooms some anonymous, nonevaluative data that focus on the current ways that teachers and students are interacting around content.

This sampling can be structured in any number of ways. For example, if you were planning on developing the strategy as a whole faculty, you might ask every member of the faculty to conduct three ten-minute observations of colleagues. If just the leadership team were going to observe classrooms, each member might observe a slightly larger number of classrooms in the same fashion, with the non-evaluative orientation and the goal of identifying areas for new learning made very clear to teachers at the outset. However you structure this data collection, evidence could be tuned to the prompts below.

1. What is the teacher doing?
2. What are the students doing?
3. What is the academic task? (See chapter 4 for a refresher.)
   ▶ What are students being held accountable for producing?
   ▶ What support or resources do they use (e.g., materials, teacher's help, other students)?
   ▶ Given the required product and available support, what must the students actually do to succeed in this class? That is, what is the actual task in this classroom?[25]

The responses to the prompts should be as fine-grained as possible to identify specific areas for learning. For example, observers might collect the following data:

▶ "The teacher sits with a group of three students for five minutes as they . . ."
▶ "The teacher reads aloud a passage from . . ."
▶ "Out of twenty-five students, eighteen are involved in reading from a textbook and are looking up answers to the following question in the text . . ."

Connecting School Conditions and Strategy

The Active Learners Elementary case study in the chapter appendix is designed to deepen your understanding of strategy and how it relates to organizational capacity. You can use this case with your leadership team or faculty to address two common challenges in strategy development: (1) developing a strategy that is well matched to the strengths and weaknesses of the organization and (2) ensuring that administrators and teachers take action to advance the strategy for improving the instructional core. By reflecting on how the experience of the school described in this case study relates to your own school or district, you can begin to identify ways to more effectively develop and carry out your strategy for improving instructional and organizational capacity in tandem.

The Active Learners case tells the story of a school with a pressing need to improve students' performance on a new and more challenging state mathematics assessment. The principal and teachers in this school developed both a short-term strategy for addressing student failure on the mathematics assessment and a longer-term strategy for improving instruction and student learning in mathematics. Like the strategy at many schools, this one is not clearly articulated in the case study. Instead, you must infer what the implicit strategy for improving the instructional core is, given the actions taken by the principal and faculty.

In addition, the case study includes graphs from the school's Internal Coherence Survey Profile, so that you can connect the organizational capacity in the school and the strategy for improving the instructional core. By reading about Active Learners, you can observe the interplay of the school's articulated strategy and the existing strengths and weaknesses in the organization, as surfaced in their internal coherence data. For example, you might note the lack of constructive criticism from the principal despite the strong relationships between administrators and teachers—an area where the school's strategy might take better advantage of its organizational strengths. Although the interplay between organizational capacity and an instructional strategy has been mentioned in this chapter and in chapter 5, this foundational experience can help to illustrate how a school's strategy for instructional improvement relates to its organizational conditions and how these relationships can be strengthened.

The case study asks readers to explore the following questions:

- ► How would you describe the school's vision for mathematics instruction?
- ► What is its strategy, or plan of action, for reaching this vision?
- ► How effective is this strategy for improving teaching and learning in math? Why?
- ► How appropriate is this strategy for the school given its Internal Coherence Survey Profile data? Are school leaders taking advantage of the school's strengths? Addressing its weaknesses?

▶ How does Principal Johnson share leadership with teachers? How effective is this approach?

Articulating the Work of Teacher Teams

Effective teams thrive within a supportive setting. As the school manager and leader, the principal is a key determinant in securing and protecting resources a team needs to accomplish its work. These resources include positive expectations, clear structures, and protected time for teams to accomplish their purpose. First, the principal must protect each team's time and space to meet. When the schedule is set for the team meetings at the beginning of the year, the teams should have enough time to engage in meaningful work with a relatively high frequency of meetings. Although the amount of time needed depends on the circumstances, teachers often cite limited time as a constraint on their work in teams. Teams that meet for only one hour once a month lack continuity between meetings, and teams that meet for thirty minutes each week do not have enough time to complete worthwhile activities.

Furthermore, leaders have responsibility for ensuring that they set a compelling direction for the work of teams. Often, leaders provide time and set the expectation for teams to meet but do not explicitly define what the teams should be doing with that time. In some cases, school leaders see this as trusting teams to act professionally—in other words, they believe that leaving the teams alone is the best way to help them do their work. This is a central dilemma that all leaders face: if leaders provide too much structure or dictate how teams should use every minute of their time, the educators might feel as if they have no autonomy or their expertise is not valued.[26] However, if leaders do not provide any direction, they increase the risk that only some teams—but not all—know how best to use their time and how to focus their efforts. It is the leaders' responsibility to establish the compelling direction for teams, align that direction with the school's goals for powerful learning, and provide resources and structures for the team.

Determining the purpose of each team's work is a component of the essential practice above. However, if leaders have not considered their teams' purpose as specifically tied to advancing an improvement strategy, some prework will be required. Leadership teams might devote a meeting to taking stock of the current state of teacher teams in the building (see table 6.2) and a preliminary pass at what the teacher teams might look like if they had a compelling purpose tied to the overarching vision for the instructional core.

Assessing the Ambitiousness of Our Strategy

Developing a strategy for improving the instructional core that will support meaningful and connected opportunities for teachers and the leaders who support them to learn to work in new ways is an ongoing process. The rubric presented inside the following protocol can be used to assess important features of your strategy, such as its connection to the instructional core and the degree that teachers and

TABLE 6.2   Taking stock of teacher teams

TEAM	EXAMPLE
Who, when, and for how long do they meet	▪ All ninth- through twelfth-grade science teachers ▪ Two Tuesdays per month ▪ 40 minutes
Current purpose	▪ Plan instruction ▪ Logistics
Current activities	▪ Create unit plans ▪ Plan field trips
More aligned purpose	▪ Develop shared units and assessments to support students' argumentative writing in science
More aligned activities	▪ Develop shared unit plan that requires students to develop an argument supported by evidence ▪ Develop a shared rubric for assessing students' argumentative essays and identifying student supports
Changes in team membership or meeting time needed to be successful with this new purpose and activities	▪ Weekly meetings ▪ Monthly support from instructional coach

leaders across the organization feel ownership for this strategy. Using this rubric repeatedly and with individuals across the organization can help you fine tune your strategy over time. The following protocol is adapted from Rachel Curtis and Liz City's *Strategy in Action: How School Systems Can Support Powerful Learning and Teaching.*[27] The activity can help you evaluate whether your strategy will truly support ambitious learning for both adults and students.

PROTOCOL
RATING YOUR STRATEGY

Objective. Use the rubric that follows to consider the degree to which your plan represents a strategy for realizing your vision for the instructional core. The purpose of analyzing the plan first as individuals and then as a team is to uncover different perspectives for discussion. This protocol will help you revisit and further strengthen your plan.

Time: 30 minutes

1. **Individual Assessment** [10 minutes]

Rate your school's strategy using the following rubric. Highlight where you think your strategy falls in each domain. What seems important to address?

2. **Group Discussion** [20 minutes]
   - Go through the rubric, and share how you rated your strategy and why. Are there areas where you or your team members disagree with one another? Why?
   - What areas would be important to strengthen?
   - How might you make this strategy more effective for realizing your vision?

Rubric for rating your school's strategy

ASPECT OF AN EFFECTIVE STRATEGY FOR IMPROVING THE INSTRUCTIONAL CORE	STRATEGY RATING			
	1 (low)	2	3	4 (high)
Instructional core	The strategy focuses primarily on operations and student support.	Some aspects of the strategy focus on improving instruction.	The strategy focuses primarily on improving instruction and student learning.	All elements of the strategy focus on improving instruction and student learning.
Focus	There are many discrete initiatives.	There are multiple areas of focus. Some are related; others are in conflict or competition.	There is more than one focus area, but they are related and focused on improving instruction and student learning.	All elements of the strategy are tightly connected, complementary, and critical for improving instruction and student learning.
Both visionary and problem solving	The relationship between the strategy, the vision, and current problems and conditions in the school is unclear.	Initiatives focus on solving problems or pursuing a vision for instruction and student learning, but not both.	Pursuing the strategy addresses some problems and will support us in reaching a vision for the instructional core.	Pursuing the strategy addresses problems we have identified and will support us in reaching an ambitious vision for the instructional core.
Ownership	There is no strategy or the people in the school do not know about it.	Key leaders in the school talk publicly about the strategy, but others do not talk about or clearly understand the strategy.	All administrators and leadership team members can describe the strategy and their role in advancing the strategy. They know how to talk about the strategy.	All members of the school community understand the strategy and their role in it. Decision-making at every level of the organization (teacher, team, administration) connects to the strategy.

CONNECTING TO CLINICAL INSTRUMENTS

Using the Internal Coherence Developmental Rubric and the Internal Coherence Survey, leaders and teachers can evaluate the degree to which members of the organization understand and contribute to the development and ongoing revision of the strategy for instructional improvement, and whether and how this strategy connects learning across individuals and teams in the school or district. When administrators and teachers use these tools collaboratively, all the participants can help identify specific steps they can take to shift responsibility for developing and enacting the strategy from a lone leader to everyone in the organization.

The Internal Coherence Developmental Rubric: organizational strategy

BEGINNING	EMERGENT	PROFICIENT	EXEMPLARY
▪ Leaders lack understanding of relationship between organizational structures, processes, and ability to reach instructional vision. ▪ Teachers perceive that professional learning is disconnected from the instructional vision or purpose of teams' work.	▪ Leaders are starting to connect professional learning and work of teacher teams to instructional vision. ▪ Leaders are beginning to develop a system of supports to focus the work of teacher teams. ▪ Teachers have limited understanding of connection between teamwork, professional learning, and instructional vision.	▪ Leaders clearly communicate an improvement strategy that aligns professional learning offerings, work of teacher teams, and instructional vision. ▪ Leaders clearly articulate purpose of teams' work aligned with the improvement strategy. ▪ Teachers are involved in developing the improvement strategy.	▪ Leaders and teachers routinely reflect on the improvement strategy and vision, in light of organizational data. ▪ Leaders and teachers revisit and adjust professional learning offerings and focus of teams' work according to progress toward vision.

In addition to items explicitly relating to a strategy, or a whole-school improvement plan, Internal Coherence Survey items relevant to strategy tap teachers' perceptions of their involvement in instructional decisions, and their opportunities to work with colleagues on planning improvement, evaluating the curriculum, and voicing professional needs and goals. The survey questions also ask teachers to reflect on the quality of their professional development experiences, the degree to which they are connected to an overall improvement plan, and the extent to which they are paired with opportunities for reflection in context.

Internal Coherence Survey Items: Meaningful Professional Development

Several specific questions in the Internal Coherence Survey relate directly to teachers' opportunities for professional development.

ASSESSING MEANINGFUL PROFESSIONAL DEVELOPMENT

▶ My professional development experiences this year have been closely connected to my school's improvement plan.

▶ My professional development experiences this year have included enough time to think carefully about, try, and evaluate new ideas.

▶ My professional development experiences this year have been valuable to my practice as a teacher.

▶ My professional development experiences this year have been designed in response to the learning needs of the faculty, as they emerge.

▶ My professional development experiences this year have included follow-up support as we implement what we have learned.

Often during strategy setting, leaders focus on identifying what kinds of professional development are needed rather than on how opportunities for professional learning are connected to practice and deepened over time. Discussions of teachers' responses to the items about their professional development can help you identify areas for greater connection across learning experiences and improve the coordination between teachers' and students' needs and opportunities for professional learning.

Internal Coherence Survey Items: Collaboration Around an Improvement Strategy

A shared strategy for instructional improvement requires awareness and ownership among the full faculty. These items from the survey can help you assess whether the strategy is clear to the essential members of the organization—the instructional faculty—and connected to the programs and initiatives in place in the school.

ASSESSING COLLABORATION AROUND AN IMPROVEMENT STRATEGY

▶ Our school has an improvement plan, of which we are all aware.

▶ We focus our whole-school improvement efforts on clear, concrete steps.

▶ We coordinate our curriculum, instruction, and learning materials with our school improvement plan.

▶ The programs or initiatives we implement connect clearly to our school improvement plan.

Internal Coherence Survey Items:
Teachers' Involvement in Instructional Decisions

Teachers' involvement in strategy development includes not only a discrete plan for improvement but all the essential "puzzle pieces" that are coordinated as part of this plan. Engaging teachers in decisions about curriculum, instructional practices, and professional development is an ongoing process that can help to connect the instructional program at the school to emerging teacher and student needs. The set of statements below reveals how involved teachers are in overarching instructional decisions in any particular school.

ASSESSING TEACHERS' INVOLVEMENT IN INSTRUCTIONAL DECISIONS

▶ Teachers work collectively to plan school improvement.

▶ Teachers work collectively to select instructional methods and activities.

▶ Teachers work collectively to evaluate curriculum and programs.

▶ Teachers work collectively to determine professional development needs and goals.

▶ Teachers work collectively to plan professional development activities.

▶ As a full faculty, we work toward developing a shared understanding of effective instructional practices.

▶ As a full faculty, we regularly revisit and revise our thinking about the most effective instructional practices we can use with our students.

Internal Coherence Survey Items: Support for Teams

As the school manager and leader, the principal is a key determinant in securing and protecting resources the team needs in order to accomplish its work, beginning with time and space. Importantly, the principal must also orchestrate the coherence of programs and priorities across the school. This coherence connects the team's work to the teachers' individual work and to the school as a whole. The survey items assess the level of support offered by the principal at any particular school.

ASSESSING SUPPORT FOR TEAMS

▶ The principal provides teacher teams with the right balance of direction and independence.

▶ The principal gives teacher teams a clear and meaningful purpose for their time together.

▶ The principal provides adequate time for teacher teams to meet.

▶ The principal ensures that teacher meeting time is protected and maintained consistently throughout the year.

▶ The principal supports teacher teams in following through on instructional decisions made by the group.

Internal Coherence Survey data about educators' involvement in, and understanding of, the strategy for improving the instructional core and their rating of the strategy domain of the Internal Coherence Developmental Rubric may fluctuate as participants change their ideas. Educators may develop different thoughts about what constitutes a powerful professional learning experience or a team purpose that connects to the goals of the larger organization. In chapter 7, we investigate the kinds of instructional conversations that must take place within teacher teams to generate interdependent or joint improvements to the instructional core.

Case Study:
Continuous Improvement at Active Learners Elementary

In 2012, Texas introduced new state assessments designed to measure students' readiness for college and career: the State of Texas Assessments of Academic Readiness (STAAR). This case describes how a school with a history of high student performance responded when a group of students failed to pass these new and more rigorous state assessments. The case study raises several questions: How can school leaders develop a strategy that takes into account both short-term and longer-term goals for improving teaching and learning? How can school leaders involve teachers in figuring out how to address problems of practice?

A SCHOOL COMMITTED TO ACTIVE LEARNING

Active Learners Elementary, a school of choice, was founded on a vision for learning. In this vision, students actively construct and apply their learning to real-world issues.[28] Principal Diane Johnson describes the goal of the school as developing students who can think, understand, and "apply what they've been learning to a new situation—hopefully a real-world situation—that's what [project-based] learning is about." The school's mission emphasizes a child-centered environment where

141

students have choices, make decisions, accept responsibility, and engage in meaningful learning experiences, such as project-based learning.[29]

The school's curriculum reinforces its student-centered, constructivist approach to learning. Using Teachers College Reading and Writing Workshop and the Investigations math curriculum from TERC, students apply what they have learned in teacher-led mini-lessons as they read books of their choice, create original writing pieces, explore numbers, or engage in math games with their peers.[30] In addition, teachers use a positive-discipline approach that encourages students to take responsibility for their choices and work with peers to resolve conflicts.[31] This approach supports the collaborative nature of project-based learning. The school has had a history of success supporting student learning, particularly in reading and writing.

Teachers and administrators report that the faculty and families are committed to their vision of active learning. The teachers describe the students as diverse in background but sharing an eagerness to learn (table 1). Because it is a school of choice, families apply to have their child attend the school and are chosen by lottery. This process helps develop a community committed to its vision for teaching and learning.

The collaborative hiring and training processes reinforce the commitment of the faculty to this vision. A panel of teachers determines whether each teacher is a good fit for their school before the principal gives final approval to a candidate. Once hired, teachers receive training in the school's positive-discipline approach and project-based learning, and they undergo Gifted and Talented teacher certification. Teachers are expected to incorporate project-based learning in the curriculum, and all new teachers participate in a weeklong training each summer for three years to support this work.

Leadership for Learning

Principal Johnson was one of the first teachers at Active Learners Elementary when it was founded twenty years ago and has been the principal for eight years. Teacher John Nolan describes Johnson as the best leader with whom he has ever worked: "She gets it. She understands that when leaders take care of their people, the people will accomplish the mission. Our mission is educating children." Johnson leads the school, together with part-time assistant principal, Janice Franklin. In this position for five years, Franklin describes herself as a support person who helps carry out Johnson's vision for the school. Teachers report that the administrators at the school treat them as professionals and trust them to make decisions about what is most appropriate for their students.

Johnson believes that treating teachers like professionals entails providing regular feedback on instruction while giving teachers the authority to determine the most effective approach to meet their students' needs. Johnson and Franklin regularly visit the classrooms. A recent district mandate required each administrator to complete a total of ten classroom visits and three face-to-face conversations with the faculty each week. Teachers describe being observed by the principal as a helpful and safe process. Teacher Linda Ball describes this feedback: "[Administrators] are there to help us be better teachers. They are not there to sit and critique us and tell us everything we are doing wrong. When they come into our classrooms and observe us, they are always looking for the positive in what we are doing. We are very supported."

Teacher Julia Lopez describes the principal's feedback as very complimentary. She added that it might be "hard for her to find something that we're not doing well or that we should do better." First-year teacher Hannah Rodriguez describes how the principal's feedback encourages the teachers to reflect on their practice individually and with colleagues rather than being directive. For example, Rodriguez asked her colleagues for ideas on how to support young learners with visual cues after getting feedback from Johnson. Through discussion with colleagues, Rodriguez learned about another teacher's approach to using visual aids, which she implemented and found successful for supporting students' independence in her classroom.

TABLE 1   Student demographics at Active Learners Elementary

Total students	394	White	58%	Economically disadvantaged	20%
African American	6%	Asian	2%	Special education	5%
Hispanic/Latino	30%	Two or more races	4%	Limited English proficiency	6%

Johnson says that what she is most proud of is the faculty's ongoing efforts to improve instruction. "We are constantly raising the bar as far as what we believe best practices are. We base that on professional development—mostly professional development that our colleagues get during the summer." Thanks to donations from their generous PTA, the teachers enjoy enough funding to attend training and conferences, including institutes with the Teachers College Reading and Writing Project and the National Council for Teachers of Mathematics (NCTM). The principal explains that the Teachers College work "is the standard we would yearn for, so we're constantly reading what they're reading, hearing what their research is showing, and we give it a go here." Teachers describe their summer professional development as opportunities to learn from the best of the best, experts who are involved in the latest research on instruction.

The principal and teachers consider the faculty a community of learners. Johnson actively cultivates this culture of adult learning by encouraging multiple points of view and bringing in research from experts in the field for discussion. Ball explains that Johnson wants teachers to be problem solvers, actively seeking out challenges to student learning and approaches for improving student learning. For example, teachers are responsible for pursuing new opportunities for professional learning and sharing promising approaches with their colleagues. Teachers take this responsibility seriously, preparing presentations about new ideas, relevant research, and resources their colleagues could use in their classrooms.

At a recent faculty meeting, two teachers presented three instructional approaches they had learned from a recent district professional development session on Singapore Math.[32] Johnson explains that the presenters were inspired by a session on this math instruction program at the NCTM conference. The teachers planned to continue sharing their knowledge as they completed the training. They handed out an article to their colleagues, explaining that a study by Barry Garelick found that young students made dramatic improvements in number sense and problem solving after engaging in the Singapore program.[33] Johnson notes that students have struggled with these mathematical tasks on a recent state test.

Working Together to Advance a Shared Vision for Instruction

The faculty works together to agree on best practices. The members have developed what they jokingly call a "Book of Answers," where they record best practices in every content area (see table 2 for an example in mathematics). They record what each practice looks like, sounds like, what the teacher is doing, and what the students are doing. Johnson explains, "One of our mission statements is about creating lifelong learners in our children, but it's really important for us to demonstrate that as well. We think of it as leading scholarly lives, wanting to know and read and try." During faculty meetings, the participants have also discussed their summer learning. They plan to revisit their best practices to see if they need to revise, add, or remove anything, in light of this summer learning.

TABLE 2   Best practices in teaching mathematics

WHAT DOES IT LOOK LIKE?	WHAT DOES IT SOUND LIKE?
Students and teachers ■ communicating mathematical understanding ■ collaborating in pairs and other small groups to share ideas	Students and teachers ■ using accountable talk ■ using mathematical vocabulary ■ engaging in questioning and discussion
The classroom has ■ student work posted ■ math word wall ■ rubrics	The classroom is ■ noisy ■ quiet

WHAT IS THE TEACHER DOING?	WHAT ARE THE STUDENTS DOING?
■ selecting task with learning goal in mind ■ sharing essential new skills through communication and modeling ■ establishing classroom culture ■ ensuring that ideas are valued ■ encouraging risk ■ conferencing with individuals and small groups of students ■ ensuring that the task meets the needs of a range of learners (differentiated task) ■ selecting activities that help students develop problem-solving procedures and computational proficiency	■ engaging in learning mathematical ideas (active participants, discussing with peers) ■ using manipulatives (tools of many kinds) ■ working with partners taking risks ■ listening to one another choosing their own strategies, and justifying their answers ■ practicing their newly acquired knowledge ■ making and learning from mistakes

There are clear structures in place to involve teachers in making instructional decisions. One teacher from each grade participates in each vertical content team in ELA, math, or science. The teachers meet at the beginning of the year, look at the state test data from the end of the previous year, and conduct item analysis to see how students did schoolwide. Johnson explains, "Those teams guide their portion of our campus improvement plan. It's their job to develop a plan for how to address the difficulties we're seeing in that data."

Similarly, Johnson sets the direction for each grade-level team meeting but leaves the teachers in charge of running their meetings. Each grade meeting has a clear agenda and a facilitator. This grade-level leader is responsible for making sure the team accomplishes what it has planned for each meeting. The facilitator role rotates among teachers each year, giving all the teachers a chance to take on this leadership role. Teachers share their agenda and any questions with Johnson after each meeting. The administrators, working to give teacher teams greater control over their meetings, have asked current grade-level leaders to participate in a five-day training on teacher leadership. Correspondingly, the administrators have been reading the research on leading teams. In a recent meeting, they discussed an article about how to support teacher teams without micromanaging them.

The teachers in the school generally have a clear idea of what they need to accomplish during their grade-level meetings, and they work diligently to meet these goals. In their most recent meeting, Johnson asked each grade-level team to discuss how the teachers record the strategies they employ to differentiate instruction for Gifted and Talented students and determine which students would be asked to attend an intersession for additional support. In addition to using the response-to-intervention process for supporting struggling students, the school has changed the school schedule to include a fall and spring semester intersession. Most students use the intersession time as a vacation, but struggling students are invited for additional small-group instruction.

Teachers also discussed their plans for the coming week during the grade-level meetings. In some teams, teachers plan jointly after school. In others, teachers share the responsibility for planning—each taking responsibility for a different part of the curriculum—and share the week's lesson plans at their meeting. In a couple of teams, teachers plan individually and check in about where they are in the curriculum during their weekly meeting.

In one team meeting, teacher Helen Wolf spends a couple minutes sharing how she has started using Singapore Math resources in her classroom after hearing a teacher discuss the approach in the faculty meeting. She explains how she included the folders that the students can choose from during math centers. She gives the other two teachers in the team a copy of each of the papers that she now uses in her classroom. These handouts include number-recognition sheets that the students color, dot-to-dot games that require counting by twos and threes, and a chart game that uses hundreds.

Mathematics Instruction at Active Learners Elementary

Walking into each classroom at Active Learners Elementary, the students are actively engaged in mathematics games and problem solving. In one second-grade class, the students play a game with coins in groups of three. They roll a die, collect the number of cents in coins, and exchange coins for higher-value coins as they try to accumulate $1.00 worth of coins. Students work in heterogeneous groups, some students quickly calculating in their heads the value of their combined coins and others struggling to count coins of different values. In one group, a student tells another student that he can exchange his coins for a quarter and asks if she can help him count his coins. The teacher circulates to different groups, encouraging students to count and exchange their coins for coins of higher value. The teacher explains that two students developed this game and taught it to their class.

In a fourth-grade class, the students have a very large, blank 10,000 chart from the TERC Investigations curriculum in front of them and are working in groups of four to locate specific numbers on the chart. In one group, a student has taken a leadership role and asks the other students in her group to take turns locating one number each and checking each other's work. In another group, a student asks her group to slow down and explain what they are doing. One of the students has labeled the chart in one way, and two other students have labeled it differently, making it unclear where each number would fall on the chart. The teacher checks in with this group and asks, "What are you having trouble with?" One student says that she feels as though she has been left out and she does not understand what the others in her group are doing. The teacher notes that they are working on the chart in two different ways and suggests that they work together to choose one approach for using the chart. She then leaves them to figure out a solution on their own and checks in with the other groups.

A New Challenge in Mathematics

Although Johnson says the faculty members have been happy with the students' language arts performance, the students' math performance fell sharply when the new and more challenging STAAR was administered last year (tables 3 and 4). Each year, fifth-grade students have three tries to pass the fifth-grade state mathematics assessment. They must pass the ELA and math assessments to be promoted to the next grade. Johnson describes the recent challenge with students' math performance:

> It fell tremendously short last year on the first administration [of the new state test]. When I saw the scores, I was taken aback. We had twenty-one students not pass, and never in the history of the school were there that many students not passing. I turned it over to the staff and said, "This is our problem. What are we going to do?" Everyone without a classroom ended up tutoring those kids. It was amazing to me. I was tutoring. Our [assistant principal] was tutoring . . . Our counselor was tutoring. Our multimedia specialist was tutoring . . . Everybody pitched in. It was not acceptable that our kids were not passing, and we got it down to four not passing.

TABLE 3   State of Texas Assessments of Academic Readiness (STAAR) at Active Learners Elementary, 2012–2013

GRADE	PERCENTAGE OF CHILDREN WHO ARE PROFICIENT	
	Reading	Math
3	90	64
4	86	77
5	96	89

TABLE 4   State of Texas Assessments of Academic Readiness (STAAR) at Active Learners Elementary, grade 5, 2012–2013*

SUBJECT	1ST ADMINISTRATION OF TEST		2ND ADMINISTRATION OF TEST		3RD ADMINISTRATION OF TEST	
	Percentage of students scoring unsatisfactory	Percentage of students scoring satisfactory	Percentage of students scoring unsatisfactory	Percentage of students scoring satisfactory	Percentage of students scoring unsatisfactory	Percentage of students scoring satisfactory
Reading	12	88	5	95	4	96
Math	35	65	19	81	11	89

*Note: In the 2012–2013 school year, all fifth-grade students were expected to pass the reading and mathematics state assessments to advance to the sixth grade. Students had up to three tries to pass each assessment. The percentage of students scoring satisfactory (or unsatisfactory) at each administration represents the cumulative proportion of students at that performance level, taking into account students who performed satisfactorily on previous administrations and those who performed satisfactorily after retaking the assessment at the most recent administration.

Examining the data from last year's STAAR, the faculty found that students had the most trouble with number sense and quantitative reasoning. On the other hand, the educators noticed that there was an increase in students scoring at the advanced level—from fourteen to twenty-five last year. Johnson reflects on this: "Something we were doing appealed to our high-achieving math kiddos."

The campus goal this year is to support at least 75 percent of fifth-graders in meeting or exceeding the Numbers, Operations, and Quantitative Reasoning standard on STAAR (see table 5). The first-grade teachers are exploring how Singapore Math might strengthen their math program. In addition, three new staff members participated in a six-week online course on their Investigations math curriculum, by TERC. Johnson explains, "Our three new teachers took the course over the summer . . . Two staff meetings from now, we'll be hearing from them about how it went. If all three of them think it really went well, then we will probably put our whole staff through the online course."

During their classroom visits, the administrators have also noticed that the teachers are using different problem-solving approaches with the students. Johnson is concerned that some students may be overwhelmed by learning a new approach to problem solving each year. In addition, some of these approaches may be more effective than others for supporting their lower-performing students.

TABLE 5   Campus improvement plan at Active Learners Elementary

SMART goal: By June 2014, at least 75 percent of all fifth-grade students will meet or exceed standards in the Numbers, Operations, and Quantitative Reasoning category, as measured by the 2014 STAAR math test.*

IMPLEMENTATION ACTION STEPS	PERSON(S) RESPONSIBLE	PROJECTED DATE	ACTUAL DATE	FUNDING
Analyze STAAR data and released math test items to inform instruction for all grade levels in mathematics	Teachers, data and leadership teams	September 2013		N/A
Provide staff development for math vertical team at NCTM conference in summer of 2013, debrief during campus professional development at beginning of school year	Vertical team, leadership team	August 2013		PTA provided funding
Utilize intervention guide from Investigations/Envision curriculum and school scope and sequence to teach specific standards not addressed in the curriculum, especially in the Numbers, Operations, and Quantitative Reasoning category of STAAR	Teachers, leadership team	June 2014		N/A
Provide fall intersession interventions to address students' identified weaknesses in numbers, operations, and quantitative reasoning	Teachers, leadership team	October 2013		N/A
Provide year-long small-group interventions for Tier II and Tier III students who did not meet fourth-grade state standards in math, 45 minutes weekly, in place of technology class	Science lab assistant, reading tutor, leadership team	June 2014		PTA grant for math tutor
Create word walls in each classroom with common words expected to be seen and used on math assessments	Teachers, leadership team	June 2014		

*Note: NCTM = National Council for Teachers of Mathematics ;
SMART = specific, measurable, attainable, realistic, and timely;
STAAR = State of Texas Assessments of Academic Readiness.

Johnson describes her strategy for addressing this challenge. First, she plans to ask each grade level to discuss its problem-solving approach. Then she will turn over this challenge to the math vertical team. Johnson explains, "There is someone from each grade level on [the] team, so they can demonstrate the process and choose one." She expects the vertical team to share its decision with the full faculty before a final decision is made. Johnson continues, "That will go in our revised campus improvement plan—teach X problem-solving strategy at every grade level." She adds that the approach may be different in the lower and upper grades. The vertical team has had additional training in this area, so Johnson feels "comfortable turning that problem over to them."

TEACHING NOTES

The Active Learners case describes the tension that principals face in responding to the realities of the high-stakes accountability environment while also working toward an ambitious vision for teaching and learning as a school. Principals influence instruction indirectly by setting a direction for improvement and creating structures and conditions to support teacher learning and collaboration.[34] Thus, challenges in student learning require changes in the direction of the school's improvement efforts and the organizational structures and conditions in which teachers work and learn. Researchers argue that teachers are more invested in these improvement efforts when these professionals are a part of seeking out and solving problems of practice.[35] The following questions explore the role of principals and teachers in improving student learning:

- ▶ How would you describe the school's vision for mathematics instruction?
- ▶ What is its strategy, or plan of action, for reaching this vision?
- ▶ How effective is this strategy for improving teaching and learning in math? Why?
- ▶ How appropriate is this strategy for the school, given its Internal Coherence Survey Profile data (figure 1)? Are the leaders taking advantage of the school's strengths? Addressing its weaknesses?
- ▶ How does Principal Johnson share leadership with teachers? How effective is this approach?

This case study can be used in graduate classes in educational leadership and administration as well as professional development for district and school-level leaders.

FIGURE 1   Active Learners Internal Coherence Profile data: average teacher responses on items related to each factor of team-level organizational processes*

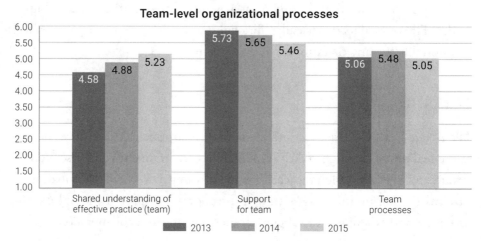

*Average response from twenty-one teachers, where 1 = Highly inaccurate, 2 = Inaccurate, 3 = Somewhat inaccurate, 4 = Somewhat accurate, 5 = Accurate, 6 = Highly accurate.

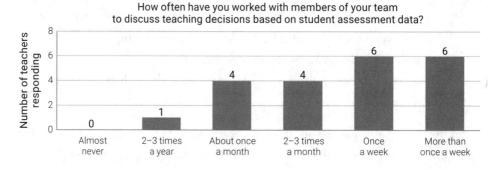

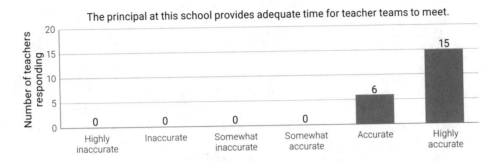

The principal at this school provides adequate time for teacher teams to meet.

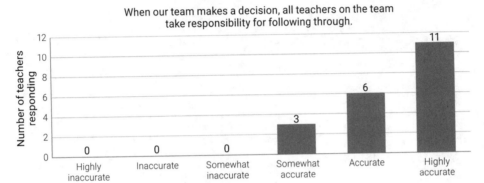

When our team makes a decision, all teachers on the team take responsibility for following through.

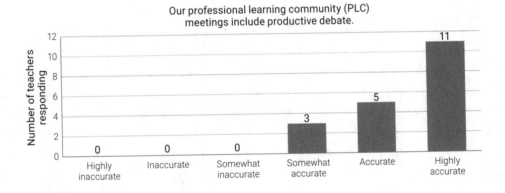

Our professional learning community (PLC) meetings include productive debate.

Supporting Teams' Shared Learning

The fourth-grade teacher team at Glenwood Elementary School sat down for its regular forty-five-minute weekly meeting. Some teachers arrived on time, and a few others arrived up to ten minutes late. The principal at Glenwood had made teams a priority in the school and had designated her assistant principal, Teresa, to be the team leader at every meeting. Teresa saw her role as making sure the team was spending time looking at data to create the next steps for instruction. On this day, she began the meeting by handing out the results from the students' latest mathematics progress monitoring assessment. Teresa asked the group to look at the results for five minutes and then talk about what they noticed.

After two minutes, one teacher observed, "I know that my class did not complete the unit on decimals, so they didn't even see these items that came up on the assessment." Another teacher pointed at the questions toward the end of the data report, saying, "I don't think students understand how to respond to the multistep problems." Teresa reminded the teachers to keep looking at the data, asking, "What skills do you think the students have trouble with?" One teacher noticed that the fourth-graders as a group did not perform as well on one or two questions that dealt with equivalence between fractions and decimals. After this observation, the teachers stopped looking at the data and began discussing how difficult this topic was for students. A common observation was, "Oh, they have trouble with that every year."

> *At this point, the team was interrupted by an announcement from the main office about the busing schedule for the upcoming field trip. The announcement led to a five-minute conversation about field trip chaperones. Teresa looked at the clock and decided that with ten minutes left, it was time to focus the group on instructional next steps. She asked, "OK, let's go back to the progress monitoring assessment. What is your plan to reteach equivalence between fractions and decimals?" A few teachers said they would start their next class with some review problems on that topic. One teacher mentioned that she wasn't ready to do review, because she had planned a special project that related fractions to cooking with recipes, and she was behind in covering the regular curriculum. Other ideas emerged, such as "I wanted to go back to having them draw equivalent models," and "Can we have them practice with calculators?" Despite many ideas being shared, no one took notes. One teacher was called out of the room to address an issue with one of his students. Teresa said, "Those are great ideas. You should update me on how it goes next week." She concluded by making a few quick announcements about the upcoming parent night as the teachers packed up their materials.*

WHY DO WE FOCUS ON SHARED LEARNING?

Today, teachers are expected to meet in teams and are often given time to do so, but the level of productivity and quality of instructional conversations on those teams is still developing. Two common problems arise on teacher teams. The first is fragmented, unfocused team discussions, leading to the common lament of "too much to do, too little time." Teams in schools are expected to meet to look at data, discuss student learning, and plan instruction. These multiple objectives underestimate the amount of time and the focus needed to pay sustained attention to the connection between data and specific instructional decisions that affect what and how students learn. As a result, team meetings often feel rushed and disconnected, and rarely does one team meeting build on where the previous meeting left off. Discussions in team meetings are often not documented for later review. Instead, each team meeting is an entirely new—and disconnected—experience for teachers.

The second problem is a lack of interdependence in teams—a problem evident in the predominance of individual sharing during meetings and a paucity of what the research calls *joint work*. Educators are good at generating instructional ideas, but teachers often feel authorized to pick and choose among the ideas on the table, rather than to agree on a shared instructional decision that all team members fully understand and implement. Team facilitators might see their role as helping the team move through the inquiry process, but, typically, facilitators have little experience supporting the development of deep instructional discussions in teams to address questions such as "How will you address the needs identified in the data?" Consequently, one-directional sharing of instructional approaches predominates. Ideas and information flow outward from each teacher to the group, but those ideas are not connected to a larger cycle of inquiry or action. While sharing suggestions can support the voluntary cross-fertilization of ideas within teams, it does little to support the more intentional development of knowledge, skills, and commitments so that teacher teams can achieve their full potential for schoolwide improvement.

At Glenwood Elementary School, teachers readily discussed their data and shared ideas about how to respond to students' needs. While the discussions were interesting and collegial, rarely did they lead to changes in teaching and learning. In the chapter-opening vignette, when Teresa asked what the team might do to support the students' mathematical understanding of fractions and decimals, many ideas were shared, but there was no consensus about which strategy to try or what it would look like in classrooms. Instead, after looking at evidence of student learning, the team members focused on identifying topics to review or sample problems for student practice. They overlooked *how* they were teaching these topics or using particular materials with students and *why* their instruction had failed to produce the desired student learning the first time around. In other words, the teachers were able to talk about elements of the instructional core in isolation—what they saw in the student assessment data, what skills and concepts they needed to "reteach," or what instructional strategy they might employ—but they didn't consider the critical interactions among these elements that determine what students actually learn.

As illustrated by the case study of Fran and Kevin (see chapter 4), it is precisely how teachers interact with students around content that drives the learning experience students have.[1] At Glenwood, the administrators had established an expectation of teamwork, but had not developed the teachers' facility with digging deeper into the how or why of the data or with committing to changing their interactions with students and content in the future. Consequently, conversations in the team remained superficial and disconnected from any clear, collective plan for action. The teachers and principals were spending a great deal of time meeting in teams but were seeing few benefits in terms of changes in teaching and learning.

Although much has been written about various teamwork structures that have their own protocols and guidelines—for example, professional learning communities and communities of practice—we refer more generally to *teams* as groups of educators who have been given a common time to meet together and are supposed to accomplish a collective purpose.[2] In schools with internal coherence, teams are considered the engine for enacting the school's improvement strategy and vision because they are where teachers work together to make sense of new instructional practices and their impact on students' understanding.

Teams that function like the Glenwood team are not positioned to drive whole-school improvement. Some teachers came to the meeting late, the team members had no means of documenting or reflecting on their work together, and the agenda was loose and covered a wide range of topics. Such a way of working might lend itself to *individual* learning: teachers come; they share or listen and perhaps leave with an idea that resonates or are otherwise inspired to try something new. However, building internal coherence advances the knowledge and skill of *every* teacher in an organization through both individual and group learning. Group learning reduces the variability in the quality of academic tasks across classrooms and builds efficacy around a shared standard of ambitious teaching and learning. Ideally, learning on teams takes place for both the individual teacher and the team as a collective. From a social-learning perspective, group or team learning is a set of social processes through which both individuals in a group and the group as a whole share information and construct, store, and retrieve knowledge.[3]

The two critical aspects of teamwork covered in this chapter are less frequently discussed in the literature but are essential to team learning. First is Judith Warren Little's concept of "interdependence" or "joint work," which describes what happens when teams meet and engage in tasks that require collaborative problem solving and collective action. The second aspect draws on Susan Henry's research about how to support the quality of instructional conversations on teams so that teachers spend most of their time building understanding of the interactions between teachers, students, and content as well as pushing one another to greater levels of collective inquiry. The essential practice in this chapter adapts an analytical tool that Henry designed to help teams reflect on their conversations by using a framework of powerful instructional talk. The foundational learning experiences build on material presented earlier about the instructional core and psychological safety, two critical parts of productive team discussion and debate. These experiences will help educators continue to build up to higher-level practices like peer observation and constructive conflict.

This chapter describes how leaders can support focused and productive team work in two ways:

▶ Provide direction so that teams do tasks that require *interdependent work*, rather than simply individual work.

▶ Strengthen the *depth and relevance* of teams' instructional conversations so that they progress to greater levels of complexity and remain focused on the instructional core.

WHAT THE RESEARCH SAYS

Traditional Frameworks from the Management Field

There are several frameworks from which you can consider the conditions of effective teamwork. One of the most popular comes from Richard Hackman, who studied how organizations and teams function.[4] The conditions Hackman proposes in his *Five Qualities of Effective Teams* include the following: clear boundaries to delineate membership and the authority to enact a shared task; collaborative norms and ways of working to facilitate team process; access to expert coaching to bolster knowledge or skill; and the organizational conditions and resources to accomplish the team's work.

However, because much of the research on effective teams comes from business or management scholarship, several unique aspects of teamwork in education prevent these ideas from being easily translated into a school setting. For one, the implicit norms of professional behavior in education, developed over centuries of teachers working in relative isolation with few incentives for deep collaboration, make even the idea of an interdependent task difficult. Further, as we have emphasized throughout this book, educators are more likely to describe what they are teaching in terms of topics, curriculum chapters, or instructional strategies in isolation, rather than as the dynamic interactions between students, teachers, and the instructional core—interactions that actually determine what students are required to know and do. Without this skill set, conversations among teachers remain peripheral to what drives student learning.

Consider the vignette above. The team from Glenwood Elementary School had many of Hackman's factors in place. Committed to supporting her teacher teams, the principal had created the organizational conditions, like protected time, that allowed the teams to work together within the school day. All team members knew that they were expected to attend the meetings, so team membership was clearly defined, and there was an administrator present to introduce the topics for discussion and facilitate the process. However, the way this typical meeting played out implies that the team members lacked both a clear, shared direction for their time together and any strategies to ensure that their discussion culminated in progress toward a collective goal.

Interdependent Teamwork

To supplement the limitations in existing scholarship in the unique context of K–12 education, the internal coherence approach draws on Little's conception of joint work.[5] She describes interdependent or joint work as teachers enacting tasks that require not only a group process but also a group outcome. Little and others have argued that there tends to be *low task interdependence* in the teaching profession—teachers rarely are asked to create group products, but instead readily engage in weaker forms of collaboration like storytelling and sharing. In contrast, tasks with high interdependence would require team members to contribute reciprocally, so that the result of their work is greater than what any team member could have accomplished by acting alone. Glenwood Elementary School is an example of low task interdependence: teachers shared ideas about topics to review, but then planned independently whether and how they would teach these topics to their students. Nevertheless, the explicit formulation of joint tasks is still challenging for leaders. Table 7.1 presents examples of how teacher teams typically work (independently) and how they might work interdependently (i.e., include both a group process and a group outcome).

In addition to expecting that teachers will spend team time on a process that culminates in a collective outcome, leaders need to support the substance of teachers' work in teams. By helping teachers ground their discussion in the instructional core, leaders maximize the potential that when educators engage in joint tasks, they delve into what truly matters for student learning.

TABLE 7.1   Examples of independent and interdependent tasks in schools

INDEPENDENT	INTERDEPENDENT
Teachers agree on the content and standards to teach in the next month and work separately to write and prepare lessons.	Teachers agree on the content and standards to teach in the next month and collaboratively plan lessons that they will all use.
Teachers each bring data from their last unit assessment to the team for a data discussion, and each person shares a summary of how many students passed the assessment criteria.	Teachers sit in a classroom as a lesson is taught, and they develop a summary document based on their observations. They then develop shared conclusions about what the students are understanding and not understanding, and the teachers draft potential instructional next steps.
Teachers look separately at student work from their own classrooms and, in a later meeting, report on how their students are progressing with essential content and standards.	Teachers use a protocol to collectively examine a cross-section of student work samples from all classrooms across the grade or department and develop a common rubric to assess future work.

Instructional Conversations

Susan Henry, a colleague from the Harvard Graduate School of Education and a practitioner with deep expertise in teacher learning, has focused her research on the following question: how do some team discussions support teachers' collective efforts to improve teaching and learning more than others? From her review of the literature on group learning, teacher teams, and professional learning communities, Henry concluded that both what teams discuss and how they discuss it appear to contribute to the kinds of benefits that teams gain from their conversations.[6] She developed the Framework of Instructional Conversations to describe broad patterns in team discourse that, if sustained, would be likely to have implications for team learning about effective instruction.[7]

Henry defines a conversation as a segment of a team meeting that focuses on a single topic. For example, a team may discuss a problem with a recent student writing prompt. Under such a definition, team conversations may be quite brief or may build on a topic as they deepen or extend their inquiry, creating a longer exchange. Henry says that well-developed instructional conversations with the greatest potential to support team learning have both instructional relevance and depth of inquiry. She then turns her Framework of Instructional Conversations (see figure 7.1) into an analytic tool that we have adapted in the Internal Coherence Research Project as a way to help educators visualize the intersection of these two dimensions and examine their own team discussions using audio recordings or written transcripts.

Each axis of Henry's framework has two separate features, each of which requires some unpacking. Because a solid grounding in this framework will help you engage in this chapter's essential practice, we examine each dimension in detail.

Instructional Relevance

Instructional relevance, the *what* of team discussion, focuses on what the teams are discussing and what they are learning through their conversation. It is defined as the extent to which team discussion focuses on the dynamic relationships between teacher, student, and content in particular terms and instructional

FIGURE 7.1   Framework of instructional conversations

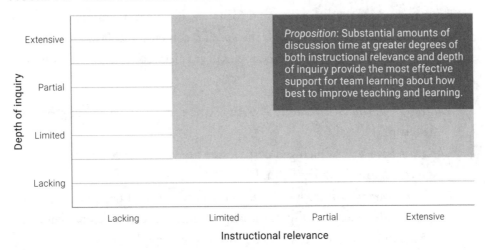

Source: Adapted from Susan F. Henry, "Instructional Conversations: A Qualitative Exploration of Differences in Elementary Teachers' Team Discussions" (EdD diss., Harvard Graduate School of Education, 2012).

Note: Both axes are intended to represent a continuum along which relevance and depth may be apparent; in team discussions, gradations are more continuous and overlapping than are represented by these categorical markers. *Depth of Inquiry*: the extent to which team discussion shows constructive challenge and progression of thought so that a team's understanding and practices are collectively examined, developed, applied, and revised over time. *Instructional relevance*: the extent to which team discussion focuses on multiple relationships between teachers, students, and content in particular terms and instructional contexts. See Henry (2012) for full explanation of both axes.

contexts.[8] Two separate features contribute to the instructional relevance of a team conversation.

Multiple Relationships.   One feature of instructional relevance is how much the conversation is relevant to the definition of the instructional core, that is, to the dynamic interactions between the teacher, the student, and the content of learning. A team conversation that does not refer to any of these components is lacking instructional relevance. A conversation with limited relevance focuses on only one element of the instructional core in isolation, such as which teaching strategy a teacher used, but without reference to the particular content that students worked with or how the students responded to a lesson. More developed, or partial, instructional relevance would be evident in a team discussion connecting two elements of the instructional core, such as which teaching strategy a teacher used to convey particular concepts or skills. And teams engaging in conversation with extensive instructional relevance would focus on the dynamic interplay between the teacher's instructional decisions, the specific content, and how the students responded. Consider the following examples of teachers' comments with different levels of instructional relevance:

> *Lacking instructional relevance:* "What is the bus schedule for this Friday's field trip?"
>
> *Limited relevance:* "Which geometry lesson are you on? I still have to do lesson three, so I think I'm behind."
>
> *Partial relevance:* "I introduced the concepts of area and perimeter by showing the difference, visually, of measuring around the outside of a shape versus looking at the amount of space inside the shape."
>
> *Extensive relevance:* "I noticed that when I was talking about finding the area of a rectangle, I still had students counting the sides around the outside of the shape. Students were having trouble seeing that area is measured in square units, instead of linear units. I decided to have them shade in the squares to find the area on graph paper."

Particular Terms and Instructional Contexts. In addition to the interaction of multiple elements of the instructional core, Henry's concept of instructional relevance also emphasizes the importance of talk that is based on specific descriptions and instructional settings. Rather than offer vague explanations, such as "Students had trouble understanding force and motion in physics," teachers need to give their colleagues a detailed, accurate representation of the interactions that are responsible for student learning outcomes. To do this, educators need to provide evidence of what happened when a particular question, based on a particular representation of content like a paragraph or a math problem, was posed to a specific group of students.

Even when teachers attend to more elements of the instructional core in their conversation, a lack of specific description reduces the team's opportunities for collective learning. For example, a teacher might say, "My students have a hard time with the first physics lab on force and motion, even if they are working in pairs, so I always introduce the topic and the first few lessons as a whole group. Then I can begin to differentiate." All three elements of the instructional core are represented here, but this teacher's colleagues lack vital information: What was the actual physics example that the teacher used to introduce the topic? What evidence did this teacher gather from the students' first physics lab? What strategies did the teacher use to differentiate instruction? Without this kind of window into the particulars of a given lesson, educators cannot dig into the discussion deeply enough to support collective problem solving or knowledge building.

Depth of Inquiry

The second dimension of Henry's Framework of Instructional Conversations, depth of inquiry, highlights the *how* of team discussions. Specifically, it involves how teams engage with topics and to what extent they build shared understanding and new knowledge that informs, and is informed by, action in the classroom. This construct considers a group's approach to inquiry; how a team investigates the relationships between teaching and learning using group processes such as sharing, examining, constructing, planning, and monitoring.[9] Henry identifies two key features that contribute to a team's depth of inquiry: the group's progression of thought, or the series of cognitive processes that shape the group's inquiry, and constructive challenge, or the tension among ideas in the discussion that can help a group reconsider and revise its shared beliefs and practices.

Progression of Thought. One feature of depth of inquiry centers on knowledge-building processes—sharing, examining, constructing, planning, and monitoring—and how much a team uses these to collectively develop, test, and revise its understanding and practices. Many schools and districts are familiar with the inquiry or improvement cycle, where they analyze data, plan for action, assess the results of that action, and then begin again.[10] The linear representation of a progression of thought is not intended to be used in place of an inquiry cycle but is meant to more fully elaborate the idea of interdependence within a cycle. Teams that use and collectively build on the ideas brought to the table are more interdependent than those that share ideas without substantive follow-up. Teams often fail to connect one step to the next during a superficial implementation of an inquiry cycle. For example, a team might commit to making changes to an academic task but might not follow up by digging deeply into the evidence of student learning that resulted. Consequently, teachers are left on their own to make sense of students' performance and its relationship to their instruction. Consider some examples of various levels of inquiry employed in a team:

Lacking depth of inquiry: The team leader makes a series of announcements about when parents' night is scheduled, what time teachers are expected to arrive, and where to obtain sign-in sheets.

Limited depth of inquiry: A teacher describes his struggle with how to structure an upcoming chemistry lab, so the other teachers in the science department offer suggestions about how they have taught this lab in the past.

Partial depth of inquiry: Three science teachers examine and compare students' laboratory notebooks to see how students have documented their use of the scientific method during the past unit. Together, the teachers analyze and chart the students' strengths and needs, using a review of the lab notebooks.

Extensive depth of inquiry: The science department and a specialist who works with English language learners discuss, create, and commit to teaching a series of lessons incorporating new ways to teach scientific academic vocabulary and to assess students' use of new vocabulary. Teachers bring the results of a brief student assignment back to the team for further examination and discussion.

The knowledge-building processes such as examining, constructing, and planning shift team conversations away from individual sharing toward collective knowledge building. When teams engage fully with these processes, which are represented along the upper levels of the depth-of-inquiry axis in figure 7.1, their work becomes interdependent and, ultimately, more effective.

Constructive Challenge. The level of constructive challenge is the amount of tension or interplay among ideas in the discussion at every phase of the knowledge-building process.[11] Just as teams can discuss all aspects of the instructional core but minimize the impact on group learning by talking in vague or general terms, teams can also progress smoothly through an entire inquiry cycle without digging into ideas or subjecting them to collective interrogation. Teams able to move into more advanced inquiry hash out ideas at the table. They engage in constructive challenges that may include checking assumptions and the interpretations driving colleagues' contributions. Participants will play devil's advocate with ideas, will identify why ideas being considered conflict or agree with other ideas or will clarify or reframe what the group understands before committing to a shared action. When teachers collectively subject ideas to a degree of debate before settling on a solution or an action step, they are more likely to generate new ideas and engage in interdependent work that produces outcomes stronger than any one teacher could produce alone.

Chapter 3 focused on building psychological safety to lay the groundwork for the critical but difficult practice of constructive challenge. In one foundational learning experience that follows, we suggest that teachers revisit the protocol "Employing Constructive Challenge" in chapter 3 as a team. Repeating this protocol can help the team build skills to revise their current beliefs and practices, and ultimately gain greater depth of inquiry from their team discussions.

TURNING RESEARCH INTO PRACTICE

This essential practice is based on Henry's Framework of Instructional Conversations, used first as a way to document a team conversation as it occurs and then to analyze the conversation to understand the extent to which depth of inquiry and instructional relevance are supporting opportunities for team learning. The essential practice helps teams understand how their current discussions relate to an analytic tool and encourages teams to reflect on what, if anything, they would like to do to strengthen their instructional conversations.

While it is important for a team to understand how members feel about the quality and productivity of their team time, it is equally important to examine hard evidence of how the team actually spends that time. Teachers need to capture and transcribe a segment of a team meeting, where a group is focused on one topic for five to fifteen minutes, as data for the essential practice. To generate this transcription someone can record the team conversation as it unfolds or capture an audio recording and transcribe it afterward. These data can connect teachers' perceptions of how their teams are functioning with the reality of what actually transpires.

ESSENTIAL PRACTICE
CHARTING THE DEPTH AND RELEVANCE OF INSTRUCTIONAL CONVERSATIONS

Teams can observe and analyze the extent to which their conversations show instructional relevance and depth of inquiry. Doing so can help teams understand whether they are optimally positioned to generate interdependent work.

Objective. Develop a shared understanding within your team about the actions you can take to engage in more instructionally relevant, inquiry-focused, and action-oriented instructional talk by analyzing a transcript of a typical team conversation against an analytic tool.

Time: 60 minutes

Have the following materials ready for this essential practice: handouts or a large poster with Susan Henry's Framework of Instructional Conversations, sticky notes, and a transcript or other written notes from one of your team's discussions.

1. Read and Annotate [10 minutes]

Individually, read the transcript from your team's discussion. Using sticky notes or color coding, identify two or three conversational exchanges that represent evidence of the various points on the instructional-relevance axis and depth-of-inquiry axis of the Framework of Instructional Conversations (see figure 7.1).

2. Plot Data Points on Framework [15 minutes]

Together as a group, read aloud each example, and decide how to plot this example along each dimension on the framework.

3. Group Discussion [25 minutes]

- To what extent does this team's conversation show instructional relevance?
  - What relationships between the elements of the instructional core, if any, do the participants address in their conversation?
  - To what degree were conversations based on particular interactions in specific contexts?
  - What might team members have said or done to raise the level of instructional relevance?
- To what extent does the team develop depth of inquiry in its discussion?
  - What knowledge-building processes are evident? How, if at all, does the team build and connect these processes to gain greater depth?
  - Where is there evidence of productive challenge or debate?
  - What might team members have said or done to increase the depth of the inquiry?

4. Group Reflection [10 minutes]

- What did we notice in this particular excerpt from our team meeting?
- What do we think is the typical level of instructional relevance in our team conversations?
- What do we think is the typical level of depth of inquiry in our team conversations?
- What might we do differently to raise our potential for sustained team learning?

Developing the Essential Practice Over Time

By collecting these data and analyzing them against the Framework of Instructional Conversations, educators think concretely about the quality of the conversations they are having in teams. In an internally coherent organization, conversations that are focused on the instructional core occur at every team meeting, topics predictably recur on a team's agenda across meetings, and teachers understand how conversations progress and connect over time. Teachers learn as individuals because they consider how to use an instructional strategy in their own classrooms. But they also learn collectively because they work to build and record new insights from the wisdom and expertise of the full group, and they are able to connect this work to initiatives and priorities in the school.

While the preceding essential practice provides a starting point for a team to understand the instructional relevance and depth of inquiry of its instructional conversations, a *practice* requires routine participation in an activity or a way of thinking over time. Teams that develop a practice of monitoring their instructional talk have routine ways to document and reflect on their discussions. For example, teams can assign a note taker to make a transcript—or write word-for-word—a section of the meeting so they can examine it later. The team facilitator can then print a copy of the conversation to be used with the discussion questions listed above. Alternatively, a team can assign a process observer to jot notes about the instructional relevance and depth of inquiry of the team's conversation for a brief report and reflection at the end of the meeting. Teams can also commit to audio-recording a team conversation and then listening to it and discussing it together.

Teams that have a solid practice of analyzing their own instructional conversations have ways of checking in with each other about their dialogue. Some teams find it useful to refer to a poster-sized version of the framework of instructional conversations to visually represent how their conversations are shifting to higher or lower levels of relevance and depth as they move through the meeting. An observer in one of these meetings might see the facilitator allocating the first ten minutes to new business or logistics, followed by a very purposeful shift toward instructional planning for specific students. To examine instructional relevance, the team members might ask themselves whether the meeting started out with mostly noninstructional business and then moved to a discussion of specific teacher-student interactions during a complicated lesson. If so, how did the team shift from a noninstructional focus to a focus on the interrelationships between students, teachers, and the content of instruction?

To examine its depth of inquiry, the team might ask whether the conversation stayed at the level of sharing or whether all team members developed shared understandings, committed to actions or changes to their instruction, and, further, committed to reexamining the results of these changes at a later meeting. What contributed to team members' public commitment to try something new? What encouraged the team to set aside time to sustain an inquiry across two or more meetings? By charting and revisiting the specific questions, conversational moves, and discussion prompts that pushed the team to greater instructional relevance and depth of inquiry, the team can learn what to say and do to strengthen its instructional conversations over time.

FOUNDATIONAL LEARNING EXPERIENCES

This chapter focuses on more advanced team practices. In many organizations, the basic conditions for effective teams—like protected meeting time, basic processes, or effective facilitation techniques—require attention as well. Because ample resources on these topics exist, we do not cover them here.[12] Rather, we provide ways to help educators think about their team's purpose and conversations in terms of interdependent work focused on the instructional core. The following foundational learning experiences provide additional opportunities for teams to reflect on the purpose of their time together. These experiences enable educators to analyze a sample transcript before attempting to do so with their own data and to use the highly scaffolded protocol presented in chapter 3 to safely develop the habits of constructive challenge in their own team situation. The final foundational learning experiences in this chapter encourage educators to collect peer observation data as a support for advancing instructional relevance and depth of inquiry. In these experiences, educators revisit the team discussion from the case study of Fran and Kevin in chapter 4 and imagine what peer observation might look like if it were a tool for team learning.

Assessing the Purpose of Teamwork

Because a truly interdependent goal for teamwork is not as intuitive in the field of education as in business or management, and because teachers often do not view their team time as a vehicle for driving collective changes to beliefs and practice, we recommend that you engage in a straightforward exercise to consider yourself in these terms. Specifically, all members of the team can write down on a sticky note their responses to the question "What is the main purpose of our team's work?" and place their responses on a spectrum from *independent work* to *interdependent learning*. It helps to draw this continuum on a poster, with each concept at either end of a line or an arrow. Once all responses have been placed, the team can collectively review the individual sticky notes to gain greater specificity and to agree on where the team currently perceives itself to be. For example, if the team finds that its members believe that they meet together to "update each other on where they are in the curriculum" or "review the schedule for assessments," those responses might indicate that teachers feel fairly independent and are using the team meeting time to catch up on business and logistics. However, if team members explain that the purpose of their meetings is to "jointly plan lessons based on a shared analysis of student work," they probably have more faith in the value of their collaborative efforts.

When we conducted this activity with our partners in California, the participants raised an important point. Despite the teams' regular use of discussion protocols intended to support collective learning, this intention was undermined by the teachers' discomfort with pushing back on each other's ideas. In other words, they were not moving beyond the "land of nice." The teachers' discomfort with constructive challenge or productive debate had rendered their work closer to the independent end of the spectrum, despite the sophistication of their collective protocols. If team members disagreed with a hypothesis or an action step advanced by a colleague, they would remain silent rather than contribute a different perspective or hypothesis, and they would simply continue to act on their personal beliefs in their own classroom. This disconnect between the intent of the protocols and the results was a useful insight for the California teams. We urge facilitators to incorporate all four features of Henry's multidimensional criteria when analyzing the *what* and *how* of team talk.

Building Facility with Individual Dimensions of the Framework of Instructional Conversations

Because her framework is multifaceted and complex, Henry recommends scaffolding practitioners' facility with the two dimensions one at a time. If the essential practice is to be useful, teams need a clear and shared understanding of each dimension first. Using sample conversational segments from actual team meetings or representative segments created for the purpose of this exercise, start with one dimension at a time.[13] The following is a fifteen- to twenty-minute warm-up protocol that Henry uses as a guided experience in separating instructional relevance from depth of inquiry, developing the extent of each, and plotting them appropriately on the framework:

- ▸ Participants read three or four sample conversational segments individually (see sample transcripts below).
- ▸ Using either instructional relevance or depth of inquiry, participants discuss the extent of the dimension present in each segment, specifically considering each dimension's two distinct features.
- ▸ The team jointly determines where each segment should be placed on the axis.
- ▸ The process is repeated for the other dimension.

Sample Transcript: Glenwood Elementary Fifth-Grade Team Meeting

The fifth-grade team at Glenwood Elementary School is meeting to review its curriculum at the start of the year. Teresa, the assistant principal and facilitator of all team meetings, passes out copies of the fifth-grade curriculum map and the fifth-grade standards. The team members have brought their teachers' manuals and materials for the literacy block.

TERESA: Let's reflect on the fifth-grade curriculum map. What worked? What didn't work? I remember we did biographies last year and feature articles . . .

SHEILA: I did a professional development workshop called "History Makers" at the John F. Kennedy museum. It taught the kids how to cite different sources and then write biographies. We can tie the biographies into whatever we're doing in social studies.

DIEGO: One of the things that my kids were proud of was their biography posters.

ANNE: I'm hesitant to take things out of the curriculum, but two months for poetry . . . and feature articles . . . that was too long.

SHEILA: My students loved reading the feature articles, but not writing them!

TERESA: How about changing the format that you're using? Last year, it was difficult because of the concern about reading levels—so many kids couldn't understand what they were reading—so maybe sticking to the same theme but using different activities?

ANNE: We did a lot of generating ideas for the writing, but not the mechanics. Over the summer, I took a course about written expression, and it was about subjects and predicates with symbols and hand signals. It gives teachers and students a common language to discuss grammar.

DIEGO: Maybe that fits with how we start the readers and writers workshop routine this year?

ANNE: We always started writers workshop going over mechanics and usage, editing marks. In October, you can hit the ground running.

SHEILA: They have writing right from the beginning, but you choose what skills you want to focus on. I used to use a journal sticker, where you could check off what you're looking at. October could be the month of punctuation, then verb-tense agreement . . .

MARKUS: In the last school where I worked, they do this all together, so in the first grade, you know what they're doing. It's vertical planning. The whole school would be working on one skill at the different grade levels at the same time.

TERESA: Let's make a list of all the topics we'd like to focus on during our first month of team meetings and prioritize them.

The team members move into a discussion about their weekly schedule and how much time they have for team meetings.

Sample Transcript: Glenwood Elementary Second-Grade Team Meeting

Teresa, the assistant principal, meets with the second-grade team as the participants look over their data from the recent district-provided math assessment. When the meeting starts, a few of the teachers are explaining their frustration with some of the test questions.

TERESA: I know there are some items that were worded strangely or not like we taught it. Let's think about those bigger concepts. How could you teach it, so students master it?

Jackson, a teacher, is looking at a sheet that shows the items each student missed. He starts up the conversation with his fellow teachers.

JACKSON: All my students had trouble with the standards on fact families and items with missing numbers—algebraic expressions. I have two students I don't see passing math, so I'll have to hit it in small group.

LORI: I have one little sweetheart in my class who—this is like a foreign language to her.

TANYA: That student will be tested and have it read aloud in the future.

LORI: I think my students were distracted.

TANYA: Well, for Jessica [a student], I think it was a language issue. She's in the English as a Second Language class.

TERESA: Let's look at problem number three. There was a big difference between how students in each class did.

JACKSON: We have been reviewing fact families in our daily morning routine.

TERESA: So the odd and even and the fact families are things that you're going to work on.

Teresa gives each teacher a sheet for data analysis and reporting and asks the teachers to complete it and document when they are next going to work on the math content for review.

TERESA: The majority of yours did really well, Tanya. For a lot of questions, your students scored over 90 percent.

TANYA: I was joking with them, saying, "I'd better see those strategies, or you'll be eating lunch with me in the classroom!"

TERESA: Regardless, if it hadn't been taught well, they wouldn't have done it. Let's take another look and see which other standards we missed on this assessment.

The teachers mark on the data analysis and reporting sheet the standards that had items mostly correct or many wrong. They begin making lists with the names of the students who missed specific items.

Practicing the Constructive Challenge Protocol

The degree to which team members push back on, and hash out, their understandings and develop action steps as they proceed through the phases of an inquiry cycle is a critical determinant of group learning. If some team members sit quietly and let their more energetic or more opinionated team members steer the discussion, the quality of the ideas generated, the level of commitment for individual follow-through, and the degree of interdependence is compromised. Because constructive challenge is a critical but difficult skill to learn, we developed a protocol from Henry's work explicitly designed to scaffold this approach. This protocol is introduced as "Employing Constructive Challenge," in chapter 3, as well as an imagined dialogue from a team that uses constructive challenge. We highly recommend that each teacher team revisit this topic and use "Employing Constructive Challenge" to develop psychological safety for this critical practice.

Discussing the Importance of Classroom Observation Data for Interdependent Learning

Effective teams have a clear, shared understanding about what good instruction looks like in their classrooms. Without this shared understanding, team members might think they are working toward common goals, but in reality, they are working in ways that are counter to one another's efforts. If teams are having trouble moving to greater instructional relevance, and their conversations are not focused on the instructional interactions between the teacher, the students, and the content being learned, the teams might need to gather evidence of teaching and learning as a starting point for team conversations. Most teams *think* they talk about instruction, but without seeing the lesson itself, teachers can find it difficult to comment when colleagues report back on how a lesson went.

In the section "Stated Versus Enacted Task Experience: The Case of Fran and Kevin" (chapter 4), the reader figuratively watches two teachers teach the "same" math lesson, with very different results. Fran later meets with her team and reports in broad terms what happened when she tried the lesson plan. Unlike the reader, Fran's team members did not have the benefit of watching her in the classroom, and they therefore lacked evidence to understand whatever student learning had or had not taken place. Their team conversation would probably have been different if the teachers had actually stood in Fran's and Kevin's classrooms, observing the specific instructional decisions each teacher made, how the students responded, and what the students learned or did not learn as a result. Often, teams will rightfully conclude that they need to directly observe their peers teaching in classrooms to gather specific evidence for team discussions. In addition to the prompts included in the case, team members might discuss the following questions:

▶ How might you characterize this team's discussion according to Henry's Framework of Instructional Conversations?

▶ How likely was their discussion to have an impact on the team's shared understanding of the connections between particular instructional decisions and student learning?

▶ What might the team have discussed in preparation for Kevin's lesson if they had observed Fran teach? How might this discussion have led to team learning?

Envisioning a Peer Observation Practice to Advance the Work of Teams

Another way to build readiness for, and interest in, peer observation is to explicitly reorient the purpose of the exercise. Traditionally, the purpose of observation is to evaluate or support the growth of an individual teacher, but teams in internally coherent schools also observe peers to anchor their team conversation in particular interactions in the instructional core and their impact on the stated task and on student outcomes. Numerous clinical practices describe processes for peer observation, but we do not promote a particular approach.[14] Rather, we encourage teams to develop a system in which team members spend time in a peer's classroom and document nonjudgmental, specific observations about the interactions between the elements of the instructional core and the academic task (see chapter 4 for a guide to determining the enacted instructional task in an observation).

While we hope that the benefits of peer observation are evident, the long-standing connection between observation and evaluation can make teachers nervous. We have adapted the "Fears and Hopes" protocol to allow teachers not only to express their worries but also to share their goals for peer observation.[15]

PROTOCOL:
USING HOPES, FEARS, AND COMMITMENTS FOR PEER OBSERVATION

This protocol is most effective after your teams have clarified the purpose and value of observing one another's classrooms. You might also read about how other schools have approached peer observation in a manner that supports learning.[16] As a facilitator, you can use the protocol to give the teachers a chance to be honest about how they are feeling. Then you can create an initial series of commitments to design a peer observation process that honors fears and supports their needs.

Objective. Develop a set of commitments to begin a psychologically safe practice of peer observation to advance the work of a team.

Time: 30 minutes

1. Individual Write: Hopes and Fears [5 minutes]

Each member records his or her responses to the following questions, using one sticky note for hopes and one for fears:

- If our team process for peer observation met or exceeded my hopes, what would or would not have happened?
- If our team process for peer observation confirmed my fears, what would or would not have happened?

2. Discussion [10 minutes]

Individuals can read his or her hopes and fears out loud, or people can post them on a wall anonymously and then have everyone read silently. Then, the team engages in a group discussion about the following questions:

- What do we notice about our hopes? What do we notice about our fears?

3. Group Commitments [15 minutes]

In this round, the team engages in a group discussion about creating a psychologically safe process for peer observations:

- How can we begin peer observation in a way that generates our hopes and avoids our fears?
- What will our process for peer observation be?
- What commitments will we make to each other as we begin peer observations?

Record these commitments on chart paper or a shared document.

CONNECTING TO CLINICAL INSTRUMENTS

Educators can use the data from the Internal Coherence Survey and Developmental Rubric to better understand effective teamwork, to self-reflect, to collect evidence about what is going well in their teams, and to decide on next steps. The tools also provide language for what teams can do differently to strengthen their teamwork.

The Internal Coherence Developmental Rubric: teacher teams

BEGINNING	EMERGENT	PROFICIENT	EXEMPLARY
- Teachers work in isolation from their teammates. - Teachers rarely observe instruction or learning across classrooms. - Team conversations reveal low depth of inquiry and low instructional relevance.	- Teams emphasize individual sharing without team expectations for commitment to action and reporting back to the team. - Teachers are beginning to examine instruction and learning through artifacts such as student work. Team conversations reveal either deeper level of inquiry or increased instructional relevance.	- Teams have frequent tasks that require interdependent work and follow-through. - Teachers have a routine practice of observing instruction and learning in classrooms or through video recording. - Team conversations move consistently to deeper level of inquiry and more relevance.	- Teams reflect on the impact of their interdependent work on their teaching and learning. - Teachers use their learning from classroom observations to revisit and revise their instructional plans. - Teams have a practice for periodically examining their instructional conversations over time.

In internally coherent schools, teams provide a powerful structure for educator learning, which is coordinated to benefit the learning and actions of the broader organization. Three factors in the Internal Coherence Survey address teamwork: shared understanding of effective practice and team processes, which are addressed below, and support for the teams, which is covered in chapter 6.

Internal Coherence Survey Items: Teams' Shared Understanding of Effective Practice

These survey items indicate the importance of developing a common language about learning and teaching.

ASSESSING TEAMS' SHARED UNDERSTANDING OF EFFECTIVE PRACTICE

▶ How often have you worked with members of your team to discuss teaching decisions based on student work?

▶ How often have you worked with members of your team to discuss teaching decisions based on student assessment data?

▶ How often have you worked with members of your team to evaluate curricular or assessment materials?

▶ How often have you worked with members of your team to discuss lesson plans or specific instructional practices?

Internal Coherence Survey Items: Team Processes

These survey items suggest ways for teams to support and develop their collaborative practices.

ASSESSING TEAM PROCESSES

▶ Our team meetings have an agenda, which we do our best to follow.

▶ There is always someone who has the responsibility of guiding or facilitating our team discussions.

▶ When our team makes a decision, all teachers on the team take responsibility for following through.

▶ Our team meetings include productive debate.

▶ All members of the team are actively involved in our collective learning.

▶ Team meetings connect to each other and the overarching purpose for teamwork.

In the next, and final, practice chapter, we consider how leaders can reap the benefits of all of the work thus far on safety, vision, strategy, and teams. We show how you can deliberately connect teachers' efficacy beliefs to their ability to achieve a shared, ambitious vision for the instructional core.

8

Efficacy for Instructional Improvement

The Internal Coherence Framework and professional learning series are designed to create the conditions for sustained adult learning about the instructional core to optimize the probability that teachers have successful experiences with ambitious instructional practice in their classrooms. These successful, or mastery, experiences are the most powerful source of positive efficacy beliefs among teachers, defined as teachers' confidence in their capability to generate desired student learning outcomes. When teachers witness their students succeeding on a higher level of academic task than the teachers previously thought possible and understand their students' success as a consequence of their efforts, teachers change previously held beliefs about what their students can do.

To make more tangible the relationship between mastery experiences, beliefs about capability, and teachers' willingness to set ambitious goals for student outcomes and to take responsibility for achieving them, we present the following implausible but, hopefully, illustrative thought experiment. By the end of this chapter, we hope readers will understand why an explicit outcome of the Internal Coherence Framework and professional learning series is to improve teacher efficacy for attaining an ambitious instructional vision and for continuous learning with colleagues.

> *Imagine the following: In an effort to raise district morale in the face of disappointing assessment scores, your superintendent at Seacoast School District offers a $250,000 prize to any school able to master the "We Can Do It!" challenge set for the end of the week. To master the challenge, each school will select a four-person teacher team to work together to lift the superintendent's car a full two inches off the ground. Your principal selects your middle school science team to represent the school because of your team's endless energy, positivity, and dedication to your students.*
>
> *Throughout the week, the principal has students and faculty make banners and T-shirts for inspiration, with slogans like "Seacoast Middle School Teachers Never Give Up!," "Seacoast Accepts ONLY Success!," and "We Believe in You, Seacoast Science Team!" On the day of the challenge, your team shows up well rested and ready. The members are excited to bring home the much-needed prize money for the school, which will be used to replace the depressing courtyard with a beautiful new playground. Taking your places around the car, you and your three teammates smile encouragingly at each other, look up at your colleagues, the principal, and your students cheering wildly and waving banners in the stands. Each of you takes a deep breath, and . . . nothing. With all four of you straining and pulling up on the car with everything you've got, the tires do not budge.*
>
> *"You can do it!" screams your principal from the sidelines. Cheers of support and "Don't give up!," "We believe in you!," and "Think about the new playground!" reach your ears. The team, on the count of three, tries again, with the same result. The car tires move not a millimeter. "Don't give up!" yells your principal. "Seacoast teachers expect success!" Your teammates give one more count of three and a final effort, but it's no use. As much as you care about your school, as much as you want that new playground for your students, the car is simply too heavy. There is nothing you can do.*

WHY WE CARE ABOUT TEACHER EFFICACY

Teachers' perceptions of their own and their colleagues' capability to generate desired student outcomes have an impact on the effort, creativity, and resilience teachers expend in their pursuit of instructional excellence. When teachers believe that they can generate high levels of student learning, they are more likely to engage in productive teaching behaviors like maintaining a supportive learning environment, enacting inclusive instructional strategies, and taking responsibility for student learning outcomes. As a result, teachers with positive efficacy beliefs consistently produce higher levels of student learning than do teachers without this faith in their ability to generate desired change.

As an organizational trait, positive efficacy beliefs in the capacity of the collective provide a boost to teachers' morale, tenacity, and resilience as they pursue increasingly ambitious student learning outcomes, rendering themselves more likely to achieve their goals. When teachers succeed because of their work together, the faculty's collective experience of mastery for improvement generates energy and resilience to take on its next identified challenge. By contrast, teachers with low efficacy believe that factors outside their control, like the social or cognitive needs of the children they teach, overwhelm any power they hold over their students' learning. In schools with low confidence in their capability to effect student learning, teachers dwell on past failures, diminishing the collective levels of persistence, creativity, or willingness to take responsibility for poor student outcomes. In situations like these, demoralization, low effort, and low student achievement become an ongoing, self-fulfilling cycle.

The connection between beliefs about capability and proactive behavior is a logical one: if individuals believe they lack the ability to bring about a desired goal, there is little motivating them to try to achieve it or take responsibility for it if they fail. Consider the teachers on the Seacoast science team in the vignette above. Once they realized that they did not have the ability to lift the superintendent's car, their energy and persistence for continuing to try dissipated rapidly—not because they didn't care deeply about the outcome, but because they are rational beings! If the car wasn't going to move no matter what they did, why continue to expend energy with no hope of success? But what if the principal of Seacoast Middle, upon learning the details of the challenge, had engaged the services of a professional weight lifter rather than creating motivational banners and T-shirts? The scenario would look more like this:

Taking your places around the car, you and your three teammates smile encouragingly at each other, look up at your colleagues, the principal, and the students cheering wildly in the stands. Each of you takes a deep breath, and . . . nothing. With all four of you straining and pulling up on the car with everything you've got, the tires do not budge. At this point, the principal sends over a professional weight lifter. He rearranges your positioning around the car and, one by one, adjusts your individual stances (knees this far apart, hands placed here) and traces in the air the trajectory you are to imagine as you lift. Walking around to check all of your positions a final time, he instructs that on the count of three, all four of you are to lift the car along your assigned trajectories with all your might. He is somewhat intimidating, looking each of you in the eye to confirm that you are ready.

"One . . . two . . . three!" he shouts, and each of you gives it everything you've got—lifting from the legs along your assigned trajectory, and . . . you feel the tires begin to lift! Although you don't get all four tires up the full two inches, you felt them leave the ground. The weight lifter comes around again, readjusts your stances, again points out your envisioned trajectory, makes you demonstrate it back to him, and reminds you how to hold your legs and back. He says, "This time, on my count, you lift and you scream out loud and do not stop until I say drop. Got it?" You all nod. You take a deep breath, wait for his count, and on three, you lift and yell with absolutely everything you have until you hear a triumphant "Drop!" You and your teammates have done it. You have cleared the two inches and won the prize money for your school.

What happened here? Despite how far-fetched this scenario is, it is exciting to see the teachers raise the car off the ground. That's because this encounter led the teachers to experience a crucial shift in what the research terms a *locus of control*.[1] In the first attempt, the teachers were unable to achieve their desired outcome, because the car was too heavy. No matter how much they tried or cared, control over success lay outside of them; it lay with the weight of the vehicle. On the second try, they were able to lift the car, not because the car got lighter, but because of something *they did differently*. On this try, the car was raised off the ground because they had adopted a more powerful stance, were more strategically positioned around the vehicle, and lifted at exactly the right angle. The teachers on this team not only took home prize money but the experience of enactive mastery, achieving their desired outcome as a consequence of their own actions. In so doing, they experienced the shift from an external locus of control (the weight of the car determines the outcome) to an internal one (what we do together determines our success). And this shift, according to a great deal of research, is powerful indeed.

Lifting a car is a thinly veiled metaphor for generating high-level learning experiences every day, for a class of students with abilities, learning styles, and life experiences all over the map. The complexity of this task and the high stakes for students if we fail make it absolutely critical that the conditions of teachers' work are *generative*, replenishing energy, creativity, and the drive to continue lifting an impossible-to-lift car every single day. When teachers see their students succeed on a higher-level task than they previously thought was possible, and when they recognize their students' success as a direct result of their own work with colleagues around the instructional core, they undergo a fundamental shift. They move from an external locus of control ("This curriculum is too hard for our English language learners") to an internal locus of control ("When we adapted the lesson in the following way, we got this result") over student learning.

The cognitive and behavioral changes required for teachers to reach new and ambitious standards are challenging. Teachers not only must forsake familiar practices and develop new understandings but must also acknowledge that their current practice is inadequate for reaching expectations for student learning. Rather than risking this harm to self-concept, teachers may attribute the challenges of meeting goals to their students' characteristics or abilities rather than their own instructional practice.[2] Clearly, creating the opportunities for teachers to generate mastery beliefs for ambitious teaching and learning is a much more serious project than helping teachers with a onetime weight lift. For this reason, chapters 3 through 7 go into great depth about how to create the organizational conditions associated with a school's ability to improve the instructional core. This chapter focuses on how leaders can most strategically reap the benefits of their cumulative work to create a learning environment, a vision and strategy focused on the instructional core, and the conditions for teachers to collaborate around improvement. This ocurs by deliberately directing the energy and commitment generated by educators' beliefs in their ability to bring about desired change.

WHAT THE RESEARCH SAYS

The Benefits of Positive Efficacy Beliefs

Self-efficacy is a construct from social cognitive theory that seeks to explain the way people function as the result of the dynamic interactions among their behavior; internal factors, including cognitive and affective states; and their environment.[3] Perceived self-efficacy occupies a pivotal role in this theory of human behavior because efficacy beliefs are the primary driver of human agency—an individual's proactive commitment to act for a given purpose. Evidence from research in a wide range of settings attests to the influential role that efficacy beliefs play in individual and group functioning. Positive self-efficacy is associated with improved outcomes in various contexts, including physical and mental health, work-related performance, and athletics.[4]

There is also a substantial body of research specifically on efficacy in schools, which links individual teachers' efficacy beliefs to a broad range of productive teaching behaviors, such as setting high expectations for students, maintaining on-task behavior, emphasizing student inquiry over teacher-to-student information transfer, and concentrating on academic instruction.[5] High-efficacy teachers attend more closely to the needs of lower-ability students, are more likely to use student-centered approaches, and less frequently criticize students for giving an incorrect answer—all attitudes and behaviors particularly essential with academically struggling students.[6] Finally, efficacy scholars have documented a relationship between teacher efficacy and certain qualities critical to the profession, including motivation, willingness to take responsibility for student learning outcomes, commitment to teaching, and passion for the job.[7]

Collective Teacher Efficacy

Social cognitive theory extends the idea of teacher efficacy to teachers' collective efficacy, or the perception of individual teachers that *the faculty as a whole* has what it takes to organize and execute the courses of action required to have a positive effect on students.[8] Collective efficacy is theorized to drive organizational agency, a quality reflected in schools by a faculty's purposeful decisions to engage in activities that support specific school goals.[9] As with individual efficacy, the stronger the perceived collective efficacy, the higher the group's initial aspirations and motivational investment, the stronger its staying power in the face of adversity, and the higher the group's morale and resilience to stress.

In addition, collective teacher efficacy is thought to increase teachers' commitment to interdependent action toward a shared intention, or their willingness to meld diverse self-interests into the services of common goals pursued in concert.[10] Using performance on standardized assessments as an outcome variable, prominent efficacy scholars Albert Bandura and Roger Goddard have demonstrated that the collective efficacy beliefs of a faculty are positively and significantly related to between-school differences in student achievement in mathematics and reading in elementary, middle, and high schools, even after controlling for student demographic variables and socioeconomic status.[11]

Lateral or Normative "Press"

The mechanism by which individual beliefs in the capacity of the collective are theorized to influence student outcomes are the socially transmitted expectations for action or *normative press*. In schools with a robust sense of collective efficacy, teachers learn that extra effort and educational success are the norm, or "the way things are done here." This collective expectation for action has an impact on the kind of tasks individuals will attempt in their classrooms and the persistence with which they will pursue student success.[12] The experience of the Seacoast science team can be helpful here. Imagine if the team returned to represent the school in the superintendent's challenge the following year, but at the last minute they had to replace one of the team members with a substitute teacher new to the district. If initial attempts to lift the car proved fruitless, the new teacher would probably be ready to throw in the towel rather than stand around straining to move a car she believed was clearly going nowhere. The veteran teachers, however, having had a prior mastery experience leading to an internal locus of control, would interpret the initial failed attempts as a call to go back to the drawing board and figure out what they did wrong. The veteran teachers would be energized to try again after repositioning, checking stances and trajectories, and agreeing to scream until the car is off the ground. Imagine these veterans' response to a half-hearted effort from the skeptical new member standing between them and a valuable prize!

High-efficacy teachers do not take kindly to weak efforts from a colleague when they know success lies within their grasp, and they often exert pressure on those who would undermine progress made by the group. If a highly effective teacher team were checking in on its commitments, a lackluster report from a member might yield the following comments: "So, we all said we'd try this, and everyone did except for you. Can we help you in some way? Do you want one of us to come into your classroom and teach it with you or . . . ?" This lateral pressure from colleagues confident that their effort will yield success is a powerful addition to the vertical authority exercised by administration.

How Teachers Generate Efficacy

Teachers develop beliefs about their own and their colleagues' capability to generate desired outcomes by assessing the difficulty of a given task, or what it would take to attain success, against perceptions of their own and their colleagues' level of competence in areas relevant to what the task requires. Specifically, teachers generate perceptions by considering questions such as "What means or actions will be required to succeed in this situation?" and weighing this assessment against an analysis of their individual or collective skills and knowledge. Further, because efficacy beliefs focus on future capability, an individual's assessment of whether the abilities required for successful task completion are innate or can be acquired or improved may be relevant to their efficacy belief formulation as well.[13]

Scholars of social cognition assume that past, or *enacted*, mastery experiences are the most powerful generators of beliefs about efficacy: an individual's success or failure on comparable tasks in the past provides the most compelling evidence of capability (or lack thereof) for the future. The second-most powerful source of efficacy beliefs is theorized as vicarious experience, in which individuals observe the task being performed by someone else and uses that person's experience to inform their beliefs about their own capacity.[14] When teacher teams are able to focus their talk on the instructional core and incorporate some form of observation data into their collaboration process, the team structure will not only support efficacy by maximizing the potential for individual teachers to experience mastery in their own classrooms, but afford opportunities for efficacy building through vicarious experience as well.

Personal Views Versus Collective Deliberation

Education scholar Jal Mehta argues that K–12 education in the United States constitutes a loosely coupled bureaucratic hierarchy rather than a full-fledged profession such as medicine or law. He contends that three characteristics of these professions are absent or not fully realized in education: (a) a well-developed knowledge base that practitioners must have, (b) internal mechanisms to ensure that members entering the field meet initial standards of quality, and (c) common norms and standards of practice to ensure that continuing teachers meet the standards of the field.[15] In the tradition of Dan Lortie's *Schoolteacher*, Mehta also notes the consequential impact of long-standing K–12 teaching norms of individualism and autonomy, which have worked against the collective development of standards of practice or efforts to guide teachers' work once the individual is in the field.[16]

Over time, the disconnect between individual teachers' practice and systemic oversight, and the atomization of teachers' work, has resulted in a consistent pattern among teachers in schools: widely divergent levels of skill from one classroom teacher to the next and instructional strategies dependent on what each individual teacher can master, with experience serving as the main source of knowledge.[17] Education scholars Richard Elmore and Susan Fuhrman make a similar point in their paper on the response of schools and teachers to external accountability mandates. They argue that individual teachers' instructional decisions are powerfully influenced by preconceptions about the traits of particular students, families, and communities instead of being informed by "systematic knowledge of what students might be capable of learning under different conditions of teaching."[18]

Efficacy judgments hinge on individual teachers' assessments of their own and their collective competence relative to the task of achieving a specific student outcome goal in a particular context. However, if the outcome goals teachers set for their students are low-level, teachers' beliefs about their own capability to achieve them are inconsequential. To harness the many benefits of positive efficacy beliefs to the core work of raising the bar for student learning, teachers must generate confidence in their ability to create the kinds of academic tasks that lead to ambitious student outcomes. All of the essential practices and foundational learning experiences in the book thus far have been designed to help groups of educators systematically determine what students should be able to learn and be able to do, and collectively analyze the interactions among the instructional core required to generate these ambitious outcomes. This final essential practice is designed to help leaders explicitly attach the generation of positive efficacy beliefs in their school or system to these collectively derived understandings of high-level teaching and learning.

TURNING RESEARCH INTO PRACTICE

Because efficacy beliefs are a perception of competence rather than an empirical level of ability, the critical factor in the generation of future efficacy beliefs is not success or failure against an objective standard. Rather, it is an individual's cognitive interpretation of, and reflection on, a particular experience. This interpretation is the process in which various sources of information are weighed and integrated to form perceptions of efficacy. The essential practice in this chapter is designed to help leaders deliberately support the formation of teachers' efficacy beliefs around a collectively determined standard of ambitious instruction. And because schools and systems must become engines of continuous improvement, this practice is also designed to help build members' collective confidence in their ability to engage powerfully in the processes that teachers need to improve in their work.

Leaders can influence practitioners' interpretation of events by directing their attention to factors that leaders consider important or to those that teachers might otherwise have overlooked or dismissed. For example, a veteran teacher taking a leap of faith by turning over a degree of control to students during a lesson might perceive the experience to have been a disaster, owing to the level of chaos that erupted in her normally well-behaved classroom. Left to her own devices, the teacher's reflection on the experience might lower her faith in her ability to successfully employ a student-centered approach and might strengthen her resolve to proceed with her traditional methods. Here a leader or colleague observing her classroom might intervene in the appraisal by directing her attention to the unprecedented level of engagement among her students or the energy and excitement in the room. This deliberate cultivation of capability around a more powerful idea of success might lead her to reevaluate her experience, and her improved feelings of efficacy might bolster her resolve to try again.

Conversely, some efficacy beliefs may actually be counterproductive for improving teacher practice, such as teacher confidence for low-level or outdated practices or a teacher's unshakeable confidence derived from an inability to learn from experience.[19] In these cases, leaders benefit from actively disrupting positive efficacy beliefs by making clear what the interactions between elements of the instructional core would have to look like to generate a truly successful academic experience for students. In so doing, leaders may replace complacency with uncertainty, which can advance teachers professionally by encouraging them to improve. In a parallel fashion, leaders can establish an organizational standard for public adult learning and can orient practitioners' efficacy beliefs around this standard. For example, leaders can reinforce a positive appraisal for a teacher who was brave enough to open up his or her classroom for peer observation by reframing aspects of the lesson that did not go smoothly as critical opportunities for collective growth.

In this essential practice, leaders and groups of educators consider both their ambitious vision for the instructional core and their processes for collective learning to reach their vision during an improvement cycle. This practice is designed to tie together all of your previous work on instructional and organizational capacity, to actively promote an internally coherent understanding of powerful instruction and instructional improvement, to reflect on what worked, and to make changes going forward.

ESSENTIAL PRACTICE
REFLECTING ON YOUR TEAM'S LEARNING

This essential practice is designed to support groups of educators in generating efficacy for a collectively defined standard of instructional practice and process of improvement. By reflecting on both the classroom outcomes and the learning process at the close of an improvement cycle, leaders can direct faculty beliefs about their joint capability to enact high-quality academic tasks and continually deepen teaching and learning at their school.

Objective. Cultivate efficacy beliefs for ambitious instructional practice and ongoing instructional improvement.

Time: 45 minutes

1. **Reviewing Our Vision for Ambitious Instructional Practice** [10 minutes]
   - Have your team spend five minutes discussing its vision for instruction, using concrete and specific details to describe what your team was trying to do.
   - Record the vision on paper.

2. **Diagraming Progress** [15 minutes]
   - Using the diagram as an example, determine the appropriate time frame that would match when you started to work on this vision, and label the x-axis appropriately (i.e., days, weeks, or months, as needed). For the y-axis, consider the amount of learning that occurred, with high levels of learning indicated by the top of the axis.

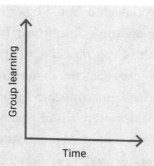

- Give each person a few minutes to quietly think about the major accomplishments that were made during this time and that related to accomplishing the vision. Then, have each person write one accomplishment on a sticky note and place it near the appropriate time on the x-axis. Each person should individually determine how much learning occurred because of that accomplishment and place the sticky note accordingly on the y-axis.
- Repeat the process above, but invite each person to think about any setbacks or challenges and to write them on sticky notes and place them accordingly.

3. Reflecting on Learning [20 minutes]

Have your team reflect on and discuss the following questions about learning:

- For all the high points, how did we work together to achieve the gains we did? What process did we use? Why did we see this as learning?
- For all the low points, what challenges did we face? What could we have done differently, if anything?
- Did any challenges result in high levels of learning?
- As a result of our work, what has changed in our school?

Developing the Essential Practice Over Time

Positive teacher efficacy for ambitious instruction and instructional improvement is an *outcome* of the Internal Coherence Framework rather than a quality we seek to intervene on directly. Although it would be expedient, exhorting teachers to raise their expectations for students is insufficient, because beliefs about students' capabilities stem from teachers' experiences of what they have accomplished with students in the past. The essential practice in this chapter is designed to help leaders direct the focus of teachers' efficacy beliefs, as a means to harness all the virtuous qualities associated with perceptions of capability to the right standards for the instructional core and research-based processes by which teachers improve in their work. However, the practice will have meaning only in conjunction with all the other essential practices and foundational learning experiences in the book. Only after leaders have actively cultivated psychological safety for public learning, a shared understanding of a vision for the instructional core, and substantive support for teachers' work in teams will teachers be positioned to enact higher-quality instructional practice and witness deeper student learning as a result.

In their regular practice, leaders can contribute to educators' opportunities to experience efficacy-boosting mastery experiences by keeping in mind the following:

▶ *Set goals that are articulated in terms of the interactions between teachers, students, and content.* Articulate goals not in terms of student outcomes, such as proficiency on standardized assessments, but as a vision for what the teaching and learning will look like in classrooms when it meets the collectively negotiated standard for instructional practice.

▶ *Emphasize the value of processes that create a shared understanding of the cause-and-effect relationship between teaching and learning.* For teachers who perceive processes like instructional rounds, team-based inquiry cycles, or peer observation as critical to the improvement of practice, access to these opportunities may contribute to positive efficacy beliefs.[20]

▶ *Enable practitioners to exert influence over instructionally relevant school decisions.* If teachers are to believe that their collective actions can make a difference, they need the opportunity to exercise collective agency and participate in frequent and formal collaboration around curriculum and instructional goals.

▶ *Forcefully disrupt efficacy beliefs that are based on an unacceptable standard of what students can do.* If leaders explicitly articulate success in terms of a collectively determined standard and afford teachers access to exemplars of best practice, teachers with less effective practices may question their own approaches and therefore be motivated to reflect on them and change.

▶ *Define capacity as a function of a willingness to learn and change.* Leaders need to cultivate teachers' beliefs that the competencies required to increase student learning can be acquired or improved through training or experience and are not a function of intrinsic qualities or an excessive devotion of time.

▶ *Cultivate not only perceptions of capacity but actual capacity by providing teachers with critical knowledge and competencies.* Leaders enable mastery experiences that provide the basis for personal change by providing teachers with access to expert support and modeling to increase the content and pedagogical knowledge teachers need for professional growth.

FOUNDATIONAL LEARNING EXPERIENCES

The previous chapters help leaders create the organizational conditions conducive to teachers' ongoing learning about the instructional core and provide opportunities for mastery of increasingly ambitious instructional practice. The following learning experiences will help educators develop a shared understanding of what success looks like in classrooms and the specific collaborative processes that generate this success.

Multiple Understandings of Success

Qualitative research by one of the authors in a high school that had conducted regular cycles of observation and analysis, precisely to create common understandings around teaching and learning, revealed that teachers still had highly varied ideas of what constituted successful student outcomes.[21] For example, two teachers in the same grade had markedly different levels of aspirations for their students. A foreign language teacher expressed hope that by the end of the year, his students would be able to put together a short paragraph on "the basics," like time, numbers, or the seasons. A colleague teaching English in the same grade strove for student outcomes including the ability to write fluently and clearly, make a claim and support it with evidence, and develop robust vocabularies. These two teachers might both possess positive efficacy to achieve their desired goals, but these individually derived beliefs would have very different implications for actual student achievement.[22]

Discussions among educators about their aspirations for students, the aim of setting a shared vision for the instructional core, can help reveal whether these expectations truly represent meaningful goals for students and create opportunities for challenging low expectations. The benefits of positive efficacy beliefs, including the resultant energy, creativity, resilience, and willingness to sublimate individual goals to the pursuit of the collective, are useful only if they can be connected to the right goals for student learning. The internal coherence professional learning series is designed to generate teacher confidence in making improvements toward a desired goal for student learning, but the goal must be anchored in the most ambitious, systematic thinking in the organization. It cannot be driven by lesser ideas of what individual teachers believe students to be capable of.

A nice way to start the process of alignment for what matters is simply to acknowledge that a single school will have many interpretations of meaningful student outcomes. To make concrete the need to calibrate a group of educators' concepts of success, leaders can engage in some form of anonymous, internal data collection using questions like the following:

1. In general, what outcomes do you hope to achieve with your students in their time with you? What skills, knowledge, or qualities are you most concerned with fostering in your students?

2. How do you gauge whether you have been successful with your students, on any given day, unit, or semester? Can you give an example of a time you felt like you had achieved real success?

3. Do you think other teachers in the school have goals for their students that are aligned with yours? How do you know?

Using any procedure by which teachers can respond anonymously and post their responses in a shared public space, surface multiple ideas about how educators currently understand success. This same process can be used with leaders in schools or districts to reveal their aspirations for students. Give teachers and leaders time to make sense of all that they see; have them consider the implications of the variability for generating a shared sense of capability for enacting ambitious instruction.

Efficacy for the Process of Improvement

The field of efficacy research is overwhelmingly composed of quantitative studies linking high levels of collective efficacy to school performance on standardized assessments. A rare example of qualitative research comes as an unintended by-product of a study by Laurel Puchner and Ann Taylor. They looked at the impact of the Japanese lesson study model in a middle school on participants' mathematical teaching practice.[23] Although teacher efficacy was not the focus of the research, its importance emerged in the analysis of the evaluation data:

> The data indicate that lesson study revealed to all four teachers that in-depth planning and attention to a lesson can bring about student engagement and learning that they had not previously felt was in their power . . . Three aspects of their reaction are particularly important: the teachers' amazement at how successful the lesson was; the apparently very low expectations that all four teachers had held for this particular group of students prior to the lesson; and their belief that it was all the hard the work they had put into the lesson that had led to the students' performance exceeding their expectations.[24]

Presumably, prior to the experience of the lesson study, these four teachers believed that the social or cognitive needs of these particular students overwhelmed the power that they the teachers held to control the outcomes of their instruction. After the lesson study, they emerged with the belief that the reinforcement of their teaching efforts, in the form of student learning and motivation, was within their control and specifically was a function of their hard work in planning.

Having your team read the section of Puchner and Taylor's analysis devoted to efficacy beliefs would deepen their understanding of the connection between beliefs about capability and beliefs about the productivity of their work with colleagues.[25] This short reading is well suited to a discussion protocol for text such as Save the Last Word, from the National School Reform Faculty.[26] Alternatively, you might have a team review the aforementioned section by Puchner and Taylor using the following discussion prompts:

- How would you describe the nature of the teachers' collaborative work?
- How do teachers' understandings, attitudes, or beliefs change as a result of this collaboration?
- How would you explain the assertion by one of the teachers that the group's feelings about the work would not have been different even if the lesson had *not* been successful?

Joint Inquiry as a Driver of Collective Efficacy Beliefs

One of the authors followed teachers in three high-poverty urban schools to learn from their efforts to integrate the Common Core State Standards into their instruction. She found that teachers who conducted *joint inquiry*, that is, working with colleagues to investigate their instruction and students' work and to determine the changes they would need to make to support students in meeting standards, changed not only their practice but also their fundamental beliefs about what they and their students could do. One team worked to teach a standards-based curricular unit that the teachers had all initially viewed as too difficult for their students. After witnessing their students' success, a special education teacher on the team described the experience this way:

> We did a curriculum unit last year on child labor that was based on the Common Core . . . The students had to look at political cartoons. They had to read articles. My first thought was, "This is way too hard for my students." But our grade-level team spent months on it. We just picked apart every article . . . We used graphic organizers. Then my students were able to meet those Common Core Standards of writing opinion pieces using evidence from the articles. I was very shocked at how well my students did. I feel like the Common Core holds you to these high standards and these high expectations. You'd be surprised what you can do and what your students can do if you stick to these standards.[27]

What is especially helpful about this research is that it details the specific team processes educators cited as able to generate heightened beliefs about their own and their students' capacity. Stosich's report, "From Sharing to Joint Work," presents a clear explanation of how a group of teachers used their time together to investigate instruction and students' work, and determine the changes they would need to make to support students in meeting standards.[28] Joint inquiry helped teachers change the way they thought about instructional planning, the kinds of questions they asked students, and the role of students in the learning process. Specifically, teachers analyzed the curriculum with support from experts and colleagues, developed or revised the curriculum to meet the new standards, and used inquiry protocols to support their learning and practice. In addition, teachers mentioned the importance of opportunities to observe an expert demonstrate how to use the new curriculum with students. Finally, teachers who generated efficacy for attaining the Common Core State Standards said that looking at models of instruction, curriculum, and student work was especially helpful for learning about the standards when doing so was paired with opportunities to reflect on how these models related to their current practice with colleagues. In addition to using any text-based discussion protocol to structure a shared reading experience with Stosich's report, leaders might ask participants the following questions:

▶ What were the specific processes that teachers cited as helping them translate abstract ideas about standards into specific instructional practices?

▶ How do these efficacy-building practices of joint inquiry compare with the practices we use currently in our teacher teams?

▶ Are there practices we might adopt for our teams in the future?

CONNECTING TO CLINICAL INSTRUMENTS

Teachers' confidence in their own and their colleagues' ability to generate desired student outcomes like engagement or meaningful learning is the definition of teachers' collective efficacy. However, the degree to which these beliefs are anchored in an understanding about what students and teachers need to be doing with content depends on the opportunities that teachers are afforded within their organization. One of the authors has argued elsewhere for a new construct, called *efficacy for instructional improvement*, to more tightly connect teachers' beliefs about capability with collectively determined outcomes for ambitious student learning, as well as for the processes that teachers need to improve in their work.[29] If teachers generate beliefs about capability against individually derived standards of effective practice or evaluate the capability of their colleagues according to effort or rapport with students, then the connection between efficacy beliefs and powerful instructional practice is diminished.

The Internal Coherence Framework and professional learning series are designed to create the conditions for educators to generate a shared standard for ambitious instruction, the language and the processes for interdependent learning about the instructional decisions that truly have an impact on what students learn, and the impetus for incorporating observation data into cycles of adult learning. By engaging in the professional learning series, educators come to understand how the interactions among the instructional core relate to student learning. Further, they recognize that their collective actions, rather than conditions beyond their control, determine whether students learn at higher levels.

The Internal Coherence Developmental Rubric: collective efficacy

BEGINNING	EMERGENT	PROFICIENT	EXEMPLARY
■ Teachers do not believe that control over what students learn lies with them, the teachers. ■ Teachers generate beliefs about capability against individually derived standards. ■ Teachers' perceptions of their colleagues' capabilities are informed by data peripheral to the instructional core.	■ Teachers begin to connect instructional decisions with student learning. ■ Teachers are moving closer to a collective standard for ambitious practice. ■ Teachers are developing interest in observing classrooms to inform discussions of student data.	■ Teachers have mastery experiences with more ambitious instructional practice as a consequence of learning with colleagues. ■ Teachers consistently look to colleagues as sources of learning. ■ Teachers interact under norms of effort, positive expectations, and persistence.	■ Teachers' mastery experiences raise beliefs about what they, their colleagues, and the students are capable of. ■ Teachers hold themselves and their colleagues accountable for student outcomes. ■ Teachers view improvement as a collective challenge and peer observation as a tool for collective growth.

Organizations with high coherence are learning organizations, in continuous pursuit of ambitious instructional practice and student learning. Therefore, an ebb and flow in teachers' responses to questions about efficacy on the Internal Coherence Survey may not be a cause for concern. As practitioners establish higher standards for constructs like student motivation or meaningful learning, their assessment of current capability may diminish. Encounters with more-sophisticated instructional approaches may have the same effect. This is an indication of organizational learning and a cause for satisfaction, not frustration.

Internal Coherence Survey Items: Collective Efficacy

The survey items about collective efficacy assess whether teachers feel that all faculty members at their schools have the requisite knowledge, skills, and beliefs to bring about powerful instruction and support student learning. However, in order for these survey items to generate meaningful data, teachers must have opportunities to develop shared mental models for what constitutes meaningful student learning, evidence of student motivation, or instructional approaches.

ASSESSING COLLECTIVE EFFICACY

▶ Teachers are confident they will be able to motivate their students.

▶ Teachers have the skills needed to produce meaningful student learning.

▶ If a child doesn't learn something the first time, teachers will try another way.

▶ Teachers believe that every child can learn.

▶ Teachers are skilled in various methods of teaching.

▶ Teachers have what it takes to explore new instructional approaches to help underperforming students meet standards.

The Internal Coherence Framework and professional learning series are designed to grow educators' beliefs in their collective ability to improve the learning experiences that all students encounter in classrooms. It is our hope that by engaging in this shared adult learning journey, teachers and leaders will find intellectual challenge and satisfaction in their own work and in the ever-more-ambitious learning outcomes they are able to generate for their students.

Insights from the Field

ROSALIE BAKER, VIRGINIA BORIS, AND LINDA HAUSER

The purpose of this epilogue is to share the insights that we have garnered over the past three years as leaders of three internal coherence learning cohorts—the joint Clovis Unified School District pilot project, led by Richard Elmore, Michelle Forman, Elizabeth Leisy Stosich, and Candice Bocala; our first independent internal coherence learning series with twelve new Clovis Unified School District schools spanning grades K–12; and our most recent launch with the ten schools in the Dinuba Unified School District. We are committed to this work and have seen the positive impact it can have on teaching and learning schoolwide.

Building internal coherence is a professional learning journey that reorients the culture of a school. At the core of this work, fundamental shifts must occur. The principal must nurture a trusting relationship with the faculty and step back, allowing teachers to take the lead in instructional improvement and professional learning. Teachers must step up and embrace the opportunities that leadership roles create for improving their own professional relationships, instructional practices, and student learning. Most significantly, the principal and faculty must embrace a schoolwide response to improvement, breaking down the traditional grade-level and classroom silos and creating articulated systems that guarantee successful learner outcomes. Throughout the internal coherence learning series, school teams are given a wide variety of tools and processes to help them fully implement these shifts. Each time we have presented the internal coherence work to a new cohort of schools, we discover better ways to guide their transformational journey.

BACKGROUND

The Central Valley Educational Leadership Institute (CVELI) was organized in 2002 to bolster the professional learning of educational leaders in California's Central Valley in support of their efforts to improve student learning outcomes and to close the historical achievement gap among the valley's students and their higher-income peers across the state. In 2008, Virginia Boris and Linda Hauser joined the Fresno State University faculty and the work of CVELI. In the fall of 2009, the CVELI team formed a network of eight small rural school district leaders with the intent of bringing university resources to these underserved educational leaders. Superintendent Rich Merlo, a founding member of the CVELI's Rural Network, introduced instructional rounds to CVELI; in 2011, Rural Network superintendents and CVELI leaders undertook the work of rounds in partnership with the California Rural Network for Instructional Rounds. The network hosted two events featuring Richard Elmore. It was at these events that Boris and Hauser first heard Elmore describe the internal coherence work.

Boris and Hauser were drawn to Elmore's description of his work in Australia, where highly coherent schools were deeply invested in their journey of continuous improvement. The Internal Coherence Survey data and Internal Coherence Developmental Rubric resonated with CVELI leaders, who had realized that the key to improving Central Valley's schools was not through one intervention at a time but through deep cultural transformation. Elmore's vision of a highly coherent faculty with the capacity to significantly raise student learning across all classrooms over time—and the belief that they could do it—aligned with CVELI's commitment to systems thinking, team building, and collaboration. Elmore shared a draft of a two-year professional development proposal that he and his graduate students Michelle Forman, Elizabeth Leisy Stosich, and Candice Bocala, were piloting in Boston and in Fort Worth, Texas. In the fall of 2012, Boris and Hauser traveled to Boston to meet with the Internal Coherence Research Project team and explore a partnership between CVELI and the Harvard Graduate School of Education to implement Building Coherence for Instructional Improvement (BCII) in the Central Valley.

Armed with descriptions of the BCII two-year Internal Coherence Professional Development plan, the Internal Coherence Survey instrument, and key research documents, Boris and Hauser returned to California to seek a district partner for this work. They were drawn to the Clovis Unified School District because of the district's political stability and commitment to high standards and clear goals; they also had strong professional relationships with district leaders. Rosalie Baker, assistant superintendent for the Clovis East High School feeder system, was particularly interested. The Clovis East High School area served the district's high-poverty neighborhoods and their achievement data consistently lagged behind that of their higher-income sister schools. Baker was particularly intrigued by Roger Goddard's research demonstrating that schools with high collective efficacy overcame the traditional negative impact of poverty on student outcomes.

The spring of 2013 was a time of great change. The epicenter of these shifts at school sites was the implementation of the Common Core, which was happening with great speed. Uncertain about the focus of content, the emerging level of rigor, textbooks, support resources, and assessment, even highly experienced principals and teachers felt insecure and unfocused. Boris met three times with Baker's eight principals to present and discuss the Internal Coherence Framework, the theory of action, and the BCII professional learning series. The principals were trusting, innovative, and in search of high-impact strategies to curb teachers' stress and to propel student learning; they all agreed to participate in the two-year project. The principals believed that BCII would provide a logical and research-based platform for leading during these times of great change. That same spring, the Internal Coherence Survey was administered at all eight campuses; the data were shared in the first BCII session held that autumn.

Each Clovis East Area school site committed to form a BCII leadership team (the principal and six to eight lead teachers), to attend every BCII full-day meeting, to take the information back to the faculty, and to pay for the required substitutes. CVELI agreed to form a partnership with Elmore, Forman, Stosich, and

Bocala through the Strategic Educational Research Partnership (SERP). The institute committed to fund the SERP contracts and sought community partners to underwrite the work. The Fresno County Office of Education; Lozano Smith, Attorneys at Law; and the S. H. Cowell Foundation were critical partners in funding and supporting this work.

BCII is not an initiative—it is *the* initiative. It must be the centerpiece of a district's or school's leadership work. The work is complex, the ideas are transformative, and the need for patiently building understanding is critical. Therefore, frequent dialogue among stakeholders enhances and accelerates the work. There were multiple participants in these conversations—BCII leaders, school facilitators (including Baker, Hauser, Boris, and several of their colleagues), district leaders, principals, and teacher leaders. When we began the work as BCII leaders, we underestimated the importance of these clarifying conversations. As the work evolved, we created a variety of formal and informal opportunities for participants to engage within and among the participating school teams.

In the beginning, the BCII presenters met with the Central Valley facilitators the day before each BCII seminar. The presenters reviewed the planned program, key activities, important concepts, and team actions. Dialogue was brisk and candid. Because the BCII leaders came from across the country, this agenda was a logical model. Additionally, we made no effort to engage the principals in the content before the learning sessions, assuming that they could learn with their teacher leaders.

By the end of two sessions, we had two key insights. First, teachers have a limited exposure to leadership concepts and theories so the BCII model was not at all self-explanatory. By starting the internal coherence team training with leadership constructs, the training did not immediately connect to the world of classroom teachers. Second, principals were very uncomfortable learning alongside their teachers. They felt foolish when confused teachers turned to their principal for clarity and the principal was unable to respond with clarity.

These two insights led us to rethink our program model. In planning the third session, the BCII presenters held a video conference with the principals, district leaders, and Boris. In the first of many of such conferences, presenters reviewed key program content and activities, and principals offered candid input, modifying activities to better facilitate learning for all internal coherence team participants. This forum afforded principals the opportunity to ask their own clarifying and probing questions about both the immediate content and the overarching BCII concepts. The video conferences lowered principals' anxiety, accelerated their professional learning, and shifted the role of principal from one of learner to one of learning leader.

As the project gained momentum, the following meeting pattern emerged. At the end of each BCII seminar, internal coherence site teams were given time to create a plan of action to bring the new learning to their campuses. Between each seminar, the site teams met at least once and often more frequently to plan the next steps for their work with their faculty colleagues. Site facilitators attended at least one of these meetings and offered insight and clarity. Early on, only a few site teams felt ready to roll out their learning in a faculty meeting. However, as the sessions progressed, the sites often held a BCII faculty session between each BCII seminar. To deepen the learning and support action, Baker facilitated a monthly principal meeting to share actions, discuss challenges, and envision next steps. Because these discussions were a high priority for the assistant superintendent, they were given adequate time and resources. The BCII leaders continued to meet with the facilitators the day before each seminar to review and polish the program.

TEACHERS AS LEADERS

A critical aspect of the internal coherence learning model is the responsibility of each school's internal coherence team members to build the capacity of their faculty peers, facilitating schoolwide understanding and mastery of internal coherence concepts and tools. Although teachers exercise leadership skills every day when they provide instruction to groups of students, we found that most teachers on these leadership teams were surprisingly uncomfortable facilitating their colleagues' learning. Great care and support should be given to team members, as most teams were initially overwhelmed by this role.

In the pilot internal coherence learning series, psychological safety was addressed amid several other topics. In our most recent kickoff, we placed psychological safety in the center of our work on day one, lowering the affective filters of team members and easing them into their new leadership roles. Trainers discussed the value of icebreakers in building interpersonal staff relationships. Familiar with icebreakers, most teachers felt comfortable facilitating such activities with their colleagues. We also introduced the Compass Points activity on day one, generating positive energy and promoting dialogue about the diversity of peoples' working styles.[1] Because internal coherence is a major shift in the way teachers do their work, protocols to foster psychological safety set a positive tone for the value of all faculty members and establish a comfortable platform for emerging teacher leaders.

An interesting finding that rose from our internal coherence work is that a faculty's perceived coherence is often based on personal camaraderie, not on professional work relationships. Many teachers and principals think coherence is the close personal relationships they already enjoy. Passing pleasantries, sharing stories about family, and emotionally supporting each other are their coherence tools. We have learned that few faculties have a schoolwide culture of professional relationships. As Elisa MacDonald notes, school faculties have lived comfortably in the "land of nice," avoiding the stress of challenging colleagues to change current practices on behalf of student learning.[2] As internal coherence team members assume the mantle of leadership, they become agents of change, a precarious leadership role that may stir up conflict.

To help team members take on leadership roles and feel less stress in their emerging work as change agents, we offer the following suggestions:

▶ Provide enough time for teams to discuss their new leadership roles during the internal coherence learning sessions.
▶ Give principals and coaches a clear protocol, promoting honest discussion and psychological safety, for the teams to use as they consider their new roles as leaders and agents of change.
▶ Give the teams an opportunity to share with other internal coherence teams during learning sessions.

- ▶ Assure the teams that each site is on its own journey and that some schools will roll out new learning faster than others.
- ▶ Encourage the teams to practice their presentation before their faculty debut.
- ▶ Don't let the principal or coach "rescue" the team by doing the leadership work for him or her.

By considering these suggestions, internal coherence facilitators will provide strong support for the team members as they assume their new roles as leaders.

TEACHERS AS LEARNERS

At the heart of a highly coherent faculty is a strong commitment to professional learning. In the absence of such a culture, many teachers feel that the source of professional learning comes from expertise outside their campus. In our internal coherence learning, we convey three critical messages:

- ▶ The most important professional learning events are the daily decisions made by the faculty to influence and improve their students' learning.
- ▶ They, the faculty, are the world-class experts on their students; there are no others who know or can learn which curriculum and instruction works best for the students on their campus.
- ▶ Everything we need is available through our relentless ingenuity to determine what works and to seek solutions to challenges we identify. When the faculty calls on an outside expert, it does so to answer a need the faculty identified, not a need identified by a third party.

These three ideas set the foundation for faculty beliefs and capacity; they uplift the concept of teachers as learners. Teachers are no longer a passive workforce that needs to be fixed by someone *out there*. They are a dynamic team of problem solvers who know how to continuously improve the effectiveness of their work.

For teacher learners, there are several lighthouse moments in internal coherence learning. We encourage you to recognize, emphasize, and linger at these critical stops along the internal coherence journey. The power of establishing a *common language* for teaching and learning through the instructional core cannot be overstated. The internal coherence teams that embraced the instructional core, discussed it in their team meetings, shared it with colleagues, and kept it in the center of their professional conversations accelerated their collaborative work. Sharing the story of Fran and Kevin (see appendix C) became a seminal moment in the work of our pilot internal coherence schools. By reflecting on this case study, teachers were able to form some critical insights—teachers fail to reflect on the numerous decisions they make throughout a daily lesson, and these decisions vary the nature and rigor of the task. If teachers fail to use the instructional core, deeply discuss the task, and consider the nature of individual students' involvement with the task, there is considerable variance among teachers' execution of any given lesson. We offer the following suggestions for leaders as they prepare internal coherence teams to share these experiences with their faculty peers:

▶ Don't rush through the instructional core. Emphasize the power of a common language of teaching and learning.
▶ Provide adequate time during the learning to discuss and reflect on these concepts.
▶ Develop a tentative rollout plan at the learning sessions, and provide time to share ideas among the internal coherence teams.
▶ Design a follow-up activity that the teams can do at their site meetings to reinforce these critical ideas.
▶ Revisit the importance of the instructional core at several subsequent meetings to encourage dialogue, deepen reflection, and provide practice using this new language.

By building the team's capacity to function as learners, team members will be better prepared to recognize, model, lead, and engage in meaningful learning opportunities in their daily work.

Sometimes the principal inadvertently limits the capacity for teachers to take charge of their own learning. In *The Principal: Three Keys to Maximizing Impact*, Michael Fullan asserts that it is the principal's job to create the conditions for learning—the learning of both teachers and students.[3] This observation is in stark contrast to the past decade's expectation that the principal be the leader of all instructional improvement. For some principals, this is the only role they've known. They fail to realize that if they control the learning, the learning is limited by the capacity of a single individual. During the internal coherence sessions, presenters need to remind principals and teachers that we create the conditions for collaboration so that professional learning becomes the shared responsibility of every faculty member.

PEER OBSERVATION

During the BCII sessions, learning experiences about the instructional core and the focus for instructional improvement establish a critical foundation for the concept of internal coherence: a faculty's belief and capacity to engage in deliberate improvements in instructional practice and student learning across classrooms over time. However, a deeper understanding of internal coherence and the need for transforming the way our schools do their work is actualized with the integration of schoolwide peer observation. In developing a peer observation model that fosters and supports the work of building schoolwide coherence, we found five critical criteria that practitioners should consider in selecting a peer observation model:

▶ View and conduct peer observation as a schoolwide process, not confined to grade levels or courses.
▶ Develop a strategy that, over time, involves all faculty members in the observation process.
▶ Frame the model around the instructional core.
▶ Use the instructional focus as the lens for data collection—translate the instructional focus into a relevant and timely problem of practice and essential questions that guide data collection.
▶ Understand the importance of collecting nonjudgmental data, and train teachers and administrators in this skill.

▶ Culminate with an all-school faculty debrief, which turns schoolwide peer observation data into information that drives teacher decisions; collectively, teachers commit to the next-best instructional action to improve teaching and learning.

As peer observation became an integral strategy that cycled throughout the school year at a predictable and appropriate time frame, teachers acknowledged the importance of viewing their role as part of a collective unit. Teachers no longer defined or limited themselves by grade-level or course-specific affiliations, but viewed learning as a schoolwide norm, something they must do collectively to take appropriate and effective actions on behalf of their students as a system.

SCHOOLWIDE RESPONSE

Schoolwide peer observation is a springboard to actualizing a whole-school response to the instructional improvement focus. As teachers begin to view learning as the *work we do together*, they move from individual teacher or unconnected grade-level responses to a schoolwide response to improvement—reducing the likelihood that there would be only pockets of excellence instead of a quality response or action for every child. Schoolwide peer observation, framed by the instructional core and the school's instructional focus, along with a schoolwide faculty analysis and debriefing, are watershed experiences that shift professional thinking from the siloed work of an individual teacher or grade level to the collective work of the school. Critical elements of a schoolwide response include collective teacher decisions on next-step actions based on data, collective teacher commitments to the actions, and collective responses in all classrooms. We found that moving to a schoolwide response required rethinking the mental models held by both administrators and teachers, including the time, space, and process for holding critical conversations about teaching and learning.

A schoolwide response requires a shift in the traditional role of the principal and the way the school operates. We observed that principals had to learn what it really meant to create the conditions for learning. It required them to step back at times and let go of some things they had traditionally held very tight; in this way, they helped develop the collective capacity of their teachers to learn and lead. Many principals will tell you that letting go is not easy; however, it is the tipping point of unleashing the collective capacity and power of the school team to do great things for kids.

THE PRINCIPAL AS LEARNER AND TEACHER

The most critical learner and teacher in this work is the principal; we are still learning how to fully support this essential position. Early on in the pilot, the principals shared with us that they felt confused and ill prepared to support the learning of their teachers, since they too were on such a steep learning curve. After two sessions, we instituted a preliminary meeting with the principals to share the content of the upcoming meeting, seek their input, and address their concerns. Although the preliminary meeting continues to be an important aspect of the internal coherence learning journey, even this meeting fails to engage principals in a deep, reflective dialogue about the work. We would encourage district implementers to organize a monthly opportunity for principals to reflect on and share the work. Such a network formed among the pilot principals, who reported that their formal and informal discussion was critical to their long-term implementation.

The internal coherence coach plays a key role in advancing the principals as both learners and teachers. We encourage this facilitator to hold a one-on-one conversation with the principal at least once a month to monitor and stretch the principal's understanding of internal coherence and how to roll out the work to the faculty. We noted a strong correlation between the principal's personal understanding of the work and the speed at which it was deployed schoolwide. As the principal embraces internal coherence as a learner, his or her confidence to be an internal coherence teacher grows. Although all the team members eventually become presenters, the principal is still a critical teacher. If the principal does not understand and model psychological safety, a common language of instruction, the power of the instructional core, or the importance of the instructional focus, the implementation founders.

We offer readers the following tips to support principals as they become public learners and teachers on the school campuses:

- ▶ Emphasize to the site coaches the importance of the principal's roles as both learner and teacher. Provide probing questions for the coach to pose to stimulate dialogue and reflection.
- ▶ Provide explicit language, in professional learning sessions and written communications, about the role of the principal as a learner and teacher.
- ▶ Provide explicit statements in session materials that articulate key learning, the importance of the learning, and its impact.
- ▶ Provide role-alike table talk so principals have opportunities to talk among themselves during professional learning sessions.
- ▶ Work with district leaders to facilitate principal networks around internal coherence professional learning, establishing opportunities for principals to engage in dialogue about the work between sessions.
- ▶ Provide models and discussion for principals during professional learning sessions to reinforce what they should know and be able to do in terms of psychological safety, instructional core, instructional focus, and other critical internal coherence efforts.
- ▶ Encourage the principal to take an active role as an equal member of the site internal coherence team.
- ▶ Urge the principal to be a visible learner and teacher in all peer observation work.

Few principals are comfortable being vulnerable in front of their faculty. For this reason, program leaders and facilitators must be in close contact with principals, answering questions, checking for understanding, and developing a trust relationship. Do not underestimate the significant change that internal coherence poses particularly to principals who did not previously view themselves as either teachers or as learners.

THE PRINCIPAL AS LEADER:
WHERE FEW HAVE GONE BEFORE

One of the most interesting leadership paradigms we discovered in this work is the compulsion of leaders to give professional learning efforts a one- or two-year focus and then move on to something new. In fact, principals believed that they were derelict in their duties if they dwelled on an instructional focus too long, fearing that other areas were being neglected. About two years into the pilot, the principals and teachers began to ask when they could move on to reading; the teachers had mastered all the math techniques. We responded with guarded joy: "Oh, 85 percent of your students are consistently passing the math tests?" Their response was a forlorn "no." And then the light turned on: "We are not done with the instructional focus until the majority of our students are mastering grade-level work. This effort is not about teachers' mastery of instructional pedagogy; it is about students' mastery of the rigorous Common Core State Standards." Then the real work began!

Principals need to stay the course and lead the faculty to the real problems of practice. We wonder why so many initiatives fail. It is because at this critical moment, when the adults are bored and don't know how to dig deeper, they move to a new initiative. Internal coherence is not an initiative; it is a way of life. It is a way of thinking that compels the faculty to constantly revisit the work until the content is mastered by teachers and students. This approach requires tremendous leadership. Principals will need to persevere and challenge the faculty to think in new ways, learn new techniques, and unlock new doors.

We keep searching for silver bullets. The only silver bullet that we discovered in the internal coherence work is its transformative power. Schools can accomplish amazing things when leaders understand that their job is to unlock the capacity of the entire instructional team to relentlessly serve students.

CLOSING THOUGHTS

Learning about internal coherence guides a fundamental shift in the way educational professionals engage collaboratively in the challenging work of educating all students. Professional development events are replaced by a culture of professional learning that happens in real time throughout the school year. The internal coherence experience transforms school faculties into collaborative cultures guided by the relentless pursuit of an instructional focus. The faculty's capacity to improve its instructional focus is supported by a peer observation process. Using the information generated through both traditional professional learning communities and schoolwide peer observations, teachers increase their capacity to serve the learning of all students, identifying what works and what does not. This learning cycle results in the continuous improvement of student results and the faculty's sense of efficacy, or belief that they do have the capacity to teach *all* students.

We have found internal coherence work to be the most exciting and rewarding of our educational careers. The Internal Coherence Framework is restoring the art, science, and professionalism of teachers. It is freeing principals to better lead and manage the many demands placed on them. Finally, it is creating school organizations that operate with the expectation that all students will learn at high levels because we, the faculty, know how to support that expectation. We encourage the reader to enjoy this most profound professional learning journey.

Rosalie Baker has worked in K–12 education for over thirty years, serving as a teacher, principal, and district officer. She served as the Assistant Superintendent, Clovis East Area, in the Clovis Unified School District for eight years and was a founding BCII district partner. Currently she is working as a Welty Center Associate at Fresno State University on the BCII team.

Virginia Boris brings cutting-edge practices to California's educational leaders and aspiring school administrators in support of their efforts to close historical achievement gaps and raise communities out of intergenerational poverty. With over forty years of teaching and administrative experience in K–12 education, Dr. Boris currently serves at Fresno State University as a lecturer and the Co-Director of CVELI, guiding superintendents and principals as they transform school cultures into collaborative systems characterized by strong teacher efficacy, growing internal coherence, and continuously improved student achievement.

Linda Hauser is a leader of learning who is focused on developing the organization called school by building the collective efficacy and capacity of educational leaders to provide quality, effective schoolwide responses that are based on the needs of students, improve student learning in every classroom, and increase student achievement. With over thirty-five years of teaching and administrative experience in K–12 education, Dr. Hauser currently serves at California State University, Fresno, as an Associate Professor teaching in the Educational Leadership and Administration (principal preparation) program and Doctoral Program in Educational Leadership. She is Chair of the Department of Educational Leadership, Coordinator of the Educational Leadership and Administration Program, and dissertation adviser. She is coauthor of the book The PBIS Tier One Handbook: A Practical Approach to Implementing the Champion Model.

Annotated Internal Coherence Survey

This overview of the Internal Coherence Survey shows which items fall under which domains and factors. While chapter 5 includes the response choices for each statement, here we show the topical organization of the survey and its relation to the chapters in the book. You can use this guide to identify specific chapters where you can learn more about the practices and processes described in the survey.

LEADERSHIP FOR IMPROVEMENT

Leadership for Learning [chapters 3 and 4]

- The principal invites input from faculty in discussions about teaching and learning.
- The principal asks probing questions about teaching and learning.
- The principal listens attentively.
- The principal encourages multiple points of view.
- The principal acknowledges the limitations of his or her own knowledge or expertise.
- The principal is knowledgeable about effective instructional practices.
- The principal communicates a clear vision for teaching and learning at our school.

- The principal is directly involved in helping teachers address instructional issues in their classrooms.

Psychological Safety [chapter 3]

- People in this school are eager to share information about what does and does not work.
- Making mistakes is considered part of the learning process in our school.
- If I make a mistake at this school, it will not be held against me.
- In this school, teachers feel comfortable experimenting with untried teaching approaches, even if the approach might not work.
- In this school, it is easy to speak up about what is on your mind.
- People in this school are usually comfortable talking about problems and disagreements about teaching and learning.

Meaningful Professional Development [chapter 6]

- My professional development experiences this year have been closely connected to my school's improvement plan.
- My professional development experiences this year have included enough time to think carefully about, try, and evaluate new ideas.
- My professional development experiences this year have been valuable to my practice as a teacher.
- My professional development experiences this year have been designed in response to the learning needs of the faculty, as they emerge.
- My professional development experiences this year have included follow-up support as we implement what we have learned.

ORGANIZATIONAL PROCESSES

Collaboration Around an Improvement Strategy [chapter 6]

- Our school has an improvement plan, of which we are all aware.
- We focus our whole-school improvement efforts on clear, concrete steps.

- We coordinate our curriculum, instruction and learning materials with our school improvement plan.
- The programs or initiatives we implement connect clearly to our school improvement plan.

Teachers' Involvement in Instructional Decisions [chapter 6]

- Teachers work collectively to plan school improvement.
- Teachers work collectively to select instructional methods and activities.
- Teachers work collectively to evaluate curriculum and programs.
- Teachers work collectively to determine professional development needs and goals.
- Teachers work collectively to plan professional development activities.
- As a full faculty, we work toward developing a shared understanding of effective instructional practices.
- As a full faculty, we regularly revisit and revise our thinking about the most effective instructional practices we can use with our students.

Teams' Shared Understanding of Effective Practice [chapter 7]

- How often have you worked with members of your team to discuss teaching decisions based on student work?
- How often have you worked with members of your team to discuss teaching decisions based on student assessment data?
- How often have you worked with members of your team to evaluate curricular or assessment materials?
- How often have you worked with members of your team to discuss lesson plans or specific instructional practices?

Support for Teams [chapter 6]

- The principal provides teacher teams with the right balance of direction and independence.
- The principal gives teacher teams a clear and meaningful purpose for their time together.

- The principal provides adequate time for teacher teams to meet.
- The principal ensures that teacher meeting time is protected and maintained consistently throughout the year.
- The principal supports teacher teams in following through on instructional decisions made by the group.

Team Processes [chapter 7]

- Our team meetings have an agenda, which we do our best to follow.
- There is always someone who has the responsibility of guiding or facilitating our team discussions.
- When our team makes a decision, all teachers on the team take responsibility for following through.
- Our team meetings include productive debate.
- All members of the team are actively involved in our collective learning.
- Team meetings connect to each other and the overarching purpose for teamwork.

EFFICACY BELIEFS

Collective Efficacy [chapter 8]

- Teachers are confident they will be able to motivate their students.
- Teachers have the skills needed to produce meaningful student learning.
- If a child doesn't learn something the first time, teachers will try another way.
- Teachers believe that every child can learn.
- Teachers are skilled in various methods of teaching.
- Teachers have what it takes explore new instructional approaches to help underperforming students meet standards.

Protocols and Readings by Chapter

Chapter 3

National School Reform Faculty, "North, South, East and West: Compass Points; An Exercise in Understanding Preferences in Group Work," protocol, National School Reform Faculty, Harmony Education Center, accessed September 12, 2016, www.nsrfharmony.org/system/files/protocols/north_south_0.pdf.

Jonah Lehrer, "Groupthink: The Brainstorming Myth," *New Yorker*, January 30, 2012, www.newyorker.com/magazine/2012/01/30/groupthink.

Patricia Averette, "Save the Last Word for ME," protocol, National School Reform Faculty, Harmony Education Center, accessed September 12, 2016, www.nsrfharmony.org/system/files/protocols/save_last_word_0.pdf.

Betty Achinstein, "Conflict Amid Community: The Micropolitics of Teacher Collaboration," *Teachers College Record* 104, no. 3 (2002): 421–455, https://cset.stanford.edu/publications/journal-articles/conflict-amid-community-micropolitics-teacher-collaboration.

Chapter 4

Walter Doyle, "Academic Work," *Review of Educational Research* 53, no. 2 (1983): 159–199.

David K. Cohen and Deborah Loewenberg Ball, *Instruction, Capacity, and Improvement* (Philadelphia: Consortium for Policy Research in Education, 1999).

Mary Kay Stein et al., *Implementing Standards-based Mathematics Instruction: A Casebook for Professional Development*, 2nd ed. (New York: Teachers College Press, 2009).

Patricia Averette, "Save the Last Word for ME," protocol, National School Reform Faculty, Harmony Education Center, accessed September 12, 2016, www.nsrfharmony.org/system/files/protocols/save_last_word_0.pdf; for other protocols for text-based discussions, see Joseph P. McDonald, Nancy Mohr, Alan Dichter, and Elizabeth C. McDonald, *The Power of Protocols: An Educator's Guide to Better Practice*, 2nd ed. (New York: Teachers College Press, 2013).

Benjamin S. Bloom, *Taxonomy of Educational Objectives, Handbook 1: Cognitive Domain* (New York: Longman, 1956/1984).

Robert J. Marzano and John S. Kendall, *The New Taxonomy of Educational Objectives* (Thousand Oaks, CA: Corwin Press, 2007).

Norman L. Webb, "Depth-of-Knowledge Levels for Four Content Areas," unpublished paper, March 28, 2002, http://schools.nyc.gov/NR/rdonlyres/2711181C-2108-40C4-A7F8-76F243C9B910/0/DOKFourContentAreas.pdf.

Chapter 6

Rachel E. Curtis and Elizabeth A. City, *Strategy in Action* (Cambridge, MA: Harvard Education Press, 2009).

Chapter 7

Mary Kay Stein, Margaret Schwan Smith, Marjorie A. Henningsen, and Edward A. Silver, "The Case of Fran Gorman and Kevin Cooper" in *Implementing Standards-Based Mathematics Instruction: A Casebook for Professional Development*, 2nd ed. (New York: Teachers College Press, 2009).

Joseph P. McDonald, Nancy Mohr, Alan Dichter, and Elizabeth C. McDonald, "Fears and Hopes," in *The Power of Protocols: An Educator's Guide to Better Practice*, 2nd ed. (New York: Teachers College Press, 2013).

For resources to prepare educators to engage in classroom observations, see Elizabeth A. City et al., *Instructional Rounds in Education: A Network Approach to Improving Teaching and Learning* (Cambridge, MA: Harvard Education Press, 2009); Kathryn Parker Boudett, Elizabeth A. City, and Marcia K. Russell, *Key Elements of Observing Practice: A Data Wise DVD and Facilitator's Guide* (Cambridge, MA: Harvard Education Press, 2014); and Kathryn Parker Boudett and Jennifer L. Steele, "Unlocking the Classroom," in *Data Wise in Action: Stories of Schools Using Data to Improve Teaching and Learning*, ed. Kathryn Parker Boudett and Jennifer L. Steele (Cambridge, MA: Harvard Education Press, 2007).

Chapter 8

Laurel D. Puchner and Ann R. Taylor, "Lesson Study, Collaboration, and Teacher Efficacy: Stories from Two School-Based Math Lesson Study Groups," *Teaching and Teacher Education* 22, no. 7 (2006): 922–934, doi: 10.1016/j.tate.2006.04.011.

Patricia Averette, "Save the Last Word for ME," protocol, National School Reform Faculty, Harmony Education Center, accessed September 12, 2016, www.nsrfharmony.org/system/files/protocols/save_last_word_0.pdf.

Elizabeth Leisy Stosich, "Joint Inquiry: Teachers' Collective Learning About the Common Core in High-Poverty Urban Schools," *American Educational Research Journal* (in press).

Protocol
The Case of Fran and Kevin

The following step-by-step approach uses the example of two teachers, Fran and Kevin, and their different approaches to the same instructional content. The case was originally presented by Mary Kay Stein and her colleagues in their book *Implementing Standards-Based Mathematics Instruction*.[1] We use this case study and the series of steps below as a foundational learning experience in chapter 4 to generate understanding of the instructional core and the stated versus enacted task. Pairing the case with this guided experience will concretize for educators how critical classroom observation data are for understanding student learning. We revisit this case study again in chapter 7 when we focus on team instructional conversations and interdependent team learning. Page numbers in the instructions refer to Stein and colleagues' book.

Step 1: Have the participants read through "Fran's Setup" (pp. 56–59) in advance. These pages describe what Fran and Kevin hoped to accomplish with their students as well as the lesson plan they designed together. If you are using this case in your team meetings, give the participating teachers—particularly those who are not mathematically inclined—enough time to process the task that Fran and Kevin will give the students and what the children are supposed to understand by the end of the lesson. Make sure the participants understand these points before they read the case. When you convene, give the participants fifteen minutes or so in small groups to calibrate their understanding of the lesson plan and the intention of its authors, including the difference between conceptual understanding and traditional algorithms, the idea of multiplication as "x of y," and the unit whole—ideas that are discussed in Stein and colleagues' text.

Step 2: Give participants about twenty minutes to read about Fran's classroom, from "Fran's Setup" through "Fran's Implementation" (pp. 56–63). Ask them to write down or annotate the interactions or instructional decisions that seem important. (*Note:* At this point, do not have participants read the section titled "Shared Meeting Time" (p. 63), because you will return to this section when you work specifically on the instructional talk in teacher teams.)

Step 3: As you did for Fran, have the teachers read the pages on Kevin's classroom, from "Kevin Talks About his Class" through "Kevin's Implementation" (pp. 64–67), and again have them mark the interactions of interest.

Step 4: Let each participant decide to analyze either Fran's or Kevin's class. Distribute pieces of chart paper or other handouts showing the instructional core triangle. In groups of four or five, the participants should map out the interactions between the instructional core elements that they highlighted during their reading. For example, Fran selected one of her best students to demonstrate at the board, and the child posted the example without a single mistake. Fran stopped at every desk to make sure that everyone was doing the problem correctly. Kevin sent a struggling student to another student's desk and asked the second student, who had initially had trouble, to explain how he resolved his confusion about the problem. Give the participants about twenty-five minutes to discuss the various decisions their teacher made and the implications of those decisions. Provide another ten minutes to answer the following discussion questions for the teacher they selected:

- What would your experience as a student be like in this class? How would you be spending your time and attention?[2]
- At the end of the class, what would you have learned?

- How would you describe the actual task in this classroom? How did it compare with what Fran and Kevin intended?

Using a gallery walk, presentations, or an open discussion, have the group discuss the differences in what the students in each classroom would have learned given the nature of the enacted task in each room.

NOTES

CHAPTER 1

1. Anthony S. Bryk et al., *Organizing Schools for Improvement: Lessons from Chicago* (Chicago: University of Chicago Press, 2010); Richard F. Elmore, *School Reform from the Inside Out: Policy, Practice, and Performance* (Cambridge, MA: Harvard Educational Press, 2004); Michael Fullan and Joanne Quinn, *Coherence: The Right Drivers in Action for Schools, Districts, and Systems* (Thousand Oaks, CA: Corwin Press, 2015); Ben Levin, *How to Change 5000 Schools: A Practical and Positive Approach for Leading Change at Every Level* (Cambridge, MA: Harvard Education Press, 2008).

2. Ronald H. Heck and Philip Hallinger, "Assessing the Contribution of Distributed Leadership to School Improvement and Growth in Math Achievement," *American Educational Research Journal* 46, no. 3 (2009): 659–689; Kenneth Leithwood et al., *Review of Research: How Leadership Influences Student Learning* (New York: The Wallace Foundation, 2004); Viviane M. J. Robinson, Claire A. Lloyd, and Kenneth J. Rowe, "The Impact of Leadership on Student Outcomes: An Analysis of the Differential Effects of Leadership Types," *Educational Administration Quarterly* 44, no. 5 (2008): 635–674.

3. W. Norton Grubb, *The Money Myth* (New York: Russell Sage, 2009).

4. Hilda Borko, "Professional Development and Teacher Learning: Mapping the Terrain," *Educational Researcher* 33, no. 8 (2004): 3–15; David K. Cohen and Deborah Loewenberg Ball, *Instruction, Capacity, and Improvement* (Philadelphia: Consortium for Policy Research in Education, 1999); Linda Darling-Hammond et al., *Professional Learning in the Learning Profession* (Washington, DC: National Staff Development Council, 2009).

5. Amy Edmondson, "Psychological Safety and Learning Behavior in Work Teams," *Administrative Science Quarterly* 44, no. 2 (1999): 350–383; David A. Garvin, Amy C. Edmondson, and Francesca Gino, "Is Yours a Learning Organization?," *Harvard Business Review* 86, no. 3 (2008): 109; Helen M. Marks and Susan M. Printy, "Principal Leadership and School Performance: An Integration of Transformational and Instructional Leadership," *Educational Administration Quarterly* 39, no. 3 (2003): 370–397.

6. For distributed leadership, see James P. Spillane, Richard Halverson, and John B. Diamond, "Investigating School Leadership Practice: A Distributed Perspective," *Educational Researcher* 30, no. 3 (2001): 23–28. For leadership for learning, see Philip Hallinger, "Leadership for Learning: Lessons from 40 Years of Empirical Research," *Journal of Educational Administration* 49, no. 2 (2011): 125–142.

7. Eric M. Camburn, James P. Spillane, and James Sebastian, "Assessing the Utility of a Daily Log for Measuring Principal Leadership Practice," *Educational Administration Quarterly* 46, no. 5 (2010):

707–737; Richard F. Elmore, *Building a New Structure for School Leadership* (New York: Albert Shanker Institute, 2000); Jason A. Grissom, Susanna Loeb, and Benjamin Master, "Effective Instructional Time Use for School Leaders: Longitudinal Evidence from Observations of Principals," *Educational Researcher* 42, no. 8 (2013): 433–444.

8. Karen Seashore Louis et al., *Learning from Leadership: Investigating the Links to Improved Student Learning* (New York: Wallace Foundation, 2010); Marks and Printy, "Transformational and Instructional Leadership"; Susan M. Printy, Helen M. Marks, and Alex Bowers, "Integrated Leadership: How Principals and Teachers Share Transformational and Instructional Influences," *Journal of School Leadership* 19, no. 5 (2010): 504.

9. Larry Cuban, *Inside the Black Box of Classroom Practice: Change Without Reform in American Education* (Cambridge, MA: Harvard Education Press, 2013).

10. Elizabeth A. City et al., *Instructional Rounds in Education: A Network Approach to Improving Teaching And Learning*; Cohen and Ball, *Instruction, Capacity*; (Cambridge, MA: Harvard Education Press, 2009).

11. City et al., *Instructional Rounds*. David K. Cohen and Carol A. Barnes, "Pedagogy and Policy," in *Teaching for Understanding: Challenges for Policy and Practice*, ed. David K. Cohen, Milbrey W. McLaughlin, and Joan E. Talbert (San Francisco: Jossey-Bass, 1993), 207–239; Cohen and Ball, *Instruction, Capacity*; Elmore, *School Reform*.

12. David K. Cohen, Stephen W. Raudenbush, and Deborah Loewenberg Ball, "Resources, Instruction, and Research," *Educational Evaluation and Policy Analysis* 25, no. 2 (2003): 119–142.

13. Cohen and Ball, *Instruction, Capacity*.

14. Elizabeth Leisy Stosich, "Building Teacher and School Capacity to Teach to Ambitious Standards in High-Poverty Schools," *Teaching and Teacher Education* 58 (2016): 43–53.

15. Paul Cobb and Kara Jackson, "Analyzing Educational Policies: A Learning Design Perspective," *Journal of the Learning Sciences* 21, no. 4 (2012): 487–521; Chrysan Gallucci, "Communities of Practice and the Mediation of Teachers' Responses to Standards-Based Reform," *Education Policy Analysis Archives* 11 (2003): 35; Judith Warren Little, "Organizing Schools for Teacher Learning," in *Teaching as the Learning Profession: Handbook of Policy and Practice*, ed. Linda Darling-Hammond and Gary Sykes (San Francisco: Jossey-Bass, 1999), 233–262; James P. Spillane, Brian J. Reiser, and Todd Reimer, "Policy Implementation and Cognition: Reframing and Refocusing Implementation Research," *Review of Educational Research* 72, no. 3 (2002): 387–431.

16. Cohen and Barnes, "Pedagogy"; Elmore, *School Reform*.

17. Elizabeth Leisy Stosich, "Leading in a Time of Ambitious Reform: Principals in High-Poverty Urban Elementary Schools Frame the Challenge of the Common Core State Standards," *The Elementary School Journal* (in press).

18. Bryk et al., *Organizing*.

19. Donald Boyd et al., "The Influence of School Administrators on Teacher Retention Decisions," *American Educational Research Journal* 48, no. 2 (2011): 303–333; Dan Goldhaber, Lesley Lavery, and Roddy Theobald, "Uneven Playing Field? Assessing the Teacher Quality Gap Between Advantaged and Disadvantaged Students," *Educational Researcher* (2015): 0013189X15592622; Matthew A. Kraft and John P. Papay, "Can Professional Environments in Schools Promote Teacher Development? Explaining Heterogeneity in Returns to Teaching Experience," *Educational Evaluation and Policy Analysis* 36, no. 4 (2014): 476–500.

20. Thomas R. Guskey, "Professional Development and Teacher Change," *Teachers and Teaching: Theory and Practice* 8, no. 3 (2002): 381–391.

21. Ibid., 384.

22. Elizabeth Leisy Stosich, "Joint Inquiry: Teachers' Collective Learning About the Common Core in High-Poverty Urban Schools," *American Educational Research Journal* (in press).

23. Hugh Burkhardt and Alan H. Schoenfeld, "Improving Educational Research: Toward a More Useful, More Influential, and Better-Funded Enterprise," *Educational Researcher* 32, no. 9 (2003): 3–14.

24. Kathryn Parker Boudett, Elizabeth A. City, and Richard Murnane, eds. *Data Wise: A Step-by-Step Guide to Using Assessment Results to Improve Teaching and Learning* (Cambridge, MA: Harvard Education Press, 2005); City et al., *Instructional Rounds.*

25. Marks and Printy, "Transformational and Instructional Leadership"; Printy, Marks, and Bowers, "Integrated Leadership."

26. Meredith I. Honig, "District Central Office Leadership as Teaching: How Central Office Administrators Support Principals' Development as Instructional Leaders," *Educational Administration Quarterly* 48, no. 4 (2012): 733–774.

CHAPTER 2

1. Bay Area School Reform Collaborative, "Teacher Survey" (online survey and website) (Oakland, CA: Manpower Demonstration Research Corporation and Center for Research on the Context of Teaching, spring 2002), www.stanford.edu/group/suse-crc/cgi-bin/drupal/sites/default/files/survey/BASRC-teacher-survey2002.pdf; Consortium on Chicago School Research, "Survey of Chicago Public Schools, High School Teacher Edition" (online survey and website) (Chicago: Chicago School Research, 2009); David A. Garvin, Amy C. Edmondson, and Francesca Gino, "Is Yours a Learning Organization?" *Harvard Business Review* 86, no. 3 (2008): 109–116; Sherri Gibson and Myron H. Dembo, "Teacher Efficacy: A Construct Validation," *Journal of Educational Psychology* 76, no. 4 (1984): 569; Roger Goddard, "A Theoretical and Empirical Analysis of the Measurement of Collective Efficacy: The Development of a Short Form," *Educational and Psychological Measurement* 62, no. 1 (2002): 97–110; Yvonne L. Goddard, Roger D. Goddard, and Megan Tschannen-Moran, "A Theoretical and Empirical Investigation of Teacher Collaboration for School Improvement and Student Achievement in Public Elementary Schools," *Teachers College Record* 109, no. 4 (2007): 877–896; Mid-continent Research for Education and Learning, "Balanced Leadership Profile" (online survey and website) (Aurora, CO: Mid-continent Research for Education and Learning, 2005); John A. Ross and Peter Gray, "School Leadership and Student Achievement: The Mediating Effects of Teacher Beliefs," *Canadian Journal of Education/Revue canadienne de l'éducation* (2006): 798–822; Megan Tschannen-Moran and Anita Woolfolk Hoy, "Teachers' Sense of Efficacy Scale," Ohio State University, Columbus, accessed May 31, 2011, http://people.ehe.ohio-state.edu/ahoy/files/2009/02/tses.pdf.

2. Elizabeth Leisy Stosich, "Measuring School Capacity for Improvement: Piloting the Internal Coherence Survey," in *Using Data in Schools to Inform Leadership and Decision Making*, ed. Alex Bowers, Bruce Barnett, and Alan Shoho (Charlotte, NC: Information Age Publishing, 2014).

3. Linda Darling-Hammond, Gene Wilhoit, and Linda Pittenger, "Accountability for College and Career Readiness: Developing a New Paradigm," *Education Policy Analysis Archives* 22, no. 86 (2014): 1–34.

4. Michelle Forman, "Building Collective Efficacy Beliefs at a Chronically Underperforming School," qualifying paper, Harvard Graduate School of Education, Boston, 2009.

5. Philip Hallinger and Ronald H. Heck, "Exploring the Principal's Contribution to School Effectiveness: 1980–1995," *School Effectiveness and School Improvement* 9, no. 2 (1998): 157–191; Louis et al., "Learning from Leadership"; Robert J. Marzano, Timothy Waters, and Brian A. McNulty, *School Leadership That Works: From Research to Results* (Alexandria, VA: ASCD, 2005); Robinson, Lloyd, and Rowe, "Impact of Leadership."

6. Anthony S. Bryk et al., *Learning to Improve: How America's Schools Can Get Better at Getting Better* (Cambridge, MA: Harvard Education Press, 2015), 6–7.

CHAPTER 3

1. For example, see Dan C. Lortie, *Schoolteacher: A Sociological Study* (Chicago: University of Chicago Press, 1975).

2. Anthony S. Bryk and Barbara Schneider, *Trust in Schools: A Core Resource for School Improvement* (New York: Russell Sage Foundation, 2002).

3. Ibid.

4. Ingrid M. Nembhard and Amy C. Edmondson, "Making It Safe: The Effects of Leader Inclusiveness and Professional Status on Psychological Safety and Improvement Efforts in Health Care Teams," *Journal of Organizational Behavior* 27, no. 7 (2006): 941–966, doi: 10.1002/job.413.

5. James R. Detert and Amy C. Edmondson, "Implicit Voice Theories: Taken-for-Granted Rules of Self-Censorship at Work," *Academy of Management Journal* 54, no. 3 (2011): 461–488; Amy C. Edmondson and Zhike Lei, "Psychological Safety: The History, Renaissance, and Future of an Interpersonal Construct," *Annual Review of Organizational Psychology and Organizational Behavior* 1 (2014): 23–43, doi: 10.1146/annurev-orgpsych-031413-091305.

6. Amy C. Edmondson, "Psychological Safety and Learning Behavior in Work Teams," *Administrative Science Quarterly* 44, no. 2 (1999): 350–383; A. L. Tucker, "An Empirical Study of System Improvement by Frontline Employees in Hospital Units," *Manufacturing & Service Operations Management* 9, no. 4 (2007): 492–505.

7. Edmondson and Lei, "Psychological Safety."

8. Nembhard and Edmondson, "Making It Safe"; David A. Garvin, Amy C. Edmondson, and Francesca Gino, "Is Yours a Learning Organization?," *Harvard Business Review* 86, no. 3 (2008): 109–116; Amy C. Edmondson, "The Local and Variegated Nature of Learning in Organizations: A Group-Level Perspective," *Organization Science* 13, no. 2 (2002/4): 128–146, doi: 10.1287/orsc .13.2.128.530.

9. Kenneth Leithwood and Blair Mascall, "Collective Leadership Effects on Student Achievement," *Educational Administration Quarterly* 44, no. 4 (2008): 529–561; Helen M. Marks and Susan M. Printy, "Principal Leadership and School Performance: An Integration of Transformational and Instructional Leadership," *Educational Administration Quarterly* 39, no. 3 (2003): 370–397; Susan M. Printy, Helen M. Marks, and Alex Bowers, "Integrated Leadership: How Principals and Teachers Share Transformational and Instructional Influences," *Journal of School Leadership* 19, no. 5 (2010): 504–532.

10. Jean Lave and Etienne Wenger, *Situated Learning: Legitimate Peripheral Participation* (Cambridge: Cambridge University Press, 1991); Etienne Wenger, *Communities of Practice: Learning, Meaning, and Identity* (Cambridge: Cambridge University Press, 1998).

11. Edmondson and Lei, "Psychological Safety."

12. Edmondson, "Local and Variegated."

13. Matthew Feinberg and Charlan Nemeth, *The "Rules" of Brainstorming: An Impediment to Creativity?* (Berkeley, CA: Institute for Research on Labor and Employment, 2008); Garvin, Edmondson, and Gino, "Learning Organization"; Jonah Lehrer, "Groupthink: The Brainstorming Myth," *New Yorker*, January 30, 2012, www.newyorker.com/magazine/2012/01/30/groupthink.

14. A copy of this protocol is available from National School Reform Faculty, "North, South, East and West: Compass Points; An Exercise in Understanding Preferences in Group Work," National School Reform Faculty, Harmony Education Center, accessed September 12, 2016, www.nsrfharmony.org/system/files/protocols/north_south_1.pdf.

15. Garvin, Edmondson, and Gino, "Learning Organization."

16. Betty Achinstein, "Conflict Amid Community: The Micropolitics of Teacher Collaboration," *Teachers College Record* 104, no. 3 (2002): 421–455.

17. Lehrer, "Groupthink."

18. A copy of this protocol is available from Patricia Averette, "Save the Last Word for ME," National School Reform Faculty, Harmony Education Center, accessed September 12, 2016, www.nsrfharmony.org/system/files/protocols/save_last_word_0.pdf.

19. Achinstein, "Conflict Amid Community."

20. Ibid.; Jorge Ávila de Lima, "Improving the Study of Teacher Collegiality: Methodological Issues" (paper presented at the annual conference of the American Educational Research Association, San Diego, California, April 13–17, 1998).

21. Achinstein, "Conflict Amid Community."

22. John W. Gardner, *Building Community* (San Francisco: Independent Sector), 15, quoted in Achinstein, "Conflict Amid Community."

23. Susan F. Henry, "Instructional Conversations: A Qualitative Exploration of Differences in Elementary Teachers' Team Discussions" (EdD diss., Harvard Graduate School of Education, 2012).

24. Judith Warren Little, "The Persistence of Privacy: Autonomy and Initiative in Teachers' Professional Relations," *Teachers College Record* 91(1990): 509–536.

CHAPTER 4

1. The four practices are the articulation of a vision for instruction, involvement in instruction and curriculum, the promotion of teacher learning and development, and the fostering of organizational structures and conditions to support teacher collaboration. See Karen Seashore Louis et al., *Learning from Leadership: Investigating the Links to Improved Student Learning* (New York: Wallace Foundation, 2010); Viviane M. J. Robinson, Claire A. Lloyd, and Kenneth J. Rowe, "The Impact of Leadership on Student Outcomes: An Analysis of the Differential Effects of Leadership Types," *Educational Administration Quarterly* 44, no. 5 (2008): 635–674.

2. Louis et al., *Learning from Leadership*; Gary A. Yukl, *Leadership in Organizations* (Upper Saddle River, NJ: Prentice Hall, 2002).

3. David K. Cohen and Susan L. Moffitt, *The Ordeal of Equality: Did Federal Regulation Fix the Schools?*, Cambridge, MA: Harvard University Press, 2009); Larry Cuban, *Inside the Black Box of Classroom Practice: Change Without Reform in American Education* (Cambridge, MA: Harvard Education Press, 2013).

4. John D. Bransford, Ann L. Brown, and Rodney R. Cocking, eds., *How People Learn: Brain, Mind, Experience, and School* (Washington, DC: National Academy Press, 2000); Richard F. Elmore, *School Reform from the Inside Out* (Cambridge, MA: Harvard Education Press, 2004); Fred M.

Newmann, BetsAnn Smith, Elaine Allensworth, and Anthony S. Bryk, *Instructional Program Coherence: Benefits and Challenges* (Chicago: Consortium on Chicago School Research, 2001).

5. Peter M. Senge, *The Fifth Discipline: The Art and Practice of the Learning Organization* (New York: Doubleday, 1990): 146.

6. Ibid.

7. David K. Cohen and Deborah Loewenberg Ball, *Instruction, Capacity, and Improvement* (Philadelphia: Consortium for Policy Research in Education, 1999).

8. Elizabeth A. City et al., *Instructional Rounds in Education: A Network Approach to Improving Teaching And Learning* (Cambridge, MA: Harvard Education Press, 2009).

9. Walter Doyle, "Academic Work," *Review of Educational Research* 53, no. 2 (1983): 159–199.

10. Ibid.

11. For examples of learning frameworks, see Benjamin S. Bloom, Taxonomy of Educational Objectives, Handbook 1: Cognitive Domain (New York: Longman, 1956/1984); Robert J. Marzano and John S. Kendall, The New Taxonomy of Educational Objectives (Thousand Oaks, CA: Corwin Press, 2007); and Norman L. Webb, "Depth-of-Knowledge Levels for Four Content Areas," March 28, 2002, http://schools.nyc.gov/NR/rdonlyres/2711181C-2108-40C4-A7F8-76F243C9B910/0/DOKFourContentAreas.pdf.

12. Mary Kay Stein et al., *Implementing Standards-Based Mathematics Instruction: A Casebook for Professional Development*, 2nd ed. (New York: Teachers College Press, 2009).

13. Doyle, "Academic Work."

14. Mary Kay Stein, Barbara W. Grover, and Marjorie Henningsen, "Building Student Capacity for Mathematical Thinking and Reasoning: An Analysis of Mathematical Tasks Used in Reform Classrooms," *American Educational Research Journal* 33, no. 2 (1996): 455–488.

15. City et al., *Instructional Rounds*, 30.

16. Mary Kay Stein and Suzanne Lane, "Instructional Tasks and the Development of Student Capacity to Think and Reason: An Analysis of the Relationship Between Teaching and Learning in a Reform Mathematics Project," *Educational Research and Evaluation* 2, no. 1 (1996): 50–80.

17. Sandra L. Christenson, Amy L. Reschly, and Cathy Wylie, eds., *Handbook of Research on Student Engagement* (New York: Springer-Verlag, 2012).

18. Stein et al., *Implementing Standards-Based Mathematics Instruction*, 1.

19. Ibid., 56–71.

20. Problem adapted from EngageNY, www.engageny.org/.

21. Stein et al., *Implementing*, xix.

CHAPTER 5

1. Richard F. Elmore et al., *The Internal Coherence Assessment Protocol and Developmental Framework: Building the Organizational Capacity for Instructional Improvement in Schools* (San Francisco: Strategic Education Research Partnership, 2014); Fred M. Newmann, Bruce King, and Peter Youngs, "Professional Development That Addresses School Capacity: Lessons from Urban Elementary Schools," *American Journal of Education* 108, no. 4 (2000): 259–299.

2. Fred M. Newmann et al., "Instructional Program Coherence: What It Is and Why It Should Guide School Improvement Policy," *Educational Evaluation and Policy Analysis* 23, no. 4 (2001): 297–321.

3. This phrase is attributed to Paul Batalden, Dartmouth pediatrician and former chair of the Institute for Healthcare Improvement.

4. Peter Senge, *The Fifth Discipline: The Art and Science of the Learning Organization* (New York: Doubleday, 1990).

5. Elizabeth Leisy Stosich, "Measuring School Capacity for Improvement: Piloting the Internal Coherence Survey," in *Using Data in Schools to Inform Leadership and Decision Making*, ed. Alex Bowers, Bruce Barnett, and Alan Shoho (Charlotte, NC: Information Age Publishing, 2014).

6. Elmore, *School Reform*; Thomas R. Guskey, "Results-oriented Professional Development: In Search of an Optimal Mix of Effective Practices," *Journal of Staff Development* 15 (1994): 42–50.

7. Richard F. Elmore, *School Reform from the Inside Out: Policy, Practice, and Performance* (Cambridge, MA: Harvard Education Press, 2004).

8. Ibid., 5.

9. Council of Chief State School Officers, *Educational Leadership Policy Standards: ISLLC 2008* (Washington, DC: CCSSO, 2008), 14.

10. Stephen Anderson, Kenneth Leithwood, and Tiiu Strauss, "Leading Data Use in Schools: Organizational Conditions and Practices at the School and District Levels," *Leadership and Policy in Schools* 9, no. 3 (2010): 292–327; Richard R. Halverson, "School Formative Feedback Systems," *Peabody Journal of Education* 85 (2010): 130–146.

11. Anthony S. Bryk et al., *Organizing Schools for Improvement: Lessons from Chicago* (Chicago: University of Chicago Press, 2010); Philip Hallinger and Ronald H. Heck, "Exploring the Principal's Contribution to School Effectiveness: 1980–1995," *School Effectiveness and School Improvement* 9, no. 2 (1998): 157–191; Kenneth Leithwood et al., *Review of Research: How Leadership Influences Student Learning* (New York: The Wallace Foundation, 2004); Viviane M. J. Robinson, Claire A. Lloyd, and Kenneth J. Rowe, "The Impact of Leadership on Student Outcomes: An Analysis of the Differential Effects of Leadership Types," *Educational Administration Quarterly* 44, no. 5 (2008): 635–674.

12. This activity is adapted from ideas presented in Kathryn Parker Boudett, Elizabeth A. City, and Richard Murnane, eds. *Data Wise: A Step-by-Step Guide to Using Assessment Results to Improve Teaching and Learning*, revised and expanded ed. (Cambridge, MA: Harvard Education Press, 2013); and Rachel E. Curtis and Elizabeth A. City, *Strategy in Action: How School Systems Can Support Powerful Learning and Teaching* (Cambridge, MA: Harvard Education Press, 2009).

13. Cynthia E. Coburn and Mary Kay Stein, *Research and Practice in Education: Building Alliances, Bridging the Divide* (Lanham, MD: Rowman & Littlefield, 2010); Suzanne Donovan, "The SERP Approach to Research, Design, and Development: A Different Role for Research and Researchers" (paper presented at the annual conference of the American Education Research Association, New Orleans, April 8–12, 2011).

14. The Internal Coherence Survey is reproduced by permission of the Strategic Education Research Partnership. Copyright © 2010, 2015 by Strategic Education Research Partnership.

CHAPTER 6

1. Richard F. Elmore, *School Reform from the Inside Out: Policy, Practice, and Performance* (Cambridge, MA: Harvard Educational Press, 2004), 73.

2. Elmore, *School Reform*.

3. Paul Cobb and Kara Jackson, "Analyzing Educational Policies: A Learning Design Perspective," *Journal of the Learning Sciences* 21, no. 4 (2012): 487–521; Cynthia E. Coburn, "Rethinking Scale: Moving Beyond Numbers to Deep and Lasting Change," *Educational Researcher* 32, no. 6 (2003):

3–12; James P. Spillane, Leigh Mesler Parise, and Jennifer Zoltners Sherer, "Organizational Routines as Coupling Mechanisms: Policy, School Administration, and the Technical Core," *American Educational Research Journal* 48, no. 3 (2011): 586–619.

4. Stacey Childress, *Note on Strategy in Education* (Cambridge, MA: Public Education Leadership Project at Harvard University, 2004), 1.

5. David K. Cohen, "What Is the System in Systemic Reform?," *Educational Researcher* 24, no. 9 (1995): 11–31.

6. David K. Cohen and Deborah Loewenberg Ball, *Instruction, Capacity, and Improvement* (Philadelphia: Consortium for Policy Research in Education, 1999); Richard Elmore, "Getting to Scale with Good Educational Practice," *Harvard Educational Review* 66, no. 1 (1996): 1–27; James Hiebert, Ronald Gallimore, and James W. Stigler. "A Knowledge Base for the Teaching Profession: What Would It Look Like and How Can We Get One?," *Educational Researcher* 31, no. 5 (2002): 3–15.

7. Cohen and Ball, *Instruction, Capacity.*

8. Ellen Behrstock-Sherratt and Catherine Jacques, *Aligning Evaluation Results and Professional Development: Driving Systemic Human Capital Management Reform* (Washington, DC: US Department of Education Teacher Incentive Fund, 2012); Rolf K. Blank and Nina De Las Alas, *The Effects of Teacher Professional Development on Gains in Student Achievement: How Meta Analysis Provides Scientific Evidence Useful to Education Leaders* (Washington, DC: Council of Chief State School Officers, 2009); Michael S. Garet et al., "What Makes Professional Development Effective? Results from a National Sample of Teachers," *American Educational Research Journal* 38, no. 4 (2001): 915–945; Laura Goe, Kietha Biggers, and Andrew Croft, *Linking Teacher Evaluation to Professional Development: Focusing on Improving Teaching and Learning; Research & Policy Brief* (Washington, DC: National Comprehensive Center for Teacher Quality, 2012); Thomas R. Guskey and Kwang Suk Yoon, "What Works in Professional Development," *Phi Delta Kappan* 90, no. 7 (2009): 495–500; Leigh Mesler Parise and James P. Spillane, "Teacher Learning and Instructional Change: How Formal and on-the-Job Learning Opportunities Predict Change in Elementary School Teachers' Practice," *Elementary School Journal* 110, no. 3 (2010): 323–346; William R. Penuel et al., "What Makes Professional Development Effective? Strategies That Foster Curriculum Implementation," *American Educational Research Journal* 44, no. 4 (2007): 921–958; Jonathan A. Supovitz, Daniel P. Mayer, and Jane B. Kahle, "Promoting Inquiry-Based Instructional Practice: The Longitudinal Impact of Professional Development in the Context of Systemic Reform," *Educational Policy* 14, no. 3 (2000): 331–356; Marjorie R. Wallace, "Making Sense of the Links: Professional Development, Teacher Practices, and Student Achievement," *Teachers College Record* 111, no.2 (2009): 573–596; Iris R. Weiss and Joan D. Pasley, "Scaling Up Instructional Improvement Through Teacher Professional Development: Insights from the Local Systemic Change Initiative" (Philadelphia: Consortium for Policy Research in Education, 2006); Kwang Suk Yoon et al., *Reviewing the Evidence on How Teacher Professional Development Affects Student Achievement: Issues & Answers,* REL 2007-No. 033 (Washington, DC: US Department of Education, Institute of Education Sciences, National Center for Education Evaluation and Regional Assistance, Regional Educational Laboratory Southwest, 2007).

9. Garet et al., "What Makes Professional Development Effective?"

10. Jane G. Coggshall, *Toward the Effective Teaching of New College- and Career-Ready Standards: Making Professional Learning Systemic,* Research-to-Practice Brief (Washington, DC: National Comprehensive Center for Teacher Quality, 2012).

11. Andrew Croft et al., *Job-Embedded Professional Development: What It Is, Who Is Responsible, and How to Get It Done Well*, Issue Brief (Washington, DC, and Oxford, OH: National Comprehensive Center for Teacher Quality, Mid-Atlantic Comprehensive Center, and National Staff Development Council, 2010).

12. Mary M. Crossan and Iris Berdrow, "Organizational Learning and Strategic Renewal," *Strategic Management Journal* 24, no. 11 (2003): 1087–1105; Amy C. Edmondson, "The Local and Variegated Nature of Learning in Organizations: A Group-Level Perspective," *Organization Science* 13, no. 2 (2002): 128–146.

13. Fred M. Newmann et al., "Instructional Program Coherence: What It Is and Why It Should Guide School Improvement Policy," *Educational Evaluation and Policy Analysis* 23, no. 4 (2001): 297–321.

14. J. Richard Hackman, *Leading Teams: Setting the Stage for Great Performances* (Cambridge, MA: Harvard Business Press, 2002).

15. Susan Moore Johnson et al., "Ready to Lead, But How? Teachers' Experiences in High-Poverty Urban Schools," *Teachers College Record* 116, no. 1 (2014): 1–50.

16. Ibid., 8.

17. Linda Darling-Hammond, "Accountability and Teacher Professionalism," *American Educator* 12, no. 4 (1988): 8–13; Helen M. Marks and Susan M. Printy, "Principal Leadership and School Performance: An Integration of Transformational and Instructional Leadership," *Educational Administration Quarterly* 39, no. 3 (2003): 370–397.

18. Marks and Printy, "Transformational and Instructional Leadership"; Susan M. Printy, Helen M. Marks, and Alex Bowers, "Integrated Leadership: How Principals and Teachers Share Transformational and Instructional Influences," *Journal of School Leadership* 19, no. 5 (2010): 504.

19. Roger D. Goddard, "Collective Efficacy and School Organization: A Multilevel Analysis of Teacher Influence in Schools," *Theory and Research in Educational Administration* 1, (2002): 169–184; Roger D. Goddard, Wayne K. Hoy, and Anita Woolfolk Hoy, "Collective Efficacy Beliefs: Theoretical Developments, Empirical Evidence, and Future Directions," *Educational Researcher* 33, no. 3 (2004): 3–13.

20. John A. Ross, Anne Hogaboam-Gray, and Peter Gray, "Prior Student Achievement, Collaborative School Processes, and Collective Teacher Efficacy," *Leadership & Policy in Schools* 3 (2004): 163–188.

21. Roger D. Goddard et al., "A Social Cognitive Perspective on Collective Efficacy and Goal Attainment in Schools: The Roles of Principals' Instructional Leadership and Teacher Collaboration" (paper presented at the annual conference of the American Education Research Association, New Orleans, April 8–12, 2011).

22. Monica C. Higgins, Jennie Weiner, and Lissa Young, "Implementation Teams: A New Lever for Organizational Change," *Journal of Organizational Behavior* 33, no. 3 (2012): 366–388; Hans W. Klar and Curtis A. Brewer, "Successful Leadership in a Rural, High-Poverty School: The Case of County Line Middle School," *Journal of Educational Administration* 52, no. 4 (2014): 422–445; Jennie Miles Weiner, "Disabling Conditions: Investigating Instructional Leadership Teams in Action," *Journal of Educational Change* 15, no. 3 (2014): 253–280.

23. Wiener, "Disabling Conditions."

24. Elizabeth Leisy Stosich, "Measuring School Capacity for Improvement: Piloting the Internal Coherence Survey," in *Using Data in Schools to Inform Leadership and Decision Making*, ed. Alex Bowers, Bruce Barnett, and Alan Shoho (Charlotte, NC: Information Age Publishing, 2014).

25. These prompts were adapted from Elizabeth A. City et al., *Instructional Rounds in Education: A Network Approach to Improving Teaching and Learning* (Cambridge, MA: Harvard Education Press, 2009).

26. Andy Hargreaves, "Contrived Collegiality: The Micropolitics of Teacher Collaboration," in *Sociology of Education: Major Themes*, ed. Stephen J. Ball (London: Psychology Press, 2000), 2:1480–1503.

27. Rachel E. Curtis and Elizabeth A. City, *Strategy in Action: How School Systems Can Support Powerful Learning and Teaching* (Cambridge, MA: Harvard Education Press, 2009).

28. The school name and educators' names are pseudonyms.

29. B. J. Barron et al., "Doing with Understanding: Lessons from Research on Problem- and Project-Based Learning," *Journal of the Learning Sciences* 7, no. 3–4 (1998): 271–311.

30. For the Teachers College Reading and Writing Workshop, see L. Calkins, *The Art of Teaching Writing* (Portsmouth, NH: Heinemann, 1986); L. Calkins and K. Tolan, *A Guide to the Reading Workshop* (First Hand/Heinemann 2010). For the Investigations math curriculum, see Pearson Education and TERC, *Investigations in Number, Data, and Space* (Pearson Scott Pearson Education & TERC, 2008).

31. J. Nelsen, L. Lott, and H. S. Glenn, *Positive Discipline in the Classroom: Developing Mutual Respect, Cooperation, and Responsibility in Your Classroom* (New York: Random House, 2000).

32. Barry Garelick, "Miracle Math: A Successful Program from Singapore Tests the Limits of School Reform in the Suburbs," *Education Next* 6, no. 4 (2006): 38–45.

33. Ibid.

34. P. Hallinger and R. H. Heck, "Exploring the Principals' Contribution to School Effectiveness: 1980–1995," *School Effectiveness and School Improvement* 9, no. 2 (1998): 157–191; K. S. Louis, K. Leithwood, K. L. Wahlstrom, and S. E. Anderson, *Investigating the Links to Improved Student Learning: Final Report of Research Findings* (New York: Wallace Foundation, 2010); R. J. Marzano, T. Waters, and B. A. McNulty, *School Leadership That Works: From Research to Results* (Alexandria, VA: Association for Supervision and Curriculum Development, 2005).

35. Johnson et al., "Ready to Lead."

CHAPTER 7

1. Mary Kay Stein et al., *Implementing Standards-Based Mathematics Instruction: A Casebook for Professional Development*, 2nd ed. (New York: Teachers College Press, 2009).

2. Richard Dufour and Robert Eaker, *Professional Learning Communities at Work: Best Practices for Enhancing Student Achievement* (Bloomington, IN: Solution Tree Press, 1998); Etienne Wenger, *Communities of Practice: Learning, Meaning, and Identity* (Cambridge: Cambridge University Press, 1998).

3. Jeanne M. Wilson, Paul S. Goodman, and Matthew A. Cronin, "Group Learning," *Academy of Management Review* 32, no. 4 (2007): 1041–1059.

4. J. Richard Hackman, *Leading Teams: Setting the Stage for Great Performances* (Cambridge, MA: Harvard Business Press, 2002).

5. Judith Warren Little, "The Persistence of Privacy: Autonomy and Initiative in Teachers' Professional Relations," *Teachers College Record* 91(1990): 509–536.

6. Susan F. Henry, "Instructional Conversations: A Qualitative Exploration of Differences in Elementary Teachers' Team Discussions" (EdD diss., Harvard Graduate School of Education, 2012).

7. Ibid.

8. Ibid, 48.

9. Jonathan A. Supovitz and Valerie Klein, *Mapping a Course for Improved Student Learning: How*

Innovative Schools Systematically Use Student Performance Data to Guide Improvement (Philadelphia: Consortium for Policy Research in Education, 2003).

10. Anthony S. Bryk et al., *Learning to Improve: How America's Schools Can Get Better at Getting Better* (Cambridge, MA: Harvard Education Press, 2015); Sandra Park, Stephanie Hironaka, Penny Carver, and Lee Nordstrum, *Continuous Improvement in Education* (Stanford, CA: Carnegie Foundation for the Advancement of Teaching, 2013).

11. Henry, "Instructional Conversations," 83.

12. For example, see Dufour and Eaker, *Professional Learning Communities;* Hackman, *Leading Teams;* Supovitz and Klein, *Mapping a Course;* Wenger, *Communities of Practice.*

13. For a more complete description of each axis, see Henry (2012).

14. For resources to prepare educators to engage in classroom observations, see Elizabeth A. City et al., *Instructional Rounds in Education: A Network Approach to Improving Teaching and Learning* (Cambridge, MA: Harvard Education Press, 2009); and Kathryn Parker Boudett, Elizabeth A. City, and Marcia K. Russell, *Key Elements of Observing Practice: A Data Wise DVD and Facilitator's Guide* (Cambridge, MA: Harvard Education Press, 2014).

15. Joseph P. McDonald, Nancy Mohr, Alan Dichter, and Elizabeth C. McDonald, *The Power of Protocols: An Educator's Guide to Better Practice*, 2nd ed. (New York: Teachers College Press, 2013).

16. In the past, we have used an excerpt from Kathryn Parker Boudett and Jennifer L. Steele, "Unlocking the Classroom," chapter 5 in *Data Wise in Action: Stories of Schools Using Data to Improve Teaching and Learning* (Cambridge: Harvard Education Press, 2007). Their chapter clearly describes how one teacher team in Boston developed a practice of peer observation to support the team's shared learning about the core. When we use this reference, we are careful to point out that we are not advocating for teachers to recreate the exact process used at the example school, but rather are highlighting how that school used peer observation as a strategy to deepen instructional conversations.

CHAPTER 8

1. The way we use this term here is a slight departure from its definition in the field of efficacy research, where individuals are presented as having an internal or external locus of control in general, rather than for a particular task in a given context.

2. Elizabeth Leisy Stosich, "Joint Inquiry: Teachers' Collective Learning About the Common Core in High-Poverty Urban Schools," *American Educational Research Journal* (in press).

3. Albert Bandura, *Social Foundations of Thought and Action: A Social Cognitive Theory* (Englewood Cliffs, NJ: Prentice-Hall, 1986); Albert Bandura, *Self-Efficacy: The Exercise of Control* (New York: W.H. Freeman, 1997).

4. Bandura, *Self-Efficacy;* Marilyn E. Gist and Terence R. Mitchell, "Self-Efficacy: A Theoretical Analysis of Its Determinants and Malleability," *Academy of Management Review* 17, no. 2 (1992): 183–211.

5. Rose M. Allinder, "The Relationship Between Efficacy and the Instructional Practices of Special Education Teachers and Consultants," *Teacher Education and Special Education* 17, no. 2 (1995): 86–95; Patricia T. Ashton, Rodman B. Webb, and Nancy Doda, *A Study of Teachers' Sense of Efficacy* (Gainesville: University of Florida, 1983); Myron H. Dembo and Sherri Gibson, "Teachers' Sense of Efficacy: An Important Factor in School Improvement," *Elementary School Journal* 86, no. 2 (1985): 173–184; John Ross and Catherine Bruce, "Professional Development Effects on Teacher Efficacy: Results of a Randomized Field Trial," *Journal of Educational Research* 101, no. 1 (2007), doi: 10.3200/JOER.101.1.50–60; Anita E. Woolfolk, Barbara Rosoff, and Wayne K. Hoy,

"Teachers Sense of Efficacy and Their Beliefs About Managing Students," *Teaching and Teacher Education* 6, no. 2 (1990): 137–148.

6. Ashton et al., *Teachers' Sense of Efficacy*; Charlene M. Czerniak and Martha L. Schriver, "An Examination of Preservice Science Teachers' Beliefs and Behaviors as Related to Self-Efficacy," *Journal of Science Teacher Education* 5, no. 3 (1994): 77–86, doi: 10.1007/BF02614577; Larry G. Enochs, Lawrence C. Scharmann, and Iris M. Riggs, "The Relationship of Pupil Control to Preservice Elementary Science Teacher Self-Efficacy and Outcome Expectancy," *Science Teacher Education,* 79, no. 1 (1995): 63–75, doi: 10.1002/sce.3730790105; John A. Ross, "Beliefs That Make a Difference: The Origins and Impacts of Teacher Efficacy," (paper presented at the Annual Meeting of the Canadian Association for Curriculum Studies, Calgary, Alberta, 1994); Sola Takahashi, "Co-Constructing Efficacy: A 'Communities of Practice' Perspective on Teachers' Efficacy Beliefs," *Teaching and Teacher Education* 27, no. 4 (2011): 732–741; Megan Tschannen-Moran, Anita W. Hoy, and Wayne K Hoy, "Teacher Efficacy: Its Meaning and Measure," *Review of Educational Research* 68, no. 2 (1998), 202–248; Anita E. Woolfolk and Wayne K. Hoy, "Prospective Teachers' Sense of Efficacy and Beliefs About Control," *Journal of Educational Psychology* 82 (1990): 81–91.

7. Albert Bandura, "Self-Efficacy: Toward a Unifying Theory of Behavioral Change," *Psychological Review* 84, no. 2 (1977): 191; Gian Vittorio Caprara et al., "Teachers' Self-Efficacy Beliefs as Determinants of Job Satisfaction and Students' Academic Achievement: A Study at the School Level," *Journal of School Psychology* 44, no. 6 (2006): 473–490; Theodore Coladarci, "Teachers' Sense of Efficacy and Commitment to Teaching," *Journal of Experimental Education* 60, no. 4 (1992), 323–337; Dembo and Gibson, "Teachers' Sense of Efficacy"; Ross, "Beliefs"; Mark A. Smylie, "Teacher Efficacy at Work," in *Teachers and Their Workplace: Commitment, Performance, and Productivity*, ed. Pedro Reyes (Thousand Oaks, CA: Sage Publications, 1990).

8. Roger D. Goddard and Yvonne L. Goddard, "A Multilevel Analysis of the Relationship Between Teacher and Collective Efficacy in Urban Schools," *Teaching and Teacher Education* 17, no. 7 (2001): 807–818.

9. Albert Bandura, "Exercise of Human Agency Through Collective Efficacy," *Current Directions in Psychological Science* 9, no. 3 (2000): 75–78; Roger D. Goddard, Laura LoGerfo, and Wayne K. Hoy, "High School Accountability: The Role of Perceived Collective Efficacy," *Education and Educational Research* 18, no. 3 (2004): 403–425.

10. Albert Bandura, "Perceived Self-Efficacy in Cognitive Development and Functioning," *Educational Psychologist* 28, no. 2 (1993): 117–148; Takahashi, "Co-Constructing Efficacy."

11. Bandura, "Perceived Self-Efficacy"; Goddard et al., "Collective Teacher Efficacy"; R. D. Goddard, W. K. Hoy, and A. W. Hoy, "Collective Efficacy Beliefs: Theoretical Developments, Empirical Evidence, and Future Directions," *Educational Researcher* 33, no. 3 (2004): 3–13; Goddard et al., "High School Accountability"; Wayne K. Hoy, Scott R. Sweetland, and Page A. Smith, "Toward an Organizational Model of Achievement in High Schools: The Significance of Collective Efficacy," *Educational Administration Quarterly* 38, no. 1 (2002): 77–93.

12. Goddard and Goddard, "Multilevel Analysis"; Goddard et al., "Collective Efficacy Beliefs"; Robert M. Klassen et al., "Teacher Efficacy Research 1998–2009: Signs of Progress or Unfulfilled Promise?" *Educational Psychology Review* 23, no. 1 (2010): 21–43; Robert J. Sampson, Stephen J. Raudenbush, and Felton Earls, "Neighborhoods and Violent Crime: A Multilevel Study of Collective Efficacy," *Science* 277, no. 5328 (1997): 918–924, doi: 10.1126/science.277.5328.918.

13. Robert Wood and Albert Bandura, "Social Cognitive Theory of Organizational Management," *Academy of Management Review* 14, no. 3 (1989): 361–384.

14. Bandura, *Self-Efficacy: The Exercise of Control.*

15. Jal Mehta, *The Allure of Order: High Hopes, Dashed Expectations, and the Troubled Quest to Remake American Schooling* (New York: Oxford University Press, 2013), 23.

16. Dan C. Lortie, *Schoolteacher: A Sociological Study* (Chicago: University of Chicago Press, 1975).

17. Ibid.; Mehta, *Allure of Order.*

18. Richard F. Elmore and Susan H. Fuhrman, "Holding Schools Accountable: Is it Working?," *Phi Delta Kappan* 83, no. 1 (2001), 67–70, 72.

19. Karl F. Wheatley, "The Case for Conceptualizing Teacher Efficacy Research," *Teaching and Teacher Education* 21, 7 (2005): 747–766, doi: 10.1016/j.tate.2005.05.009.

20. Takahashi, "Co-Constructing Efficacy."

21. Michelle L. Forman, "Teacher Efficacy for What?: Aligning a Theory of Behavioral Change with the Core Work of Schools" (EdD diss., Harvard Graduate School of Education, 2014).

22. Ibid.

23. Laurel D. Puchner and Ann R. Taylor, "Lesson Study, Collaboration, and Teacher Efficacy: Stories from Two School-Based Math Lesson Study Groups," *Teaching and Teacher Education* 22, no. 7 (2006): 922–934, doi: 10.1016/j.tate.2006.04.011.

24. Ibid., 926.

25. Puchner and Taylor, "Lesson Study," 925–928.

26. Patricia Averette, "Save the Last Word for ME," protocol, National School Reform Faculty, Harmony Education Center, accessed September 12, 2016, www.nsrfharmony.org/system/files/protocols/save_last_word_0.pdf.

27. Stosich, "Joint Inquiry."

28. See the "Findings" section of ibid.

29. Forman, "Teacher Efficacy for What?"

AFTERWORD

1. A copy of this protocol is available from National School Reform Faculty, "North, South, East and West: Compass Points; An Exercise in Understanding Preferences in Group Work," National School Reform Faculty, Harmony Education Center, accessed September 12, 2016, www.nsrfharmony.org/system/files/protocols/north_south_1.pdf.

2. Elisa MacDonald, "When Nice Won't Suffice," *Journal of Staff Development* 32, no. 3 (2011): 45–51.

3. Michael Fullan, *The Principal: Three Keys to Maximizing Impact* (San Francisco: Jossey-Bass, 2014).

APPENDIX C

1. Mary Kay Stein et al., *Implementing Standards-Based Mathematics Instruction: A Casebook for Professional Development*, 2nd ed. (New York: Teachers College Press, 2009).

2. The first and second questions are adapted from Stein et al., *Implementing Standards-Based Mathematics.*

ABOUT THE AUTHORS

Michelle Forman, EdD, works as a consultant helping educators develop internal coherence as a learning process to support teacher agency, organizational capacity, and ongoing improvements to teaching and learning. In this capacity, she has consulted with schools, districts, networks, leadership coaches, and other providers of professional learning. While completing her doctorate at the Harvard Graduate School of Education, Michelle served as the director of the Internal Coherence Research Project of the Strategic Education Research Partnership (SERP), at the Boston field site. Michelle received her doctorate with a concentration in leadership, policy, and instructional practice, and her research focused on tightening the relationship between teacher efficacy and the core work of schools. She is a contributing author to *Data Wise in Action: Stories of Schools Using Data to Improve Teaching and Learning*. Previously, Michelle worked as a high school teacher in New York City; Oakland, California; and a small rural community in upstate New York. She holds an MA in English education from Teachers College and a BA from the University of California, Berkeley.

Elizabeth Leisy Stosich, EdD, is a Research and Policy Fellow at the Stanford Center for Opportunity Policy in Education. Elizabeth's research focuses on the school conditions and learning opportunities that help teachers engage in ambitious instruction; this support included opportunities for teachers to use curriculum, assessments, and inquiry-based practices to meet the goals of standards-based accountability policies. Her research interests include school improvement, standards-based accountability policies, teacher collaboration, and teacher preparation and development. Previously, Elizabeth taught elementary school in Oakland and San Francisco.

She received her BA in Spanish and Portuguese from University of California, Berkeley; an MA in teaching from the University of San Francisco; and an EdM in educational policy and an EdD in education policy, leadership, and instructional practice from Harvard University.

Candice Bocala, EdD, is a Senior Research Associate at WestEd and Lecturer at the Harvard Graduate School of Education. Her research focuses on the connections between educator learning and the organizational conditions that support collaboration and improvement. She has led and designed numerous professional learning workshops for educators as a senior team member of the Data Wise Project and the Internal Coherence Research Project. She is also committed to supporting educators with understanding issues related to racial and ethnic diversity and enacting pedagogical practices that promote equity. At WestEd, she serves as a program evaluator, researcher, and technical assistance provider to state and local education agencies. Candice received her EdD from the Harvard Graduate School of Education, and she holds an MAT from American University, an MA in policy analysis and evaluation from Stanford University, and a BA in government from Cornell University. Previously, she taught elementary school in Washington, DC.

INDEX